1

P9-DFE-180

A1290T 650335

WITHDRAWN

4/06

I.C.C. LIBRARY

ENDING GLOBAL POVERTY

PRAISE FOR *ENDING GLOBAL POVERTY*

Smith's book is a terrific contribution to our understanding of how to improve the well-being of impoverished people. It is accessible and informative for anyone who is interested in understanding clearly the fundamental causes of chronic poverty and the innovative responses by organizations worldwide to address them. Smith's discussion of the keys to poverty traps dispels many popular misconceptions and helps the reader understand the real issues. His profiles of successful programs designed to address those traps show the impact many organizations have already made worldwide and highlights some of the lessons they have learned in the process. This book should help raise the effectiveness of donors, organizations, and governments in their efforts to help those in need.

—Judith M. Dean,
International Economist, Washington, D.C.;
former Associate Professor of Economics,
SAIS, Johns Hopkins University;
and former Board member, World Relief.

The world's leaders have repeatedly promised to tackle poverty on a massive scale, but they always seem to find excuses for failing to mobilize the necessary resources. Stephen Smith shows convincingly that even the poorest of the poor can help themselves—with a little help from the rest of us. Anyone who wants to understand why so many remain trapped in poverty, and what they and we can do about it, should read this inspiring book.

—Ann Florini,
Senior Fellow at the Brookings Institution
and Director of the World Economic Forum's
Global Governance Initiative

ENDING GLOBAL POVERTY

A GUIDE TO WHAT WORKS

STEPHEN C. SMITH

I.C.C. LIBRARY

HL
79
.P63
S62
2005

ENDING GLOBAL POVERTY
Copyright © Stephen C. Smith, 2005.
All rights reserved. No part of this book may be used or reproduced in any
manner whatsoever without written permission except in the case of brief
quotations embodied in critical articles or reviews.

First published 2005 by
PALGRAVE MACMILLAN™
175 Fifth Avenue, New York, N.Y. 10010 and
Houndmills, Basingstoke, Hampshire, England RG21 6XS.
Companies and representatives throughout the world.

PALGRAVE MACMILLAN is the global academic imprint of the Palgrave
Macmillan division of St. Martin's Press, LLC and of Palgrave Macmillan Ltd.
Macmillan® is a registered trademark in the United States, United Kingdom
and other countries. Palgrave is a registered trademark in the European Union
and other countries.

ISBN 1–4039–6534-X hardback

Library of Congress Cataloging-in-Publication Data
Smith, Stephen C., 1955-
Ending global poverty : a guide to what works / Stephen C. Smith
    p.   cm.
  Includes bibliographical references and index.
  ISBN 1–4039–6534-X
  1. Economic assistance, Domestic.   2. Basic needs.   3. Social planning.
4. Social policy.   5. Poor—Services for.   I. Title.

HC79.P63S62   2005
339.4'6—dc22
                                                              2004061056

A catalogue record for this book is available from the British Library.

Design by Letra Libre, Inc..

10   9   8   7   6   5   4   3

Printed in the United States of America

3/06 B&T 26.95

This book is dedicated with thanks to the participants and staff of the selected poverty programs I visited. They renewed in me an optimism that I would like to share.

CONTENTS

Preface and Acknowledgments   ix

Introduction   1

PART I: EXTREME POVERTY: THE CRUELEST TRAP

1. Understanding Extreme Poverty:
    Poverty Traps and the Experience of the Poor   11
2. The Keys to Capability:
    Eight Keys to Escaping Poverty Traps   31

PART II: ESCAPING THE POVERTY TRAP: HOW THE POOR ARE GAINING THE KEYS TO CAPABILITY

3. Health, Nutrition, and Population   49
4. Basic Education   61
5. Credit for Poverty Reduction, and Insuring Opportunity   75
6. Bottom-Up Market Development:
    Assets and Access for the Poor   89
7. Entitlement to New Technologies
    and the Capability to Benefit from Them   103
8. Sustaining the Environment for Ending Poverty   115
9. Social Inclusion and Human Rights
    for the Poor and Voiceless   127
10. Community Empowerment and Development   139
11. Ten Strategies for Innovation
    in Ending Global Poverty   155

PART III: WHAT YOU CAN DO TO HELP

12. First Steps   161
13. Further Questions   171
14. Stepping Up   181

15.   What Businesses Can Do   205

                        CONCLUSION

16.   Some Closing Words: The End of Global Poverty   213

Notes and References   221
Index   251
About the Author   260

PREFACE AND ACKNOWLEDGMENTS

Poverty is a cruel trap. For many of the unfortunate people who are ensnared in this painful leg hold, escape on their own can be all but impossible. A billion human beings today are bound in poverty traps, in almost unrelenting misery.

Although it may look bleak, there is real hope. In fact, hundreds of millions of people have already broken free from poverty, gaining the assets and capabilities to sustainably support themselves and their families in decent living conditions. There have been real breakthroughs in understanding the causes of poverty traps and in designing and implementing grassroots programs that reliably provide the means of escape. Many of the best plans for breaking out of poverty traps have been devised on the ground by people from the developing world, but with much-needed assistance from outside.

This book shows how the world's poorest people, even those not fortunate enough to live in high-growth economies such as China, can escape the grind of extreme poverty. This can be accomplished in our time, through increasingly effective strategies, in a drama in which we can all play a supporting role while the poor take center stage. The book shows how we can provide the essential help for those doing the best work, as voters, donors, and active citizens.

This book began to take shape a few years ago with a simple question from my wife. Like millions of Americans, we receive letters asking for money almost every day. Renee had been collecting recent requests from groups working on poverty in developing countries. She showed me a stack of requests and asked me how we could decide if we should give to groups we had supported in the past, or whether some of the other groups were doing a better job. She had a reasonable question: We met in grad school where I was studying development economics 25 years ago, so she has heard me talk about poverty for a long time. But I didn't know how to answer this question in a comprehensive way, as a development specialist. I knew the most rigorous studies published in professional journals—but there was no reason to suppose (and some good reasons to doubt) that the best programs had been subjected to the most rigorous research. So some of the best programs likely weren't even known to most specialists. I'm sure it never occurred to her that I would say, "I really don't know, but I'll get back to you on that."

There are charity ratings, which offer some guidance, and I will talk about those later in the book. But key factors in these ratings—low reported expenses in overhead—are no guarantee of effective programs; and the right kind of overhead, such as careful evaluation, can do a lot of good. So something more was needed to answer my wife's question. But there was no book on the principles and resources that would allow a person to decide for herself how to direct her time and treasures wisely, and to get involved effectively. No one seemed to be addressing the big picture on poverty and effectiveness in poverty programs in a way that would be useful for individual donors and concerned citizens. A couple of years later, still lacking an answer for my wife, I decided I would have to write the book myself. For reasons explained in the book, I have not attempted a rating system or a comprehensive overview of key actors—I have tried to identify some clear examples of innovative and potentially effective programs addressing poverty traps and building capabilities and assets of the poor.

I decided I would also try to answer some other questions I have been asked over the years: "I am concerned about global poverty but is there really anything I can do about it besides making financial contributions?" I decided to collect all the possibilities together in one place. "Do you *really* think we could ever end poverty?" This book would also be an occasion to give a more complete explanation of why I always answered "yes." "Why can't the poor escape poverty by working harder?" "Do any of these programs really make any difference?" "Can't we solve the problem by stimulating economic growth?" I decided to take a fresh approach.

Extreme poverty is such a difficult problem because the poor are often stuck in poverty traps, but the special difficulties posed by these traps are all too often overlooked. So I decided to make these traps a focal point of the book. I also decided to primarily address problems of poverty in regions where economic growth was not rapid, and where the near-term prospects for rapid growth were not high. When found together, local traps and national stagnation make for the most intractable conditions of extreme poverty. If poverty can be overcome under these conditions, it can be overcome anywhere. But this raised the question of what capabilities the poor would need to at least escape from extreme poverty without counting on much help from national and global markets, but that well-designed poverty programs might provide. I identified eight keys that were particularly important.

Then came the problem of which programs to feature. There are on the order of one million programs around the world attempting to reduce poverty in its broad sense as used in this book. I had to develop a method of selecting some of the most effective, innovative, and promising programs from among this large pool. This selection process still goes on as this book goes to press—in fact I expect to continue with this effort indefinitely—but I identified some outstanding programs that illustrated the important points. I used three main screens: highly rigorous evidence of program impact, the winning of major juried prizes and awards for development effectiveness and innovation, and citations in systematic interviews of chief program evaluators of highly regarded private voluntary organizations, in which I placed particular weight on frequent citations by peer (or competitor) organizations. The latter method was loosely patterned on the methods used by the National Academy of Sciences in ranking academic departments. But the result is *not* a ratings scheme, nor am I in a position to offer one. Instead, I hope to offer a way to think about problems of poverty that creates opportunities for all of us to play a role in their solutions—that lets potential donors and citizens decide for themselves what problems they think are particularly important and identify actions they can take and programs they can support that make a difference while empowering the poor.

My wife never could have imagined that my answer would be so long, or so long in the making.

I would like to thank first of all the participants and staff of the specially selected poverty programs I visited. They shared their work in all its glories and its limitations with candor and kindness. They renewed in me an optimism that I would like to share.

Parts of this book were assisted with a patchwork quilt of travel support. For partial funding of travel expenses I would like to thank: the Institute for International Corporate Governance and Accountability (IICGA), Africa Project of the GW Law School (funded through Sloan Foundation), Delta Airlines through the Center for Latin American Issues, GWU; Title VI in-country travel grants, funded through National Resource Centers program, from U.S. Department of Education (GW-ESIA); and Columbian College (GW).

I have received very valuable comments and suggestions on the manuscript from Jennifer Brinkerhoff, Renee Jakobs, Shahe Emran, and Hildy Teegen. My editor at Palgrave Macmillan, Toby Wahl, helped me to stay out of the long-sentence trap and the long-book trap. Amanda Fernández, Heather VanDusen, and Rick Delaney of Palgrave Macmillan provided excellent editorial assistance. I want to thank my wife, daughter, and son for putting up with my travel schedule and many weekends spent at my laptop, and for all of your understanding and support during this project.

INTRODUCTION

Global poverty is the scourge and disgrace of our affluent era. But we can effectively end extreme poverty as we know it in our times. The starting point is the awareness of these basic facts: The dimensions of extreme poverty are enormous, but an equal amount of progress has already been made. And although an end to global poverty is not inevitable, with redoubled commitment, we can end extreme poverty in one generation. We have only to follow through and adequately fund strategies that are already working, while continuously and carefully evaluating both new and old strategies and learning from their lessons.

The story of poverty so far is one of good news and bad news—how very much progress we have already made, but also how much remains to be done.

The scale of global poverty is immense. According to the World Bank, about 1.25 billion people subsist on less than $1 per day, and some 2.8 billion—nearly half the world's population—live on less than $2 per day. Both the measures and the nature of poverty are more complicated than this, but these numbers do adjust for the fact that many services are cheaper in poor countries. Imagine trying to live in America on $2 a day, housing included, and you get some idea. Life is truly desperate for many of these people. Meanwhile, the average real income gap between the richest billion and the poorest two-and-a-half billion has widened to more than 16 to 1.

Conditions of poverty are particularly desperate in Africa. The real income of the average American is more than 50 times that of the average person in Sub-Saharan Africa. In fact, real living standards in the United States 200 years ago were greater than in many African countries today, and about 20 countries in Sub-Saharan Africa are poorer today than they were a generation ago. The number in the region living in extreme poverty has been estimated by the World Bank to have increased from 217 million in 1987 to 291 million in 1998. By 2001, some 48 percent of the population was absolutely poor, living on less that $1 per day—the highest incidence of poverty in the world.

Poverty is hunger. Some 17 percent of the world's population is classified as undernourished, or suffering from chronic hunger. Chronic hunger
is measured by a daily intake of less than about 1,700 calories and a lack
of access to safe and nutritious food. This is a dangerously low level of
calories, making a person lethargic and susceptible to disease and death.
Clearly, many of the hungry do survive, although often miserably. It is
amazing what the body can adjust to, but for children the impact is catastrophic. In many poor countries half of the children are so short for their
age as to signal severe malnutrition. These estimates of the malnourished
do not even consider micronutrient deficiency, such as low levels of iron,
Vitamin A, and other vitamins and minerals, which can also be very dangerous. Micronutrient malnutrition affects at least 2 billion people. Children are particularly vulnerable and may face lifelong disabilities as a
result. Researchers have discovered that even "subclinical" levels of Vitamin A malnutrition can cause death.

Poverty is pervasive poor health and early death. Every day, about
30,000 children in developing countries die from preventable causes—almost
11 million this year alone. Most of these children die from dehydration from
diarrhea, diseases for which there are inexpensive immunizations, and infections treatable with antibiotics such as pneumonia. The underlying cause in
more cases than not is undernutrition leading to vulnerability. The under-five
mortality rate is 126 per 1,000 live births in low-income countries, and 39
per 1,000 in middle-income countries (compared with 6 per 1,000 in high-
income countries). In some countries such as Angola, Burkina Faso, Malawi,
Mali, Mozambique, Niger, Rwanda, and Sierra Leone, more than one-fifth
of all children die before the age of five from preventable causes. In South
Asia as a whole, one child in ten dies before age five. In some of the poorest
parts of the world it is traditional not to give a newborn baby a name until
she is at least a month old—because so many do not live that long. A woman
dies during childbirth every minute; almost none of these women would have
died if they had lived in North America or Europe. Life expectancy at birth
in Sub-Saharan Africa is only 46 years, and is plunging in large part because
of the AIDS epidemic. In many low-income countries, debilitating parasites
are nearly ubiquitous. The incidence of drug-resistant malaria and TB are
dramatically worsening. Tuberculosis, AIDS, and malaria kill millions of people each year—about three thousand children in Africa die from malaria each
day. Poverty plays such a central role in most health problems faced by developing countries that it has its own designation in the International Classi-
fication of Diseases: Code Z59.5—extreme poverty.

Poverty is the loss of childhood. According to International Labor
Organization (ILO) estimates, at least 180 million child laborers are either under 14 years of age or work in conditions that endangers their

health or well-being, involving hazards, sexual exploitation, trafficking, and debt bondage. This includes 110 million children under the age of 15 doing hazardous work. Over 73 million working children are under 10 years of age. And an estimated 8.4 million child laborers are trapped in slavery, trafficking, debt bondage, prostitution, pornography, and other abhorrent conditions.

Poverty is the denial of the right to a basic education. There are close to one billion illiterate adults in the world. Nearly half of all adults in South Asia are illiterate. A child in Europe, North America, or Japan can expect to receive more than 12 years of schooling on average, but a child in Sub-Saharan Africa and South Asia can expect to spend less than four years in school, some never entering a classroom in their life. It has been estimated by the World Bank that in 2003, more than 100 million children have been unable to go to school due to their poverty—they are thus deprived of their chance to escape poverty when they grow up. According to the United Nations Development Program, in at least 16 Sub-Saharan African countries a child is more likely to die before the age of five than to attend secondary school.

Poverty is also about other conditions that are less quantifiable but no less real and oppressive. It is awareness and fear of becoming destitute as a result of a shock or catastrophic event, such as an illness, or the death of a draft animal, or theft of your land: Poverty is vulnerability. And it is the ongoing stress of trying desperately to anticipate and adapt to this vulnerability. In fact, each year perhaps three-quarters as many people fall into poverty as escape from it. The struggle against poverty may be one of four steps forward and three steps back.

Poverty is powerlessness. It is the lack of access to real markets that could offer a way out of poverty. It is the systematic exploitation, theft, and abuse not only by the rich but by the government officials ostensibly there to help: the poor must pay larger bribes, as a share of their income, than the rich just to survive. It is the debilitating and deliberately created psychological feeling of hopelessness and dependence on whatever minimal remuneration may be offered by a particular rich family in your sphere of life. It is the violence from within the family and without. It is the powerlessness to stop the things that are hurting you and your family and keeping you poor.

These conditions cry out for concerted action. But it is not easy to know what we can do about them.

As bleak as these numbers appear, it is far from hopeless. The best place to start is to appreciate the progress that has already been made—not long ago the situation was far worse. Contrary to popular impression, progress against poverty in the past few decades has been nothing short of extraordinary. This serves to remind us how bad it was in the not-so-distant past—but also to assure us that more meaningful progress can surely be made with concerted efforts.

Many students arrive in my courses with an image of the Third World that is decades out of date. They imagine a vast ocean of the poor spanning Latin America, Africa, and Asia in which, excepting a few rich landlords, politicians, and industrialists supported by the state, everyone is hopelessly impoverished, lucky to have corrugated tin rather than mud or cardboard for walls and ceiling. Certainly hundreds of millions still live in such hovels and oppressive conditions today. But there has also been tremendous progress. Partly because of the steady absorption of ideas and technologies from the West, but also due to the increasing effectiveness of poverty programs, that great featureless ocean of poverty out there has been shrinking. Think of the ground in these continents drying up, so that you can see individual pools of poverty surrounded by nonpoor land. Those in deep poverty can now be distinguished from those in relative poverty, whose incomes are much less than ours, but enough to keep their heads above the water. This makes it more possible to target efforts toward those who need help the most.

In every country one can point to the specific regions where poverty is most severe, such as Irian Jaya in Indonesia. Within impoverished regions, we can find the villages that are most deprived, and we are learning how to find the most deprived people within those villages. India is a good example. Most of its people used to suffer from extreme deprivations, and indeed two in five remain desperately poor. But today, more than half of its poor live in just four of its twenty-six states. Within cities, the poor are concentrated in readily identified slums. In some ways it will be harder to get the poorest out of poverty than it has been to help those who have emerged from poverty to date. This is because the chronically poor are often caught in poverty traps, which we turn attention to shortly. Even so, the problem seems much more manageable than it did a couple of decades ago. Although counting the poor and estimating the depth of their poverty is extremely difficult, and fraught with statistical problems, there is little doubt that the *percentage* of the world's people living on less than one dollar per day has fallen significantly since 1990. In one typical calculation, the United Nations Development Program estimated in 2002 that the percentage of the world's people living in such extreme poverty dropped from 29 percent in 1990 to 23 percent in 1999. And while the world's population has continued to grow—more than 42 percent between 1980 and 2004—the number of those living in poverty has not significantly worsened; this is in itself an achievement given the large population increase. In fact, the *number* in extreme poverty may actually have fallen by as many as 400 million people since 1981, according to a recent World Bank study by Shaohua Chen and Martin Ravallion.

The number of people with access to safe water is increasing steadily. In 1960 little more than one third of people had access to safe water, while well over two thirds have access today, again despite huge population growth in the developing world. Progress is real, even allowing that what is considered "access"—a tap 100 meters (109 yards) away shared by hundreds of people—may leave very much to be desired.

Sometimes, headlines that look alarming, and indeed should summon our renewed commitment, lead to discouragement rather than resolve because the context is missing. The United Nations Food and Agriculture Organization (FAO) reported in its November 2003 report, "The State of Food Insecurity in the World," that the number of people suffering from chronic extreme hunger increased during the last half of the 1990s by 18 million. This means that 842 million people in developing and transition countries are severely undernourished—three times the total U.S. population. This increase reversed what had been a steady drop over the previous three decades, a period in which the share of population in the developing world experiencing chronic hunger fell from 37 percent in 1970 to 17 percent in 2000. There is still much more work to be done, but experience like this shows that hunger can be eliminated.

The biggest success is China, where 58 million fewer people experienced chronic hunger in the late 1990s, largely due to the spectacular growth of that economy. However, a substantial increase of some 17 million more undernourished people was noted in India, a country that also experienced rapid economic growth—reflecting the fact that economic growth is not a cure-all for extreme poverty. The biggest disaster was in the Democratic Republic of the Congo, in which the number of the hungry increased from 12 million to 38 million in the late 1990s. At least two out of every five children in Sub-Saharan Africa are malnourished.

The problem is not that there is too little food in the world. According to the FAO, 2,807 food calories per capita were produced worldwide in 2001, in principle far more than needed for everyone to be well-nourished (estimates of the calories needed range up to about 2,500 per person, some well below this figure). According to the Worldwatch Institute, there are now actually more overweight people in the world than people suffering from calorie-deprivation. And there is still an enormous capacity to increase food production and improve food distribution within the developing world. So, the good news is that the world can produce more than enough food needed by its people. The problem is how to give the poor enough command over resources to meet their nutrition and other basic needs on a regular basis.

In impoverished regions, the poor might languish indefinitely in poverty traps. Escape is not inevitable, even with the relatively strong growth seen in countries such as India in recent years. An end to global poverty as we have known it is attainable within a single generation. But it will require more than letting growth take its course. And it will require action on environmental sustainability—the poor are potential victims of catastrophic environmental changes that threaten to reverse hard-won gains.

So is there anything that we should do, or that we can do? The answer is a resounding "yes."

The African poverty tragedy teaches us that, despite some successes in transferring health and other technology, poverty reduction is *not* inevitable. As poor as the people in this region were to begin with, average living standards are falling each year, not for the length of a recession but for 25 years. Despite this appalling experience, we have also learned, from East Asia particularly, another crucial fact: poverty reduction, and even ending poverty altogether, *is* possible. Poverty can be eliminated, in a surprisingly short time, if we focus on the problem. These two facts together—that ending poverty is possible but not inevitable—create a moral imperative for action.

It is one thing to know that people are suffering. But it is another thing to know that this suffering can go on indefinitely, is largely unnecessary, and that we could have done more to help—with potential benefits that could prove very significant for our own future.

There is a growing sense among the American people that we have a moral imperative to do more to end global poverty. To cite just one of many polls, a bipartisan poll commissioned by the Christian lobbying group Bread for the World, released in July 2002, reported that 92.7 percent of likely voters now say that "fighting the hunger problem" is important to them; and 48.5 percent said it was "very important," meaning it would affect their voting.

There has also been growing public interest in such topics as cutting the external debt owed by low-income countries, improving conditions of workers in sweatshops, reform of the World Bank and International Monetary Fund (IMF), and halting the worsening environmental degradation in developing countries. Demonstrations at the World Bank in 2000 and 2001 drew public attention to the connections between high debt levels in Africa and the continent's extreme poverty. The Africa trip of U2's Bono and former U.S. Treasury Secretary Paul O'Neill in the summer of 2002 attracted broad public interest. The March 2002 UN Poverty Summit in Mexico, and the August 2002 World Environment Summit in South Africa, which largely focused on problems of poverty, received significant public attention. Global poverty is on people's minds as never before.

The increased concern about poverty in the developing world is part of a broader renewed public interest in volunteering and social service, in "giving something back." In the United States, young people are engaging in community service in unprecedented numbers. A 1998 poll by Peter Hart Associates showed that "68 percent of young adults report that in the past three years they have been involved in activities to help their community." People say they would also like to do more to help end global poverty. There is clear interest among the public in gaining a better understanding of extreme poverty and hunger and what can be done about it. But most don't know where to begin, and many suspect that there is little that they or their country can do to help. Yet in recent years significant strides have been made in understanding the nature of poverty traps and the requirements for successful escape from these traps, and real improvements have been made in the effectiveness of poverty programs. Through this book I hope to increase awareness of this progress, and what it means for our opportunities to end extreme poverty.

This book offers several complementary ways to understand poverty and its remedies: Problems pointed to by the poor themselves; the types of poverty traps or vicious cycles of poverty pointed out by poverty researchers and programs to solve them; the capabilities needed by the poor and programs to help develop these capabilities; and the range of actions individuals can take to help end poverty.

The book has three main parts. The first explains poverty—what it means, what it is like in the words of the poor, and why it is a trap that a person or family often cannot escape by their own efforts alone. I then describe the eight "keys to capability" for escaping poverty traps. The second part of the book lays out strategies and programs (generally run by non-governmental/nonprofit organizations but sometimes sponsored by governments or companies) helping to build capabilities and assets among those in extreme poverty and leading to real improvements in the lives of the poor. The third and final part of the book offers a guide to the concrete steps we can each take, as individuals and groups, to help end global poverty. It shows how to be part of the solution, and how not to inadvertently contribute to the problem.

I hope you will come away from reading this book with a strong optimism that we can put an end to extreme poverty. Of course, this is a very hard problem. There are many sometimes-conflicting ideas about what causes poverty and how to end it. We are always learning more, and there is plenty of room for legitimate disagreements. Certainly I do not claim to have all the answers. We need to know much more, through better and more rigorous evaluations of poverty programs. In a real sense this book reflects the current state of a work in progress. But although even today's best programs may be greatly improved upon, particularly as technology and knowledge of problems of poverty and keys to capability improves, we do know enough to be sure that we can end global poverty in our time.

PART I

EXTREME POVERTY: THE CRUELEST TRAP

UNDERSTANDING EXTREME POVERTY

POVERTY TRAPS AND THE EXPERIENCE OF THE POOR

To understand how poverty can be ended, first we need a clear understanding of what poverty is, and what it means to be trapped in poverty.

A *poverty trap*—also called "structural poverty" because it is not a temporary problem that people can eventually escape from through sustained efforts—is much more than just the lack of income. Instead, the very conditions of poverty today make it likely that poverty will continue tomorrow.

The grim statistics cited in the introduction show that impoverished people frequently suffer from malnutrition, poor health, and illiteracy; live in environmentally degraded areas; have little political voice; and attempt to earn a meager living on small and marginal farms or in dilapidated urban slums in which conditions make significant growth of incomes exceedingly difficult. Such extreme conditions mean that the children are also likely to be trapped in poverty when they grow up.

Can't the poor pull themselves out of poverty if they try hard enough? The answer is sometimes yes but in general no. The poor are *not* "lazy," but caught in poverty traps. No one wants to be poor, and poverty is not the fault of the poor. The poor work very hard, particularly when doing so offers any reasonable chance of paying off. But they are generally unable to take entrepreneurial risks because the consequences of failure are so dire. When people are severely malnourished, they feel exhaustion and fatigue. In less extreme cases the poor are simply stuck at a minimum level of existence.

Even when the poor seem to have escaped from poverty, they often remain vulnerable, falling into the snare again—and knowing this affects the whole way they go about life. Both their immediate conditions and the deeper causes of their underlying vulnerability have to be addressed in successful poverty programs.

THE PREDICAMENT OF THE POOREST OF THE POOR: WHY IT'S A TRAP

The term "poverty trap" is very evocative. The phrase reminds us that where there is a trap there is likely to be a trapper—indeed poverty traps are all too commonly set deliberately by the rich to ensnare the poor. Yet the word "trap" also suggests that there is a way out. Indeed there is—but like many traps, escape from poverty often requires some help from the outside.

In fact, not all poverty at all times and places is a trap. Poverty may be temporary and in some cases people can and do work their way out of poverty. But poverty becomes a trap when a vicious cycle undermines the efforts of the poor, in which conditions of poverty feed on themselves and create further conditions of poverty.

Here are sixteen of the major poverty traps that keep the poor enslaved to the vicious cycle of poverty—and that the best poverty programs are working to address. It is not an exhaustive list, but it reflects the range of problems that are addressed in this book. Remember, as hopeless as these traps might sound, there are ways out of all of them.

1. Family child labor traps.
In a family child labor trap, if parents are too unhealthy and unskilled to be productive enough to support their family, the children have to work. But if children work, they can't get the education they need—so when they grow up, they have to send their own children to work. It has been estimated by the World Bank that, in 2003, more than 100 million children were unable to go to school due to their poverty. In this way, poverty is transmitted across gerenations.

2. Illiteracy traps.
Closely related to the problem of a child labor trap is the illiteracy trap. Even if the family cannot or will not send their children to work, parents may not send their children to school because they cannot afford transportation, school uniforms, or a modest school fee. If a family could borrow this money, the higher incomes received a few years later by their then-literate children could pay back these loans easily. But if the poor lack access to credit, they may not be able to get loans to finance otherwise very productive schooling. The lack of credit traps the poor in ways that were not understood until recently.

3. Working capital traps.

Lack of credit also plays a role in other poverty traps. In a working capital trap, a microentrepreneur must make do with an inventory too small to be productive—but this means she will also have too little net income to have a larger inventory in the future. For example, I met a woman in Ecuador trying to make ends meet by selling three pairs of used American jeans door to door—all she can afford to hold. But that made the chance of a sale—a matching style and size that the customers want—so low that her income was not enough to buy a larger inventory the next day. Despite the explosion over the last 15 years of microfinance institutions (MFIs) making small loans to the poor, it has been estimated by Sam Daley-Harris and his collaborators that MFIs are currently serving just 11 percent of the world's 240 million poorest families. This statistic suggests that working capital traps are still pervasive.

4. Uninsurable-risk traps.

It is often the people with the fewest assets who face the greatest chances of losing what is most important to them, such as their land, their basic nutrition, their health—the greatest uninsured risks. For example, a majority of the poorest are farmers, and they are generally unable to get any weather insurance. As a result, they have to orient their entire approach to farming to minimizing the risks of a catastrophic drought or other shock in which their families face ruin. But this approach to farming also makes it unlikely that they can take advantage of opportunities to do much better and begin to build assets that can lift them out of poverty in the long run. As a result, they are unable to change their circumstances in a way that would let them gain more security against high risks in the future. Similar distortions are found in the behavior of microentrepreneurs. Although the poor show great ingenuity in developing informal risk-sharing arrangements in their communities, the result can be considerable distortions and inefficiencies that also retard the rate of economic progress.

5. Debt bondage traps.

While credit is needed, the wrong kind of debt from unscrupulous moneylenders can also be a trap. Colluding moneylenders calibrate loan amounts and interest payments to ensure that a family can never get out of debt. Sometimes the rate of pay for impoverished people working for their creditors is so low that it is insufficient even to pay back the interest they owe. Such is the plight of tens of thousands of low-caste salt workers in rural India. Although bonded workers are allowed to keep a subsistence income so that they can survive to work (as slaves used to be), essentially all the surplus is extracted by the moneylender in an endless cycle of debt. Terms are designed so that the more you work or the more productive you become, the more you must pay to your masters: the quicksand of poverty.

All too commonly the children of the bonded laborers are themselves born into bondage, never to escape. This is slavery by another name. The non-governmental organization (NGO) Free the Slaves estimates that there are some 27 million people serving in debt bondage and related forms of effective slavery around the world today.

6. Information traps.
Impoverished day laborers, housemaids, and others among the poorest of the poor work long hours every day just to put one or two meals on the table. Even though existing alternatives may pay a higher wage, they have no time or energy to learn about what these occupations pay or how to work in them. Clearly, their employers have no incentive to help their workers learn about better opportunities, and may work to prevent it. Lack of access to information keeps the poor in poverty, and conditions of poverty prevent the poor from getting information needed to escape from poverty. I have seen this in rural Bangladesh, where people remain as low-paying day laborers simply because they are unaware of other local opportunities. And it is not difficult to imagine even from our own experiences: how often do all of us continue with our routines, with some way of doing things—at home, at work, the job itself—because we never took the time to look at our alternatives? If it happens to us, imagine what can happen to an abused day laborer or domestic worker, shielded from the world beyond her part of the village.

7. Undernutrition and illness traps.
If an undernourished person is too weak to work productively, her resulting wage is too small to pay for sufficient food, so she continues to work with low productivity for low wages. This is an undernutrition trap, an extreme form of structural poverty found in famines and deeply impoverished areas. A similar vicious cycle can keep chronically ill (but treatable) people in the bondage of poverty. And poor shelter from severe weather such as monsoons can cause sleeplessness and prolonged illness, reducing earning power along with the chance of affording better housing.

8. Low-skill traps.
If there is no employer in the region who is seeking skilled workers for, as an example, basic manufacturing jobs, then there is no visible incentive for individuals to invest in attaining these skills. But if there is no workforce available with these skills, outside investors are not likely to invest in the region. Why do so, when you can go to other developing regions where these skills are readily available? This type of trap could be described as a chicken or the egg problem—which comes first, the investment or the

skills? Governments can help with training and incentives for firms if they have resources—but when they lack resources, resulting from such conditions as a high debt burden, this may be difficult or impossible to resolve from within the trapped economy.

9. High fertility traps.

If everyone around you is having many children, and there are few decent jobs to go around, then you too must have many children, or face the likelihood that no one—no child of yours—will have the means and the willingness to take care of you when you are too old to work. If all could have lower fertility, all might be better off. But how could you, a poor, powerless woman in an obscure village, possibly be expected to make such a change?

10. Subsistence traps.

Specialization can be the key to increasing your productivity. But you can only specialize if you can trade for the other goods and services you need. If, for example, everyone in your region is practicing subsistence agriculture, there is no one to sell to, and you have to remain producing for subsistence with perhaps a little trading on the side. The alternative is to produce for more distant markets. But to do so, you must first know of them, must somehow get your product to these markets, and indeed must convince distant buyers of its quality. Middlemen play a key role by vouching for the quality of the products they sell. They are able to do this because they get to know the farmers and artisans they buy from and they specialize in the product. It is difficult to be an expert in the quality of many products, so there needs to be a sufficient number of concentrated producers with whom a middleman can effectively work. But without available middlemen that the farmers can sell to, they will have little incentive to specialize in the first place. The result can be an underdevelopment trap in which a region remains stuck in subsistence agriculture.

11. Farm erosion traps.

In farm erosion traps, the poor are so desperate for food that they have to overuse their land even though they know the results will be reduced soil fertility and productivity the next year, and eventually even desertification. In times of famine, impoverished farmers have been known to eat the seeds they have saved from the last harvest to plant in the next sowing season so that they do not starve before then. This is a metaphor for the basic problem. Even though you know you are overusing your soil and that it will degrade if you do not rest it or plant less aggressively, the degradation happens at some point in the future. You have to grow more food today to keep your family from becoming badly undernourished. But in the end, you are simply trapped into a cycle of poverty. Any gains in productivity from learning new techniques are undermined by the poorer quality of soil. And while fertilizers and other land improvements might be a good investment by conventional calculations, they are of no help if you cannot afford them or borrow to finance them.

12. Common property mismanagement traps.

Lakes are overfished, forests are not managed sustainably, land is overgrazed. Part of the problem is that community management of common resources has broken down, often a legacy of greedy colonial practices, now all too often imitated by post-colonial regimes. Once broken down, responsible use of shared resources is difficult to restore. Put in stark terms, someone in this predicament may think, "if I do not fish today even at unsustainable levels, someone else will catch those fish instead of me—either way, I will catch fewer fish tomorrow."

13. Collective action traps.

Many times a community of the poor could improve its circumstances by working together on joint projects. However, this requires a leader who has time to organize, and generally the poor do not have the time and resources to do this. Also, because the payoff of collective action goes to the group and not just the organizer, the reward rarely offsets the risk. As a result, it can be difficult for individuals to take the initial steps.

14. Criminality traps.

Youths without access to useful education and who see little future in legitimate work are drawn to gang membership and other cultures of criminality. Emotional scars from the experience of violence reinforce this trend. The resulting fights, thefts, and criminal activities then compound the community's poverty trap by destroying assets, diverting resources to provide for personal and property security, and even taking the lives of able-bodied young men. Most of the victims are innocent, and most are poor. Worsening social and economic conditions draw more people into criminality, a vicious circle that reinforces poverty.

15. Mental health traps.

Depression and anxiety are pervasive among the poor in developing countries—not surprisingly, they are in part the consequence of poverty and its associated powerlessness. Being unsure of where your family's next meal is coming from creates tremendous emotional stress. Many poor people are deeply ashamed of their poverty, even when it is not their fault. They commonly have to endure daily mocking and humiliation for their circumstances. And they usually feel terrible that they are unable to provide adequately for their children. This inability creates chronic feelings of hopelessness and anguish. Worse than that, in a real sense, depression and anxiety are inflicted on the poor deliberately, for the rich all too commonly abuse and terrorize the poor to keep them from gaining any bargaining power. Compounding this, poor women face domestic violence and abuse, along with a lack of personal identity, factors contributing to the much higher incidence of depression in women than men in countries such as India. Then, once depression takes hold, a poor person can become listless, exhausted, and unable to take initiative. Drug and alcohol abuse also becomes increasingly common—and so depression also becomes a cause of poverty. A vicious cycle ensues, making poor mental health a form of poverty trap.

16. Powerlessness traps.
More generally, the condition of powerlessness is a trap, in which it is not only the relatively impersonal forces such as the environment or even the market that keeps the poor ensnared, but the active connivance of the rich, who benefit from low wages and subservience. Poverty entrapment is poverty of, by, and for the rich. As Mohammad Yunus, founder of the Grameen Bank, discussed in chapter 5, told me when I visited him in Bangladesh, "The poor remain in poverty not because they want to, but because of the many barriers deliberately built around them by those who benefit from their poverty." He was referring to the nexus of landlords, colluding moneylenders, corrupt officials, and others who are probably among the very few in the world who will be better off if poverty continues than if it is ended. But there is a way out of these traps as well—the key is empowerment.

From the study of poverty traps we get confirmation that not only is poverty not the fault of the poor, neither are the things usually blamed on the poor, such as high fertility, the underlying cause of poverty—they are a result of poverty. And we gain insights into both general principles and the specifics of what poverty programs must do to be successful.

It is not a matter of making a simple diagnosis of what poverty traps impoverished families find themselves caught in. These traps are "pure types," not an exact description that necessarily applies to any one person. In particular, some poor people may show many of these "symptoms," and others may not appear to be affected by any. These traps are guides to general understanding, not a ready-made checklist to diagnosis and action.

Former World Bank official John Clark wrote in 2003 that, "virtually all the agencies involved [in development assistance] maintain that poverty reduction is their primary mission—but in truth all of us know little about it." Indeed we have a wealth of information about the wealthy—from the percentage of homes that have a television set to the "lifestyles of the rich and famous" portrayed on them—but in comparison we have poor information about poverty. Princeton economist Angus Deaton points out that even the reported number of the poor varies by as many as 200 million across different high-profile World Bank reports issued just a couple of years apart.

The reason for this may be the simplest one—there is more money to be made knowing about the rich and their habits than about the poor and their habits. But collectively, we do know more than a little about poverty. Agencies such as the Washington-based International Food Policy Research Institute (IFPRI) and the World Bank have invested a great deal in collecting better statistics through careful sampling of poor households in all parts of the world. A growing amount of information collected by the World Bank is now available on the Internet—although more of its survey information should be made available much more quickly and easily. Finally, many of the organizations fighting poverty that are featured in this book, such as Africare and BRAC, unquestionably know a great deal about both causes and remedies of the poverty afflicting their program participants. They know because they study poverty problems systematically, and because they listen attentively and continually to the poor.

With a blend of rigorous research and attentive listening, useful knowledge for ending global poverty is growing steadily.

VOICES OF THE POOR:
THE EXPERIENCE OF POVERTY

First and foremost we must listen to the poor on their own terms. It is impossible to talk with poor people in the worst slums and most impoverished rural areas without coming away deeply affected by the experience. Talking with the poor in their homes and workplaces and observing how they go about their lives breathes life into the whole effort to end poverty—it provides the inspiration for better policies and programs.

Prodded by advocates both inside and outside, the World Bank decided to talk and listen to the poor directly. With their huge resources, the Bank was able to do this on a global scale and in a systematic way. More than twenty thousand poor people were interviewed. The results were published in a three-volume set. (See http://www.worldbank.org/poverty/voices/.) One of the most striking findings of this global study is that the poor typically feel that they are worse off now than they were in the past. Presumably those who have escaped poverty feel differently. But those still poor feel more trapped than ever.

Some of this feeling of falling further behind may result from the natural tendency of people to compare themselves to others. As the rich (and middle class) grow richer, those who remain in absolute poverty may *feel* even poorer. In fact, in a real sense they are poorer, since social standing and differences in capabilities are part of the multidimensional nature of poverty. And as the economy around you develops, the gap between the capabilities of the poor and what is needed in regular employment grows greater and can become more difficult to cross.

But this is not all that the poor are saying, and we need to listen. Sometimes the growing misery of the extremely poor is quite basic—hunger is on the rise in India, life expectancies are falling in much of Africa, and millions have fallen into a chilly poverty in the former Soviet Union.

Some countries and regions have been almost entirely bypassed by development—and however impoverished the poor were a quarter century ago, they are still more desperately poor today. Ethiopia is one such place. Here are some of the things the poor in Ethiopia themselves say about the hardships they suffer, drawn from the *Voices of the Poor* report.

VOICES FROM ETHIOPIA—
WHAT IT FEELS LIKE TO BE AMONG THE ULTRAPOOR

we are left tied like straw
living by scratching like a chicken
what is life when there is no friend or food
life has made us ill
we are deprived and pale
we are above the dead and below the living
hunger is a hyena
a life that cannot go beyond food
we simply watch those who eat
difficulties have made us crazy
we sold everything we had and have become shelter-seekers
it is [like] sitting and dying alive
a life that is like being flogged
a life that makes you look older than your age
just a sip and no more drop is left
if one is full, the other will not be full
we have become empty like a hive

That is what life feels like from inside a poverty trap. You can sense that these are the voices of people in undernutrition and mental health traps. But the poor also have clear ideas about what would help them. Again from Ethiopia, the poor have specific ideas on what would reduce their poverty:

If there is the chance for employment
If there are credit facilities, the farmer can use them to increase production and improve his life
If the widow and landless women are given some sort of vocational training, they can make it a means of living
If the farmer is given some sort of training in the use of money he can save some his earnings to use it in days of difficulty
If people who suffer from dense settlement were able to move and settle in fertile, unsettled areas

The poor intuitively understand that they are also in working capital, low-skill, and farm erosion traps. But these traps are mutually reinforcing and all but impossible to escape without help.

Here are some more quotes drawn from the *Voices of the Poor* study, which reflect many kinds of poverty traps, but also the determination to go on—vividly expressed in the words of the poor from around the world.

Although basic foods cost very little, the poor regularly speak of problems in getting enough to eat.
"Lack of work worries me. My children were hungry and I told them the rice is cooking, until they fell asleep from hunger."
—An older man from Bedsa, Egypt.
Half the population in a region of Malawi "miss meals for many days, especially in the hungry months of January and February."
—Women villagers in Malawi
"In the evenings, eat sweet potatoes, sleep. In the mornings, eat sweet potatoes, work. At lunch, go without."
—Farmer in Vietnam
"There are many needs, but the principle one is food, which is not sufficient, and we don't have a place to live or the means to pay rent."   —Indigenous agricultural laborer, Guatemala
"How can you face your children day after day hungry?"
—A mother in Tanzania

The poor speak with disturbing regularity of lives surrounded by sickness and death.
"If you don't have money today, your disease will take you to your grave."   —An old woman from Ghana

"If you don't know anyone, you will be thrown to the corner of a hospital!"   —India
Well-being requires "a physically fit husband in the family and a son for every mother."   —A poor woman in Bangladesh
"Being poor is being always tired."   —Kenya
"I stopped sending my daughter to the . . . [daycare], because they insist on eating the 'Sattu' which is rotten and even the animals will not eat it. My daughter fell sick of diarrhea once after eating it."
—Village Jimmaur, India

The poor are well aware that their inability to read or get a basic education for themselves and their children is holding them back.
"If I did not go to school, how can I have [a say] in community matters; if I don't have money, who am I to talk?"
—A poor woman in rural Nigeria
"The school was o.k., but now it is in shambles, there are no teachers for weeks . . . There is no safety and no hygiene."
—A parent from Brazil
"If parents do not meet these payments, which are as high as Rs. 40 to 50 per month [about $1 at current exchange rates, a sizable sum for a sharecropper in a poorer area], the teachers were reported to beat the student or submit a failing grade for her/him."
—Pakistan
"[I]n the hospitals they don't provide good care to the indigenous people like they ought to, because of their illiteracy they treat them badly . . . they give us other medicines that are not for the health problem you have."   —A young man from La Calera, Ecuador
"Teachers do not go to school except when it is time to receive salaries."   —Nigeria

Lack of access to credit, for example, for working capital and home loans, causes serious problems
"The moneylender and the pawnshop are like husband and wife. One month we borrow from the moneylender and pay the pawnshop. The next month we borrow from the pawnshop and pay the moneylender."   —Indonesia
"I don't even think about saving-my earnings are not even enough to eat sufficiently."   —Indonesia
"Our [mud] home is in very bad condition. It leaks and looks like it is falling but we cannot afford to maintain it. This has made our lives more miserable."   —Malawi
"Some have land, but they can't buy fertilizer."   —Guatemala

The poor talk about their lack of land and other resources needed to access and benefit from markets.

"All our problems stem from lack of land. If we had enough land, we would be able to produce enough to feed our households, build houses, and train our children."   —Nigeria

"Poverty is because of the land; the person who doesn't have any must leave to do day labor."   —Ecuador

"The road is so bad that no public transportation reaches our village."   —Indonesia

"We think the earth is generous; but what is the incentive to produce more than the family needs if there are no access roads to take produce to a market?"   —Guatemala

"Today we're fine, tomorrow they will throw us out."
          —Isla Trinitaria (a squatter settlement)—Ecuador

The availability of safe water is probably the most pressing environmental problem of the poor.

"Water is life, and because we have no water, life is miserable."
          —Kenya

"We have to line up for hours before it is our turn to draw water."
          —Malawi

Other problems with environmental degradation and the loss of natural resources are widely noted.

"Rich entrepreneurs are now catching all the fish near the coast with trawlers and large fishing nets. They leave nothing for the poor fishermen."   —Fisherman in Indonesia

"The poor live at the whim and mercy of nature."
          —Farmer in Kenya

"The environment is dying and people don't understand that the problem comes from the fact that [the rich] man is killing the environment."   —Mother in Guatemala

"Ten years ago we harvested . . . eight sacks of maize per acre. Today, because of decline of soil fertility and rain and because we do not use fertilizer or improved seed, some of us get three or four sacks of maize while others harvest nothing."
          —Farmer in Tanzania

"The flood washed away all of our crops, and there was a lot of hunger around here, to the point that many people actually died of hunger."   —Farmer in Benin

The poor speak of their feelings of powerlessness in their lives and in their efforts to escape from poverty traps.

"Poverty is like living in jail, living under bondage, waiting to be free." —Jamaica

"If you want to do something and have no power to do it, it is *ta-lauchi* (poverty)." —Nigeria

"I want to commit suicide, I want to run out . . . because to see the kids crying, and I do not have one sucre [a few cents] to given them some bread. . . . Life is so sad." —A woman in Ecuador

"Poverty is lack of freedom, enslaved by crushing daily burden, by depression and fear of what the future will bring." —Georgia

"We poor men have no friends. Our only friend is the ground." —Man in Nigeria

"When one is poor, she has no say in public, she feels inferior. She has no food, so there is famine in her house; no clothing, and no progress in her family." —A woman from Uganda

"A poor person has to exist so he can serve the great one, the rich. God made things like that." —Man in Brazil

Whole communities, and many of those with low social influence such as women, minorities, low-caste families, and indigenous peoples, feel a lack of social inclusion and lack of access to needed services.

"Women are rarely consulted in matters of consequence." —Bihar, a very poor state in India

"Community decisions are the rights and responsibilities of men-folk. Women's role is only to accept and implement them." —Indonesia

"Even the non-government initiatives have at best provided marginal access to Gandas [an ethnic group labeled "tribal" in India]. There has been quite limited participation of Ganda women in the development activities promoted by NGOs." —India

"Far from defending us, the police mistreat us. . . . The police are just another gang." —Argentina

Many of the voices of the poor are unexpected and striking. The problems the poor cite often surprise outsiders: crime or local corruption; daily and yearly school scheduling; attitudes of health personnel; being ridiculed in public when they speak up about oppressive social conditions; thefts of wives by husbands. That surprise itself shows the value of giving the poor real ownership of poverty programs. Empowerment must start with the programs that are supposed to be empowering. Genuine authority must be given to organizations *of* the poor, not just those who would like to work *with* the poor.

Poverty, as the varied voices of the poor demonstrate, is multi-faceted. But there are common problems that underlie these vivid descriptions of the conditions of poverty. The poor themselves have some characteristics in common. And many aspects of poverty spring from the lack of key assets and capabilities.

A HOLISTIC UNDERSTANDING OF POVERTY

The importance of assets

In developing countries, the poor rarely have a steady and reliable job in the conventional sense. In understanding and combating poverty, the first step is to focus not just on the income or consumption levels of the poor, but more fundamentally on their underlying assets. Assets include any goods that enable the poor to draw a stream of income or consumption. A goat that provides milk, a cart with which to carry goods for sale, a marketplace stall, a bicycle enabling more distant commuting to find work, and arable land on which to grow crops, are all assets. In addition, a person's assets include less tangible properties that influence the income potentially received at any point in time. Health and skills are assets: With better health or nutrition, a poor person may be able to work more productively, and so be paid more as a laborer or produce more on their land. The same is true for higher levels of skill.

Assets yield a partially predictable, but variable return to their owners. For example, a goat produces an average amount of milk that sells on the market for an average price. If the price of milk temporarily rises, a poor person with three goats may temporarily rise out of poverty; but if it falls, a nonpoor person with ten goats may temporarily fall into poverty. Knowing a poor person's assets can help us understand whether she has suffered a temporary setback (a "shock") or whether their poverty is chronic (structural). Similarly, knowing a poor person's assets helps us understand whether she has permanently escaped from poverty, or has just been lucky, and is likely to fall back into poverty once conditions return to usual.

Thus a focus on assets of the poor helps us to know whether a person is temporarily poor, or stuck in a more intractable poverty trap; and it clarifies what a family would need to permanently escape from extreme poverty. Under some conditions, attaining an asset level that would enable an escape from poverty is possible through slow savings and accumulation by the poor. But under other conditions, the need for immediate consumption, the lack of access to credit and insurance, and other deprivations make it impossible for a family to escape from poverty without either direct assistance or broader economic or social change.

Many successful strategies for helping the poor escape from poverty traps begin by inventorying a family's or community's assets and then finding ways to build upon them. Some of these assets are obvious ones such as farm animals, or knowledge of a trade, but some are not-so-obvious, such as social networks and knowledge of peoples' abilities and character, which can also reduce poverty by helping people protect assets, smooth shocks to income through loans or informal insurance, and improve access to vital information. Another example is traditional knowledge of properties of food or medicinal plants.

Extreme poverty as deprivation of capabilities

A poor man from Ghana said: "Poverty is like heat: You cannot see it, you can only feel it; so to understand poverty, you have to go through it." That may be so. But it is possible to begin to understand once we appreciate that being chronically poor generally means being *trapped*. We have already seen some of the many interlocking poverty traps in which hundreds of millions of people find themselves. Impoverished families face a nexus of traps locking them into child labor, illiteracy, debt bondage, low skills, low working capital for their microenterprises, lack of access to information, undernutrition, environmental deterioration, and powerlessness.

The need for a holistic approach is clear from the fact that poverty traps afflict virtually every aspect of life. Nobel Laureate Amartya Sen argued that, at root, to be poor is to lack basic "capabilities to function"— that is, the ability to live the kind of life that one values. Sen reminds us that income and wealth are only instruments for other purposes. As Sen put it, "[E]conomic growth cannot be sensibly treated as an end in itself. Development has to be more concerned with enhancing the lives we lead and the freedoms we enjoy."

Sen argues that poverty cannot be properly measured by income; what matters is not the things a person has. Nor is well-being based on the feelings that possessions and consumption provide. What matters for well-being, Sen concludes, is what a person is, or *can be,* and does, or *can do.* In addition, what matters is not just the characteristics of commodities consumed, but what use a person can and does make of goods and services. For example, a book is of little value to an illiterate person (except as a status symbol or as cooking fuel).

Sen identifies several sources of disparity between incomes and actual advantages: personal differences such as disabilities or age; environmental differences such as heating needs or a high incidence of infectious diseases; variations in social climate such as the prevalence of crime or the strengths of social networks; relational differences, such as problems earning a living for a person who cannot afford the clothes or other resources needed for self-respect and social inclusion; and distribution within the family—when girls get less medical attention than boys, for example.

Thus, calculations of income that are not fully comparable across countries cannot suffice as a measure of well-being. One may have commodities, but these are of little value if they are not what consumers want (as with the example of the former Soviet Union). One may have income, but certain commodities essential for well-being, such as nutritious foods, may be unavailable. Even when providing an equal number of calories, the available staple foods in one country (casava, bread, rice, cornmeal, potatoes, etc.) will differ in nutritional content from those of other countries. Depending on climate, and conditions such as whether a woman is lactating, different nutritional needs affect how much well-being different individuals can get out of identical consumption. Finally, people may need food to fulfill requirements for social inclusion. As a result, measuring individual well-being by levels of consumption makes the mistake of thinking of commodities as ends in themselves, rather than as means to an end. In the case of nutrition, the end is health and what one can do with good health, as well as personal enjoyment and social functioning.

As Sen stresses, a person's own valuation of what kind of life would be worthwhile is not necessarily the same as what is desired or gives pleasure. For one thing, even malnourished people can have a happy disposition. The poor may learn to appreciate any small comforts they can find in life, such as a single breeze on a hot day, or may strive only for what seems attainable. If nothing could be done about a person's deprivation, this attitude of subjective bliss would have undoubted advantages in a spiritual sense, but it does not change the objective reality of deprivation. In particular, such an attitude would not prevent the happy but homeless poor person from greatly valuing an opportunity to become freed of parasites or provided with basic shelter.

Many critical problems of developing countries, such as the greater deprivations of health, nutrition, and education experienced by girls, simply cannot be adequately addressed by a focus on income, or even on family assets. Sen concludes that the expansion of freedom is both the primary end and the principal means of economic development. This perspective helps explain why development economists place so much emphasis on health and education and refer to countries with high levels of income but poor health and education standards as cases of "growth without development." Real income is essential, but any deeper appraisal of well-being leads to a consideration of health and education in addition to income.

COMMON CHARACTERISTICS OF THE POOR

Effective efforts to end poverty begin with an understanding of who the poor are. Throughout the world, the poor tend to share several characteristics. The poor tend to suffer malnutrition, poor health, and low levels of education; they live in environmentally stressed areas, have poor access to technology and markets, and lack personal and political power.

The poor are more likely to be rural, agricultural, and have little or no land. The poor also tend to come from large families, with few income earners. The problem of female-headed families living in poverty is growing in developing countries. Although the majority of poor households—as most households generally—are still headed by men, the share of female-headed poor families has grown steadily. In a number of countries they have already approached or exceeded 50 percent. The chances of being poor are far greater for a female-headed family. The chances that a person will be poor, if he or she is a member of a minority or indigenous group, is also far greater than if a person is from the majority ethnic group. In most countries, poverty is also concentrated within particular regions: In the northeast of Brazil, the northwest of Bangladesh, the southwest of Uganda, and the southeast of Ethiopia, one finds a higher percentage of the population living in poverty than the national average.

The failure to account for the characteristics of the poor in the design of poverty programs has led to tragic consequences. One example is the frequent focus of agricultural training on men in areas in which women do most of the farm work. Another example is the poor design of programs that, because of language or other barriers, fail to reach the indigenous populations, who often suffer the greatest poverty. A third example is the concentration of poverty programs on the urban poor, for political reasons or perhaps because those are the most visible to the policy community—domestic and foreign—even when the largest numbers of the poor, and the poorest of the poor, are found in rural areas. When the programs extend to rural areas they commonly focus on people who live near major roads, who are better off than the less visible poor who live farther away from these roads. However, the best NGOs are increasingly successful at targeting effective programs to the poorest.

One last characteristic of the poor is important to note: the poor generally come from poor countries. While this may seem like a tautology, it is not quite. Through one means or another—public assistance, NGO poverty programs, or the availability of employment opportunities—people who live in rich countries tend not to stay in extreme poverty. This is a good sign that if we can achieve higher incomes in the poor countries, we will be on the road to ending global poverty. While there will always be a need for a safety net, high average national income usually largely ends extreme poverty.

DOES INEQUALITY MATTER?

This book emphasizes problems of *poverty*, which leads to its focus on how people rise above and stay above an *absolute standard of well-being*. In contrast, the problem of *inequality* focuses on peoples' relative standing—their well-being *in relation to other people*. In a very poor country you could have perfect equality and everyone in extreme poverty, or in a very rich country you could have very high inequality but with the lowest-income citizen affluent enough so that no one is poor. Traditionally, the two notions of extreme poverty and inequality have been addressed separately.

However, the distinction between inequality and poverty is not so sharply drawn as was once believed. In fact, inequality may undermine individual opportunities, social cohesion, and community development, keeping individuals from attaining capabilities that influence poverty status in their own right and that also influence earning ability, as Amartya Sen has stressed.

Humans are also social beings, with a fundamental need to fit in to the human communities around us. To fit in requires consumption to a certain standard. Adam Smith observed in 1776 that one needed a linen shirt and leather shoes to show your face in public in London. Such fashion standards may make the poor unemployable, or may make the poor psychologically unable to look for better employment opportunities. And as the average consumption standards of communities rise, and extends to new products such as initially shoes, then radios, and then televisions, the poor may feel under great pressure to acquire these symbols of minimum standing in the community. If a poor family has no other money for a radio, they may forgo food and medical attention to remain respectable and connected to society. The drive to not fall too far behind ones peers seems as strong as the drive to eat high-calorie foods. It is difficult to blame the poor for buying a radio or bicycle when there is only enough food for one or two meals a day. The media and society at large are implicitly telling them that they are a failure if they do not own such goods. And owning a radio is observable (or audible in this case) to your peers in a way that the number of grams of protein you consume is not.

Inequality has other effects on poverty. For example, the more unequal the wealth, the larger the fraction of the population that is unable to put up collateral for a loan. Among other things, this means fewer children can attend school and fewer businesses and microenterprises can expand. The result is not only greater poverty, but also slower economic growth, as well as transmission of poverty across generations.

Although still somewhat controversial, a growing body of evidence suggests that inequality can make you sick. When comparing families of the same real income level but living in different countries, we find that such apparently equal people have worse health if they have less income than do a larger fraction of people within their own country or region. This may be due to the stress of being a low-status individual, to the attitudes of medical professionals toward the relatively poor, or to people behaving like the example above, giving up meals to be able to afford the minimum symbols of status.

We do not need to greatly reduce inequality before we can achieve basic goals, such as minimum nutrition and literacy. Indeed we are already making great progress. Illiteracy rates have been steadily falling and nutrition steadily improving on average around the world. *Some* local increases in measured inequality are merely a statistical figment of the fact that some of the poor escape from poverty before others. However, to make further progress in the struggle to end poverty it is crucial to stay attuned to social context. The health, psychological, social, and political power dimensions of poverty must be taken into account when designing programs to meet basic needs. If worsening inequality spills over to other forms of deprivation of capabilities, then either the underlying inequality or at least its poverty impact must be addressed. Clearly, world inequality has greatly increased since the industrial revolution, although there is little agreement about whether international inequality is *currently* rising. But we need to pay attention to rising local inequality, when this results from gains for the rich at the expense of gains for the poor—particularly when this leads to a worsening of poverty in the broad sense of this book.

THE KEYS TO CAPABILITY

EIGHT KEYS TO ESCAPING POVERTY TRAPS

The escape from poverty requires the keys to unlock poverty traps. In providing various kinds of freedom, the keys to capability are intrinsically valuable. They also open the door to increasing income and wealth, which can in turn provide the means for building further capabilities and assets and resiliency to the many risks and shocks that people in developing countries face. Only with sufficient capabilities and assets can a person's escape from poverty be reasonably secure over the long run. Acquiring the keys to capability can enable most people to use their resourcefulness to escape from extreme poverty, even when they do not live in high-growth countries and their standard of living remains very modest.

The keys to capability are closely interrelated. Unlocking one capability can sometimes help unlock others, but by the same token, the benefits of having one key are inherently limited if you lack the others.

THE FIRST KEY

Health and Nutrition for Adults to Work and Children to Grow to their Potential

When we count our blessings we often say "at least we have our health." Such a remark is heard much more rarely in the poorest countries. Health requires good nutrition, safe water, and knowledge, as well as access to medical care when needed. Nutrition in turn depends on health. In the poorest countries all these requirements are sorely lacking.

I remember meeting with a group of villagers in a remote area of the African bush. These were very poor people: They lived in mud huts, had no running water, no electricity, no telephones, not even battery-operated radios. The villagers' way of life was under threat. Invading land grabbers had stolen land and resources. Most of the people were illiterate, or nearly so; there was no sign of a newspaper or any reading materials for many miles around.

The village leader welcomed me through a translator and told me proudly, we are doing much better now, our lives are improving. Look at our people, he said: No one here is starving, we all have enough to eat, and as you can see all here are healthy, no one is sick. Though they lacked security, the people were healthy and well fed. Though this was not sufficient to get and stay out of poverty, they had at least temporary if precarious control of their health and basic nutrition, an essential prerequisite for doing so, and a treasured possession in its own right.

But the same cannot be said for the 842 million who are chronically hungry, according to a report of the UN's Food and Agriculture Organization in November 2003. Undernutrition is responsible for more than half of the infant and child deaths in poor countries, according to a 2004 study in the *American Journal of Clinical Nutrition*.

The poor do not need much to meet their basic nutrition. In most cases an extremely small amount of money would be enough for people to escape undernutrition traps in which they have too little nourishment to be able to work with sufficient strength. And yet, when the poor are asked what they need the most frequent answer is adequate food. To end poverty we must make it a top priority to address hunger. Good jobs can pay for food. But even without regular, formal sector jobs, if the poor are well nourished (and have the other keys to capability), they can frequently use their creativity to earn a basic living in microenterprises and other activities.

Food security is defined by the U.S. Agency for International Development (USAID) as "a state when all people at all times have both the physical and economic access to sufficient food to meet their dietary needs for a productive and healthy life." Food security has three components: food availability, food access, and adequate food utilization (knowing and providing a proper diet, safe water, and sanitation).

There is no shortage of food in the world as a whole—there is only a shortage of entitlement to food. But that does not mean the problem of hunger is best or most easily solved by shipping food from its current location to where people are hungry. It is easy to imagine that if the world is currently producing enough calories of food, the answer is to ship more food. There are times when this is possible and the correct response, such as the current crisis in Sudan.

But as a general policy, shipping food as part of foreign aid is not effective for two reasons. The first is the perverse effect it has on the rural population, where poverty is concentrated. Food shipments will generally lower the price of food in the cities, where better-off people tend to live. Very little food aid will reach the rural areas where the chronically poor live, largely because they lack the political clout to demand it. The impact may well be to make poor farmers worse off, because the greater supply of food has lowered the national food price. The second reason that food aid does not work stems from a blend of politics and markets. For example, the government of India calls the country "food self sufficient"; but this is because the *market* demand for food is met by local supply. However, the market demand is woefully low because of the impoverishment of nearly half its people.

A permanent solution is to increase the purchasing power of the poor—and create local entitlements for people when for whatever reason they cannot provide a minimum number of calories for their family. As long as most of the poor remain farmers, it is vital to improve the productivity of their farms, along with ensuring their claim on the income from that productivity. This in turn generally means helping poor farmers to gain the keys to capability.

Access to clean water, and to basic sanitation, are also critical. Benjamin Franklin famously said, "[w]hen the well is dry, we know the worth of water." Studies consistently show that women without water in or near their homes spend about two hours a day fetching it—when they do not have long waits in line. We say that time is money. For the poorest of the poor, time is survival.

If the water is not safe, we can buy bottled water, but the poor cannot. So if the water is not safe, the poor have to boil it. This uses up scarce fuel wood; and the fires create indoor and outdoor air pollution, one of the unheralded health risks in poorer countries.

If the water is not safe, people will get sick. The poor are sick many more days than the non-poor. The poor must spend a large fraction of their time fending off illness, trying to recover after illness strikes them or their children, and facing the prospect of an untimely death.

Finally, better health knowledge among the poor is critically needed. In Africa, the Andes, and elsewhere, people in isolated villages still believe that if a child has diarrhea she should not be given water, because they believe that the system is trying to "expel water." Many people believe that sex with a virgin can cure AIDS. Popular opinions about reproductive health sometimes bear little relation to modern medicine. Although enormous progress has been made, further improvements in basic knowledge are essential to improving health and nutrition. The use of radio messages in rural Kenya and elsewhere has helped; but it is difficult to make sustained progress in public knowledge where literacy skills remain limited.

Public health has improved dramatically in recent years, and with this improvement the worst forms of poverty have decreased. Yet easily preventable, debilitating illnesses continue in many countries. We can affordably provide safer and cleaner water, basic nutrition, and cooking fuel alternatives, along with health education, mosquito control, and basic medicines.

To be able to say "at least I have my health" is indeed great wealth, helping unlock the door to a good life.

⊶ THE SECOND KEY

Basic Education to Build the Foundations for Self-Reliance

In West Africa, poor people with no apparent vision problems will sometimes say, "I am blind." This startling expression means "I am illiterate." In fact, to be illiterate in the twenty-first century is truly to be blind to much of what the world has to offer.

Unfortunately, the problems of illiteracy can be subtle, and solving them is not as simple as ABC. Tens of millions of people in rural Asia, Africa, and Latin America speak only indigenous and tribal languages that are very different from the dominant language. This makes literacy difficult to attain. First, governments rarely make it easy to learn to read in indigenous languages, and even if you are one of the few around you who can do so, reading materials are limited. To learn to read, you typically first have to learn to speak the official language of the country, be it Spanish or Swahili, which may be entirely unrelated to the language spoken by everyone around you. Then, you have to learn to read and write in that strange tongue, which you find hard even to practice speaking.

Language barriers have afflicted almost all of us who have traveled extensively abroad. Being unable to read a sign in a foreign language is a window onto the world of the illiterate. The insight this situation can bring occurred to me recently when I was traveling in a van with a group of people in a remote rural area, returning from a visit to a poverty program. Two people who spoke English were present, and the conversation was being translated for me. But as we neared the end of the journey, first one of the people who spoke English was dropped off at his destination, then the other. The conversation continued, but it became opaque to me. It was as if the lights had gone out. In a way illiteracy is like trying to function after a power failure. Almost anything you try to do is blocked by the lack of electricity. Similarly, in a modernizing world almost anything you might do to improve your life is blocked by illiteracy.

When I have little chance to practice speaking a foreign language, I lose my language ability all too quickly. Although it is difficult to imagine forgetting how to read and write in your own language, experts say that this is in fact a real problem for semi-literate people.

Opportunities of literacy include being able to read signs, to fill out forms to apply for jobs, credit, or almost any service, even to use a telephone. Illiterate people find tricks to get by but will also have to avoid many situations that otherwise could be advantageous to them. People who have trouble counting coins may be laughed at and humiliated in the marketplace. Peasants frequently recount how their incomes rose when they attained basic literacy and numeracy—simply from being able to avoid getting cheated when selling their agricultural produce.

Despite the fundamental importance of basic education, even today the United Nationals Development Program (UNDP) estimates as many as 113 million primary school–age children still do not attend school at all. Many children who enroll in government schools find no desks, no books, and often as not, no teachers.

⊶ THE THIRD KEY

Credit and Basic Insurance for Working Capital and Defense against Risk

For the poor rural peasant, access to credit provides the chance to purchase tools, a draft animal, or a small tractor, and irrigation. These animals and instruments can help a farmer greatly improve her productivity, help her diversify crops, and help her move toward commercial farming. Fertilizer, once a luxury, is now essential for survival in many poor areas, where population growth has necessitated an end to traditional practices that left land uncultivated for many years to restore its fertility.

For the poor rural landless laborer, access to credit can mean a chance to purchase raw materials (such as cloth) and tools (such as a sewing machine), and eventually move from the edge of survival to becoming an established businessperson. For the poor urban peddler, access to credit can mean a chance to build a bigger inventory so that she has items on hand when customers request them, and so that she can eventually move from the insecurity of being a petty street hawker to the stability of being an established vendor.

This message—that credit can be a powerful tool for poverty alleviation—has spread throughout the world. There has been a virtual explosion of microfinance institutions, sometimes called village banks—many sponsored and supported by donors in the developed countries. Millions of borrowers have taken part, and these banks have done much good, particularly when accompanied by programs that help the poor gain some of the other keys to capability. But the spread has still been limited. To be commercially profitable, the emphasis has been on lending to the richest of the poor. It has been estimated that microfinance institutions are currently serving only 11 percent of the world's 240 million poorest families. The effort to provide credit and insurance to the poorest to help them escape from working capital traps has only just begun.

At the same time, even people seemingly well above the poverty line in many parts of the developing world are vulnerable to catastrophic events that can throw their families into destitution.

Credit and insurance are usually thought of as ways of building or protecting wealth, and they are that; but they are also important means of realizing practical freedom. Credit makes us free to build an enterprise that provides fulfilling—and remunerative—work. Credit can turn dreams into reality. Without credit, many things we could afford to do based on our lifetime resources, such as buy a home or go to college—or, in a developing country, buy a sewing machine or keep a child in primary school—can remain out of reach.

Not being able to take out insurance can distort almost everything a person does. Insurance frees people to use resources to build new capabilities and assets, rather than saving up just in case an unlikely but devastating outcome occurs. It frees people from unnecessary worries. The poor are willing to pay for credit and insurance, but in all too many cases neither has been available to the poor at any reasonable price, or at any price at all.

Small farmers try to cope with price and weather risks by diversifying their production, but this keeps them from getting the often-substantial profits that come from specializing in one or two crops. A cushion of subsistence crops provides something to eat if the market price of the cash crop collapses: this is an advantage of setting aside a small portion of your land to grow food for your own consumption. But the bad news is that this reduces monetary income. And while I often hear the opinion that it would be nicer if farmers in developing countries didn't have to produce cash crops, this sentiment is little more than a romantic illusion. The costs of the subsistence lifestyle are just too high for the poor. We know this from the statistics on the extreme poverty of subsistence farmers, and we know it from watching and talking to farmers. Farmers in America don't choose to produce primarily for subsistence, and neither would the poor in Africa if they had a real choice. The lack of price or weather insurance is needlessly holding down the incomes of the desperately poor.

But even health, education, and credit are of limited help if you lack access to markets and barriers to the accumulation of assets.

THE FOURTH KEY

Access to Functioning Markets for Income and Opportunities to Acquire Assets

On December 10, 1948, the United Nations General Assembly adopted the Universal Declaration of Human Rights. Article 17 of the Declaration asserts that: "Everyone has the right to own property alone as well as in association with others" and "no one shall be arbitrarily deprived of his property."

If every poor person had these rights, with real access to functioning markets, it would provide a great foundation—a step to equal opportunity. But many of the poor simply cannot take part freely in economic life. Opportunity includes the ability to start a business. But when economic power is overwhelmingly concentrated in the hands of elites, the natural entrepreneurial abilities most people are born with are snuffed out. The rich may find ways to skim or steal outright the newly growing assets of the poor. In Mozambique, registering a new business requires 19 steps taking over 5 months—showing that part of the problem also rests with government bureaucracy. To end global poverty reforms are needed both of government policies and of markets and the distribution of wealth.

The need of the poor for land is critical, and is also emblematic of problems gaining access to markets and productive resources. Genuine land reform on economically viable farmland is an essential part of the struggle to end global poverty. Most of the poor are still rural, often living in remote areas. If you ask the rural poor what is most important to them, what would make the biggest positive difference in their lives, they frequently say owning enough of their land to make a living, and holding it securely. This is an overwhelming concern in densely settled South Asia, but also in Latin America and Africa: Remember the Nigerian who said, "[a]ll our problems stem from lack of land." A UN study has concluded that at least a half a billion people—100 million households—depend for a living on farming land that they do not securely own, whether as day laborers, sharecroppers, tenants, or as squatters (in the eyes of the law, however long they have been farming there). When farmers have insecure land tenure rights, there is also an incentive to treat land as a short-term resource.

Unfortunately, landless farmers or those eking out a living on a tiny plot of land cannot directly purchase land from the big landowners. This is because credit markets do not function adequately enough to provide a loan. Even if they did, the price of land is too high, because the big landowners are unwilling to dilute their holdings. Ownership confers many benefits beyond the income from farming activities, such as disproportionate political influence and social prestige. Only an active policy of land reform can provide the needed changes. Land reform has failed in many countries because of either poor design or political maneuvering, but where it has succeeded, such as in Taiwan and South Korea, it has made an enormous difference for poverty reduction. Although both of these economies are better known for manufactured exports, they experienced substantial periods in which rural income growth exceeded that of urban income growth, partly because of the greater efficiency and lower inequality that followed land reform.

Even with enough land to move beyond subsistence you have to be able to sell what you produce. It is still common to come across regions in low-income countries where many farmers live on paths impassable by vehicles, miles from the nearest functional road. As a poor person in rural Ecuador said, "a community without roads does not have a way out." Roads give people essential connections to markets—and a way out of poverty.

⊶   THE FIFTH KEY

Access to the Benefits of New Technologies for Higher Productivity

Basic literacy and numeracy are of intrinsic value. But to be most effective in helping the poor to take advantage of market opportunities, raise their productivity, and escape from poverty traps, there must also be access to useful knowledge and improved technologies. Access to new technology lets a person with basic literacy become functionally literate in that branch of knowledge—connecting a poor person to some of the technologies that could lift her out of poverty.

There have already been great benefits of new technologies for poverty reduction, from contraception and medicines, to high-yielding crop varieties, to telecommunications. In India, computer-assisted learning for the poor coming to school at a somewhat older age has proven highly effective. When electrification has reached rural villages, and been distributed in a way that gives access to the poor, clear benefits have been recorded. A child who works in the fields after school can now do his homework at home after dark. Cellphones in Bangladesh have made an enormous difference. For example, you don't have to spend the whole day going to the city in order to have a conversation with someone or resolve a problem. This way people can use their time much more productively, working on their farms or businesses. But cellphones and access to the Internet do not come automatically. In many cases NGOs concerned with poverty have taken the vital first steps.

Ultimately, the poor need more than just specific job skills—these may become obsolete. They need to learn to learn, to learn how to adapt and make flexible use of new technologies. Teaching new skills in the context of immediate problems faced by the poor reinforces learning and helps participants to move to the next steps needed to escape from poverty. The contexts in which the poor learn new skills become important in themselves. Learning skills as a member of a solidarity group can also help build confidence, offer personal support, and reinforce learning.

⊶ THE SIXTH KEY

A Non-Degraded and Stable Environment to Ensure Sustainable Development

Lake Victoria beckons from the history books and the map, an apparent oasis, a great lake of Africa. Surely the people who live there, if anywhere, have a beautiful environment and a steady source of food. The reality on the ground is far different.

Watching the Kenyan boys fish along the shores of Lake Victoria, one sees some of the limits to the old catchphrase, "teach a man to fish, feed him for a lifetime." There are many impediments to making this simple solution work. Fishing skills are of limited help in a dying lake. In Kenya the human population is rising and the fish population is falling, due to a combination of overfishing and pollution. Water hyacinths, introduced from Asia, choke out other life and provide a breeding ground for malarial mosquitoes and parasites.

Just as we have an escalating pace of new diseases emerging in the world, no doubt there will be an acceleration of environmental shocks, the results of which we cannot anticipate. Some result from the accidental importation of pests, such as the Asian beetle invasion in the United States, a byproduct of increased world trade. Others, like global warming, result from accumulated choices of millions of people decentralized around the globe, especially those of us in the rich countries. Rising sea levels from increased warming threatens to inundate many islands and densely populated coastal regions of developing countries. Eight million people in densely populated Bangladesh live in coastal areas likely to be affected by rising sea levels in the next few decades. Environmental crises are looming as the biggest barrier to progress against poverty. As Walt Kelly put it so well, "We have met the enemy, and he is us."

Rapid population growth creates a race between needed and available resources. It challenges carrying capacity and can ultimately lead to ecological collapse, as indeed looms in parts of the Sahel, where desertification and other forms of environmental degradation threaten to make growth unsustainable and the cost of ecological restoration unattainable.

The poor are both victims and also unwitting perpetrators of environmental degradation. A common conjecture is that the richest billion and poorest billion people do most environmental damage. The poor have a high rate of fertility. They practice slash and burn agriculture in the tropical rainforests. They overuse soil, overforage for fuelwood. The cause is poverty.

With increasing income, the poor are able to improve their environment, through both individual and collective action. With the aid of NGOs, the poor learn how to maintain the environment, and to get help with environmental protection when it is needed. In part because of the damage that we in the rich countries are indirectly doing to the environment of the poor countries, we will have to accept that there will be a need for assistance for poor countries for some time to come.

Problems of the urban environment receive less attention than rural problems. But slum dwellers face environmental hazards that can exceed those in rural areas. The rich find ways to insulate themselves from the worst of it, although they are by no means immune, but the poor suffer the greatest impact. Urban statistics often understate problems of poverty. For example, as pointed out by Jan Vandemoortele, head of the Poverty Group of the UNDP, national statistics may count slum dwellers as having "access" to safe water as long as they live within 100 meters (328 feet) of a public water tap—assuming that one tap can serve the needs of five hundred to one thousand people in that zone, and that the tap or pump actually works.

Urban environmental problems are stark in Kibera, a shantytown of somewhere between a half million and three quarters of a million people, no one really knows more precisely. Located just a short walk from the modern high-rise office buildings and hotels of downtown Nairobi, Kibera is Africa's largest and most infamous slum. The word actually means jungle in one of Kenya's tribal languages. Most of the makeshift homes consist of a small single room, typically with a mud floor and no window, in which five people may try to survive. The lack of sanitation is legendary; open pit latrines are common. Crime is high, and at night it is unsafe even to venture outside to use them. Among the peri-urban perils of Kibera are "flying toilets." Lacking public toilets, let alone sanitation in the home, people defecate into plastic bags and hurl them out the door onto their neighbors' roofs. This would be bad enough, but apparently the hurlers often fall short of their targets. A UN study found that a majority of the landlords of Kibera were actually government officials and politicians.

Without empowerment, in many cases the poor can do little to protect their own environments.

THE SEVENTH KEY

Personal Empowerment to Gain Freedom from Exploitation and Torment

George Bernard Shaw said, "Poverty doesn't produce unhappiness—it produces degradation." Indeed it does. But degradation also works perniciously to keep you from escaping your poverty. "When one is poor, she has no say in public, she feels inferior" said the woman in Uganda.

Personal empowerment may be the most important key to capability, because it can unlock the strongbox where other keys are found. Professor Yunus, founder of the Grameen Bank said, "a $20 loan is really just a pretext to give a woman an opportunity to find out who she is, to give her a chance to open up her natural creativity."

Poverty and powerlessness are two sides of the same coin. When the poor are powerless they remain poor. Those without power find it very difficult to get the power and resources they need to make a better life. All too commonly, local elites work to reinforce this vicious cycle. When elites benefit from others' poverty or powerlessness, they often actively perpetuate both. They do this with coercive exploitation enforced with terror. When you ask the poor about their lives, they frequently speak of their feelings of impotence and fear. "Today we're fine, tomorrow they will throw us out," said the squatter in Ecuador. "If you don't know anyone, you will be thrown to the corner of a hospital!" said the man in rural India.

The *Voices of the Poor* study found that "mental health problems—stress, anxiety, depression, lack of self-esteem, and suicide are among the more commonly identified effects of poverty and ill-being by discussion groups," particularly in Latin America and the Caribbean. This is starkly seen in the woman in Ecuador who said "I want to commit suicide, I want to run out . . . because to see the kids crying and I do not have one sucre to give them some bread. . . . Life is so sad." The poor and those who live in close proximity to them are well aware of these links. In parts of Africa, people describe a mental condition associated with poverty as "madness." Mental health has deteriorated significantly in the former Soviet Union and southeast Europe, along with the general decline in health and incomes.

Depression and anxiety are often considered afflictions of affluent societies, but they are pervasive among the poor in developing countries.

These mental health problems are a consequence of poverty, but then become also its cause—another poverty trap. This is rarely taken seriously as a medical issue for the poor. Malnutrition, malaria, parasites, and other infections all are obvious, basic medical problems, while mental illness may not be. Yet mental health matters in developing countries; it is not a question of addressing other aspects of survival first before the "luxury" of psychological well-being can be addressed. Mental illness deprives the poor of "capabilities to function." Poor mental health, in addition, is also often associated with poor physical health.

In some African countries AIDS is creating a virtual generation of orphans. Over ten million AIDS orphans lived in Africa in 2000. Children whose parents died of AIDS face stigma and low self-esteem, in addition to other handicaps. Providing basic needs for these orphans, ensuring that they are not discriminated against out of irrational fears, and seeing that they are able to obtain the few years of schooling that will help rescue them from absolute poverty is a major challenge in the struggle against poverty. It is not a challenge to which Africa, with all its problems, is accustomed. Traditionally, extended family networks have provided for children who lost their parents. Because of the scope of the AIDS crisis, in some parts of East Africa this traditional family adaptation to death is on the verge of collapse. Political analysts claim conditions are ripe not only for child abuse and exploitation, but for recruiting children for guerilla armies led by unscrupulous aspiring dictators or mercenary groups. The resulting destabilization and diversion of resources can have a devastating social and economic development impact.

Thus, sometimes the outside forces causing poverty traps operate at too large a scale for individual empowerment to be sustainable. Individual empowerment must take place in a context of participation in much broader, empowered *communities*. This leads us to the final key.

☞ THE EIGHTH KEY

Community empowerment to ensure effective participation in the wider world

"Powerlessness corrupts. Absolute powerlessness corrupts absolutely."

When Harvard Business School professor Rosabeth Moss Kanter inverted the familiar aphorism of Lord Acton she was talking about the corporation. Kanter was concerned about the loss of innovation and potential in a company when many of the workers are kept powerless. Kanter concluded that it was the structure of the corporation—rather than the employee's inability or unwillingness to wield power for themselves—that prevented many, particularly women, from exercising power. While we may not fully share her optimism that "those who feel powerful are more likely to empower others," it is surely true of communities that "organizational power grows when it is shared."

Kanter's aphorism rings true when looking at the misery and denigration of life as an impoverished person or community facing what seems to be the incalculable power of the major employer or landlord. When you speak to the rich, they tell you of the listlessness of the poor, of their lack of initiative, and of their need for paternal guidance. But having power is critical to your ability to take control of your life, and to take advantage of opportunities to escape from poverty traps. The analogy with the management trend of participation and empowerment in the corporation is an imperfect one. But empowering the poor also frees them to innovate, to envision new possibilities, to become more productive, to find new ways to solve problems, and to form productive, cooperative relationships with others to achieve shared goals.

For Kanter power is two things: "First, access to the resources, information and support necessary to carry out a task; and second, ability to get cooperation in doing what is necessary." These also reflect the constraints that hold back poor communities and the individuals who constitute them.

To escape from poverty requires empowered people within a community that is empowered to function within the wider world. The poor depend on their community's security to survive, to defend their rights, and to preserve their opportunities to improve the lives of their families. Where communities and social networks are strong they need to be carefully protected; where communities are weak everything must be done to develop them.

Individual empowerment is necessary but insufficient. *Communities* of the poor must be collectively empowered: this is a basis for entitlement, and a deterrent to the communal violence against communities of the poor that reinforces their poverty. Communities must have and maintain peace to be empowered. Civil strife is still one of the greatest impediments to ending global poverty. Community empowerment is key to security.

Well-being is fundamentally individual, but it is also social. Direct participation in ones' immediate community, and indirect participation in the larger society, can affect well-being. At the basic village, neighborhood, or township level, to escape from poverty you must have a voice within your community that is taken seriously when you have a legitimate concern. Your community, or communities, however humble, must be informed, empowered to stand up for their interests, and able to defend their rights.

Self-esteem also comes from being able to help others in ones community. The poor stress their inability to help people they love as one of the worst features of their poverty.

The arbitrary application of law and regulation can also be a burden to the poor and their families. For example, without identity cards and other documents it is impossible to get benefits you are entitled to, as well as to get loans, so as to make progress. Many of the poor never had these documents—their parents could not afford them. Many others lost them—this is easy to understand given the wretched conditions under which many of the poor must live. Documents are expensive, or very difficult to get; it may require going to your place of birth. Getting new documents may require proof of your identity: a Catch–22 for those trying to get proof of their identity. Many have no idea where to begin. If the poor can obtain documents at all it is likely through strenuous efforts, squandered time, payments of bribes or fees tantamount to bribes, and humiliation. The poor need the power to enjoy the rule of law as a reality, not just an abstract right.

I was once told in a low-income country, while trying to buy an airline ticket but lacking an obscure approval stamp, "come back tomorrow. You bring something for us, and maybe we will have something for you." I saved my dignity by finding a way to get a ticket without having to bribe. But it felt insulting, and if I had paid it would have felt demeaning. Unlike most of those who are pressured to give a bribe, I had not just money but alternatives, knowledge of the world, contacts—and a U.S. passport. Following this obscure regulation to the letter by going through the process to obtain the stamp or by leaving the country by land, would have cost me two or three days (not even lost really—as I could have used the time reading and writing) and or two or three hundred dollars—a minor inconvenience for me but a cost utterly beyond the reach of the poor. It is not surprising that many of the poor do not even try to deal with the establishment. But as we shall see there are things that can be done even in these circumstances to help the poor.

As the *Voices of the Poor* study concluded, "[a]ll too often poor people report experiencing law and law enforcement not as a means to a better life, but as obstacles. They say a key challenge is staying ahead of public authorities and well-organized criminals bent on shutting them down, intimidating them, or demanding bribes." In this situation, formal legal empowerment of individuals is not enough; communities of the poor must be collectively empowered.

The poor need democracy and human rights as much as do the rich. These are not luxuries we can indulge in once we are rich enough. Amartya Sen argues that famines do not occur in functioning democracies because of the power of a free press. This may not be an iron law of political economy—Malawi has been at least a semi-functioning democracy since 1993, despite its current famine—but the empowerment of democracy and a free press can make a decisive difference by calling attention to an emerging crisis at an early stage, giving politicians an incentive to speak out and respond to it, and mobilizing society and the international community to address it.

Empowerment supports the other keys to capability. Without empowerment there may be no access to markets and land. While greater income can do much even in the short run, it cannot guarantee a sustainable escape from poverty traps if the poor are still not in a position to access education and healthcare, if they cannot demand that government provide a functioning road to a wider market, if income can only be gained in a grossly demeaning or dependency producing way, or if the poor live and work in an environment being undermined by outside forces lacking accountability. As John Clark, a World Bank official, has asked of the familiar proverb of teaching a man to fish, "Are the poor really just . . . waiting to learn how to fish? Or is the issue really one of power and poverty?"

The goals and means are often the same in the best poverty alleviation programs. Health, education, environmental sustainability, personal and community empowerment, access to economic opportunity: All these are worthy ends in themselves as well as prerequisites for escaping poverty traps. Effective poverty programs don't just deliver services—they build capabilities and sustainable assets.

PART II

ESCAPING THE CRUEL
TRAP OF POVERTY

HOW THE POOR CAN GAIN
THE KEYS TO CAPABILITY

Even in the poorest regions of the world, far from the major growth engines of the global economy, and in the face of many handicaps, good work is being done to help the poor gain the keys to capability and escape from poverty traps. Part II of the book takes a close look at innovative and inspiring programs in areas such as the Andes, Sub-Saharan Africa, and rural South Asia that remain outside the mainstream of the world economy.

Up to this point, we have looked at what poverty is, why it can be a trap, who the poor are. But what exactly is a poverty program? Many definitions are possible, but the one I use casts a fairly wide net: *A poverty program is an intentional and systematic attempt to change the status quo (or equilibrium) in a way that reduces poverty.*

Keep in mind that identification of effective or innovative programs is not a science; it relies on a combination of statistical and case study methods tempered by judgment. Moreover, there are many other excellent poverty strategies. Although chosen carefully, programs featured in this book are not necessarily superior to many others that are not covered. Instead, these cases are intended to be illustrative of the broad range of promising work now being carried out, and to encourage thinking outside the box about what could be done to meet some of the less-obvious needs of the poor.

3

HEALTH, NUTRITION, AND POPULATION

Our hopes for ending global poverty depend on better health for the poor. Health begins with safe water. But water is all too often scarce, far away, contaminated, or a combination of the three, threatening our efforts.

SOUTH AFRICA: SAFE WATER AND HEALTHY CHILDREN

In rural South Africa, the poor often live one or two miles or more from sources of water, which must be drawn from streams, or, for the lucky, drawn from hand pumps, although either method is physically straining on tired women, who are generally the ones who fetch the water. Risks of cholera and other diseases found in contaminated water are high. Needless to say, the poor cannot afford the piping and power pumps (even if they could get electricity) that are used by the rich. So the women must trudge twice a day to collect water, wasting desperately needed hours. You can often see their children following sullenly behind. When a little older, the children themselves must fetch the water. These children have generally never enjoyed the playground equipment we take for granted.

The Solution: enter Roundabout Outdoor with its ingenious invention, the Roundabout Playpump. The company developed a low-maintenance merry-go-round (also called a roundabout) for children to spin around in, started and sped up with their feet: the kind of playground staple many of us remember from childhood. But the spinning action is used as power for pumping water out of a well dug nearby, which is then sent up to a water tank a few meters above the ground. The design has an innovative way of converting the circular motion of the toy into up-and-down motion for drawing water using only two moving parts. The children get a playground toy that they really delight in. The Playpumps are often placed in schools, giving children an additional incentive to attend (at least they like the recess time). The children help their families and communities get better access to water simply by having a good time. Children at play may be one of the great renewable resources of the world. The only problem is convincing the kids to get off the Playpump when it's time to come home.

The pump is effective to a depth of about 100 meters, and at 40 meters is considered remarkably efficient—significantly better than what a hand pump could deliver even with great effort. And the water is much safer now. By pumping the water with proper plumbing and storing the water in a covered tank, waste and the risk of contamination are reduced. Environmental damage is lessened by drawing water from deeper in the water table. For all these benefits, the Playpump costs only about $5,000. That is about $12.50 for each of the approximately 400 people who benefit from each installed Playpump—an investment that is quickly returned just from the time saved in fetching water. The first two pumps were installed in KwaZulu Natal in Masinga district in 1994; they were recently replaced with new models, but the originals were still in good working condition without special maintenance since their installation a decade earlier.

Many Playpumps have been financed through grants. The project was a winner of a $165,000 World Bank development marketplace award. The government and other donors have helped to expand the program. Over 500 Playpumps have been installed to date, and over 200,000 South Africans have benefited. Roundabout is now moving into Mozambique with the planned installation of 130 Playpumps in cooperation with the World Bank and its International Finance Corporation (IFC) private sector arm. They are also soon to move into Zambia with 40 Playpumps, in partnership with UNICEF. Simple calculations show that the Playpumps are a sound social investment just on the benefits of safer water and the time and effort saved—even before we consider either the special environmental benefits, or the direct value of the playground for the children.

Though maintenance costs are low, these are not trivial to impoverished villagers. Maintenance is financed with small advertising billboards on the sites. Some contain messages to help prevent the spread of HIV, a scourge in South Africa now infecting almost a quarter of the adult population. The advertiser is designated as a sponsor of the Playpump. This way financial sustainability is more likely—an important consideration in the developing world in which the attention span of governments and development agencies seems very short. The project is clearly something that can be replicated in many parts of the world in thousands of villages, and

Figure 3.1   Play power: Merry-go-round-powered village water supply with a message. Photo: Roundabout Playpumps

interest is growing in transferring this new technology to other countries in Africa and Asia. In fact, as we toured sites in South Africa, Roundabout CEO Trevor Field told me of agreements to get amusement parks in the US, Japan, and Europe to install Playpumps, along with videos showing how they help solve problems of poverty, and providing an opportunity for parents to contribute.

FIGHTING HIV/AIDS:
THE AIDS SUPPORT ORGANIZATION, UGANDA

Now the leading cause of death of working-age adults in the developing world, if unchecked AIDS may condemn Sub-Saharan Africa, the hardest hit region, to grinding poverty for at least another generation. In 2004, some 42 million people worldwide were infected with HIV, with over 34 million of these in Sub-Saharan Africa. There the prevalence rate is now estimated at 8.8 percent of the adult population, with women representing 55 percent of the infected. The impact of the disease is approaching that of the bubonic plague of Medieval Europe.

The World Health Organization (WHO) estimates that, by 2002, nearly 22 million people had died from AIDS since the disease was identified in the 1980s, with the large majority of deaths occurring in Sub-Saharan Africa. Throughout the region AIDS is now the leading cause of death of adult males in economically active years. Although infectious childhood diseases still kill far more people in developing countries, AIDS strikes those who have successfully run this gauntlet of child killers. Their societies need the energies and skills of precisely the part of the population most afflicted.

Even today, AIDS is widely perceived in the developing world as a disease of developed countries and one primarily afflicting homosexuals. However, in the developing countries as a whole AIDS is primarily transmitted by heterosexual intercourse. In addition, infected blood and needles, both by drug abusers and in hospitals, and perinatal transmission (from mother to fetus) play significant roles. In low-income countries average survival once AIDS symptoms set in has been less than one year. Recently, the media has hailed progress in making antiretroviral medication and other expensive treatments available to low-income countries at much reduced prices, or even free of charge. Unfortunately, these lifesaving drugs are still not available to the overwhelming majority of the infected in Africa and South Asia because of limited availability of the low-priced drugs, slow implementation, and inadequate health system infrastructure to get the medicines to patients in these countries. In the absence of these drugs, treatments have generally been limited to aspirin, antibiotics for infections, and cortisone for skin rashes.

Some NGOs are responding to AIDS with innovations that have resulted in a significant humanitarian and poverty alleviation impact. Uganda was the first country to be hit hard with an AIDS pandemic, but, partly through the work of NGOs, the country became a model for how to contain such an explosion of HIV and to treat its victims with dignity. The AIDS Support Organization, or TASO, has played a crucial role in treatment, family assistance, and counseling. It has been instrumental in prodding government into action, and helping Uganda to respond to AIDS.

A Uganda-based and locally governed NGO, TASO was founded by Noerine Kaleeba in 1987, after her husband died of AIDS contracted through a blood transfusion. Its goal is to help people to "live positively with AIDS." Patient testimonials suggest that the counseling makes a big impact on how people live after learning they are HIV positive. Some of these patients have themselves become activists in the organization, and many other TASO staff and volunteers are also people living with HIV/AIDS.

Uganda-based TASO was the first indigenous NGO in Africa to respond to the needs of people living with HIV/AIDS, and it has received accolades for its pioneering and successful efforts to disseminate AIDS education to the local grassroots levels and relieve the suffering of AIDS patients. TASO won the King Baudouin International Development Prize in 1994. Recently TASO has garnered much attention, with visits by U.S. Secretary of State Powell in 2001 and by President Bush in 2003.

The AIDS Support Organization has played a crucial role in Uganda's long fight against AIDS, in the fields of treatment, family assistance, and counseling, as well as general education. It works in the areas of HIV-prevention education, counseling and family support, basic medical care for the infected, training and other support for income-generation activities of victims and their families including credit for microenterprises, and lobbying of government. Although entirely indigenous, it has received substantial outside funding. For example, USAID provided almost $2 million in support of TASO in fiscal year 2001. Recently, TASO established a permanent center in northern Uganda despite security concerns over the longstanding and, by some measures, worsening problem of civil strife in the northern region, with an insurgency by the notoriously cruel Lord's Resistance Army. Substantial funding has been received for this new effort from the European Union. Another $2.5 million has been allocated by USAID over the next five years to support at least 2,500 children of TASO clients in accessing vocational skills.

The case for fighting AIDS is slightly different from that of fighting the major childhood killers. In both cases, there is a moral imperative to help when people are needlessly suffering. With small children our obligation is primarily humanitarian. If there were a tradeoff between saving children and adults given limited funds, many would support saving the children.

We can afford to do both. Indeed, the two cannot be separated. With adults with HIV/AIDS the case for action is not only humanitarian but is also an investment in reducing future need for aid. Adults who have survived childhood diseases are the ones the children and the elderly count on for support. If Africa loses people entering the prime of their bread-winning years, children and the elderly will become even more destitute, making it that much harder to break out of poverty traps. Moreover, AIDS has tended to strike those with more education and higher productivity—thus having a disproportional impact on economic development. In many parts of Africa today, teachers are dying of AIDS faster than new teachers can be trained. Keeping an HIV+ person with basic education productive as she enters the earning years is a better way to raise national incomes and general well-being (or keep them from falling) in countries such as South Africa than most other investments.

Good work on AIDS is going on now throughout Africa. An excellent recent model developed by church groups in Zimbabwe is to utilize volunteers to visit and provide basic care for AIDS orphans in the homes where they live, which can be homes of child-headed households, foster parents, grandparents, or other relatives. These visits provide a much needed combination of emotional and material support for these orphans. But AIDS must be prevented in the first place. And modern methods of family planning need to be introduced.

POPULATION AND FAMILY PLANNING: CARE MAKES PROGRESS IN ETHIOPIA

There are more than ten times as many people living on the Earth as there were three hundred years ago. But one of the huge success stories of recent decades is the decrease in the rate of growth of world population. The growth rate peaked in the early 1960s at about 2.2 percent per year, but has now been cut in half to 1.1 percent. This is the difference between the population doubling at a rate of every 64 years in the 1960s, and every 32 years today. Although the population is still growing, the number of people added to the Earth each year (the number by which births exceed deaths) is now getting smaller. After a peak of adding 87 million additional people in 1989, in 2002 the world added 74 million people, and this figure is getting progressively smaller. Still, most of the increase is occurring in developing countries that are often already facing growing environmental pressures.

In isolated villages of rural Ethiopia, population growth has been fast and knowledge of family planning minimal. There has been very limited access to healthcare. Women have little power in the family. Fewer than 19 percent of women in the country can read, and the percentage is even lower in rural areas. On average, a woman in Ethiopia will give birth six times, a rate of fertility almost unchanged for decades. Yet the environment is becoming increasingly stressed. The population, now at 65 million, is expected to reach 88 million by 2015. The hope of ending poverty in Ethiopian villages depends on decreasing fertility. The work of CARE's Population and AIDS Prevention Project (POP/AIDS) in rural Ethiopia shows that this is possible.

The program began in 1996 with a mission to improve the health status of women and children. In CARE's program, an extension agent (or profession trainer) lives in a village for several months, working in a cluster of between four and nine villages with a local peasant's association. The goal is to help establish "a culture of family planning" and a framework for community health. The CARE agent begins by identifying and working actively with natural leaders in these villages—people CARE calls "opinion leaders" rather than "political leaders." The extension agent works to persuade these leaders of the importance of family planning. The leaders in turn play a key role as "change-agents" by convincing others, partly by setting an example through their own behavior. The CARE agent and community leaders often meet, sitting together in a large circle outdoors, to discuss family planning, health issues, or other concerns raised by participants. With the assistance of these opinion leaders, the CARE extension agent then identifies an appropriate local resident who was respected in the community and would serve as the reproductive health representative after the extension agent had transferred to another village.

In the first months after moving on to another community, the CARE extension agent makes a few brief return visits for training. After that point there is follow up from the Ethiopian Ministry of Health, including programs to involve the representatives in immunization, in an anti-polio campaign, and in the distribution of Vitamin A supplements. The involvement of the ministry is intended to help promote program financial sustainability.

CARE says it works with the tacit approval of the official leaders. In practice such approval is achieved by making courtesy calls to officials, such as introducing outside visitors who might be deemed important, symbolically demonstrating respect and acceptance of their authority. This helps the official by leaving the impression that he has something to do with the benefits that the village is receiving. However I doubt many villagers are much fooled by this symbolism.

During a five-year pilot project from 1996 to 2001, CARE extension workers trained and established 344 community representatives potentially serving some 260,000 villagers. Awareness and knowledge of modern contraception greatly improved. Contraceptive use rose from just 4 percent to some 24 percent in the Oromiya region program area south of Addis Ababa. The percentage of wives who said they discussed the number of children that they would like to have with their husbands rose from 7 percent to 34 percent according to a survey. Additionally, the program worked better when men were more actively involved in the process. Men sometimes served successfully as community representatives, in large part because of their relatively better education. The program is currently working to improve the effectiveness of women representatives.

As of the end of 2004 these village family planning representatives were still active and linked to nearby government health facilities for supplies and technical support. This linkage is an important phase in the assumption of responsibility for the program by local government.

Ensuring that an adequate, steady supply of contraceptives for the village was available after the launch period was very important to maintaining use. If costs of contraception cannot be kept very low, the villagers cannot afford them, so continued subsidies will likely be needed for some time. Consistent involvement by community based organizations and the Ethiopian government is needed to ensure the new "culture of family planning." In this way, an escape from the high fertility trap might be secured.

HEALTH MAKES EDUCATION POSSIBLE: DEWORMING IN KENYA (ICS IN BUSIA)

Worldwide, hookworm and roundworm each infect about 1.3 billion people, whipworm infects about 900 million, and schistosomiasis infects about 200 million. These parasitic infections can be debilitating. Severe infections lead to abdominal pain, anemia, protein malnutrition or kwashiorkor, listlessness, and other complications. In Africa, millions of children live in communities where parasitic infections are nearly universal. If all children in heavily infected areas were given the safe deworming treatment now available, we could control these infections for an estimated 49 cents per child per year.

In rural Kenya parasitic infections are endemic, including hookworm, roundworm, whipworm, and schistosomiasis. But with so little money available—annual government expenditure on public health in Kenya was only about $5 per person in the 1990 to 1997 period—and so many pressing problems, officials in aid agencies and in the Kenyan government doubted whether these treatments should be a priority. Now an action-research project has shown clearly that deworming is one of the most high-impact and cost-effective strategies for keeping children in school while improving their general nutrition and health.

The program is run by the International Christian Support Fund (ICS), an NGO based in the Netherlands. The programs of ICS in Kenya's Busia district involve education and health support, plus some work in the area of agricultural extension. There is a much-needed HIV/AIDS education program: Busia has a severe HIV problem, with an estimated adult infection rate of 32 percent. A large fraction of ICS programs in Busia are school-related, including child sponsorship, school assistance, teacher prizes, school meals, girls' scholarships, and early childhood development projects. The International Christian Support Fund implemented its deworming program with cooperation from the Kenyan Ministry of Health, and is working with a Harvard-MIT research team led by Michael Kremer, assessing their poverty programs using the highest standards of rigor: randomized impact evaluations.

The ICS model begins with the community, which identifies their needs. Next, ICS helps the local staff and leaders to write up a proposal, and finally forwards the proposals for possible funding to donors. The community participates directly in project implementation, and provides at least token monetary financing, and more substantial in-kind contributions to the project such as stones for constructions, and skilled and semi-skilled labor for such work as digging building foundations. Evaluations are carefully designed at the same time that new projects are being developed, making monitoring and evaluation an integral part of the whole process. The university evaluators are viewed as part of the ICS team. In fact, the researchers suggested some of the projects, but there was always extensive dialogue and participation of the beneficiaries.

In Busia district, 92 percent of schoolchildren were infected with at least one parasite, and 28 percent had at least three infections. Thirty-one percent had a moderate to heavy infection. In fact, the prevalence was likely even worse than these figures suggest, "to the extent that the most heavily infected children were more likely to be absent from school on the day of the survey," as the researchers put it.

The deworming program was one of the most rigorously evaluated poverty programs in the world, using randomized trial methods. All the schools in the target district were covered, but because of financial limitations as well as limits to the capacity of organization, all the schools could not be included from the beginning. Given this, randomizing the order of inclusion seems a fair way to respond to those limits, because it is like drawing straws. It also gives a chance to better estimate the effect of the treatment, as in a conventional medical trial. Signed or marked parental consent was required for each child to participate, and this represented a significant hurdle for showing results, as poorer parents were reluctant to come to the school if they were behind on fees. This means that, if anything, benefits of deworming were underestimated.

The results showed it to be more cost effective than virtually any known program in increasing the level of primary school attendance among very poor children. The Busia deworming project was identified by ICS as its most successful program activity in Kenya. The program cost per additional year of schooling was just $3.50, much less than the alternative methods used to increase school participation, such as subsidies to attend school. The program began as a research project at the instigation, and with the initial funding, of outside collaborating academic teams—in this case economists Michael Kremer of Harvard and Edward Miguel of the University of California at Berkeley. But ICS views Kremer and his colleagues as team members, so this is not a typical case of a program initiative driven by priorities of development agencies or foundations.

The result was a well-designed program, rigorously evaluated, with an unusually favorable cost-benefit ratio. The research showed that, by any standard criteria, deworming passes cost-effectiveness criteria by a wide margin. No other known program has such a large impact on enrollment and attendance for the expenditure involved. In fact, deworming of primary school-children turned out to cost only a fraction of any other method of boosting school participation. And it was a large boost—absenteeism decreased by a quarter, directly attributable to deworming. Treated children also reported small but statistically significant reductions in illness, and better height-for-age scores, measures of nutritional status. Neighboring school districts also felt substantial benefits of deworming. Children spread the disease across school districts when they swim in the same lake, for example. Although academic test scores did not increase significantly, this might have been due to the larger school class size that resulted from greater participation rates, thereby increasing the student to teacher ratio. The net benefit of the program is greater than the cost of hiring additional teachers to keep this ratio from rising—though this does not mean there is enough political will to do so. However, despite its large benefits, families are very sensitive to the price of the deworming treatment, suggesting that subsidies will be needed for some time. Although there is an almost knee-jerk reaction against all but short-term infusions of aid, in many cases this is unrealistic and counterproductive.

While rarely discussed in a media obsessed with high-profile problems like AIDS and malaria, defeat of parasitic worms, whose infections have such devastating effects on children, must be made a priority of the struggle to end global poverty.

Although it is not entirely obvious whether the ICS operations can be carried out on a broader regional or national level, the government of

Kenya has been sufficiently impressed that it is seriously considering a national deworming program based on the ICS-Busia model.

My interviews with teachers and students provided qualitative evidence that generally supported the quantitative evidence uncovered in the evaluation. I visited schools in rural Busia district, to meet the students and talk with the teachers. Nangina Primary School is a long row of mud schoolrooms with a tin roof and a patch of bare ground in front where the children play. Along one wall someone had planted a row of flowers. A sign painted onto the wall reads: "OUR MOTTO: HARDWORK AND DISCIPLINE LEAD TO SUCCESS." There are some wonderful and dedicated public school teachers in rural Africa, such as Wiafred Mujema. She sat with us, wearing a plain dress and a colorful headscarf, exuding love and concern for her students. "Pupils who had been miserable now became active and lifeful," she told me with obvious satisfaction. "When they were still infected, they acted dull. Then, after deworming, they had their hands up and were active in class. The number of students repeating a grade went down and there were improvements in standards [test scores], children moving from bottom to middle or top." She said that about 10 of 94 students were staying behind, less than usual but still too many, but that all of them would pass this year. There were also fewer dropouts, she added.

Teachers in Sirindiro Primary School told me of children who had been too listless to join in games at recess who were now playing enthusiastically with the other kids, of children's skin smooth and soft again instead of rough with ringworms, of children no longer constantly running to the latrines, who could concentrate during the lessons for the first time—important details that don't show up in the econometric findings. Combining qualitative and quantitative evidence helps us really understand what is happening in the field.

But Wiafred told me that the new students coming in have a lot of ringworms and other signs of infection, and overall health is deteriorating. "The children play in the streams," she said, "and so the worms are just coming back again." As we ended our discussion, she made a plea that the program be continued.

ICS has had many benefits from participating in rigorous randomized trials that extend even beyond the knowledge it gains on program effectiveness. They have received many valuable ideas from the researchers, and have acquired an international reputation for innovation and careful program assessment. It is to be hoped that many other NGOs will follow their example.

BASIC EDUCATION

In rural areas, and among the poorest families, even with the abolition of primary school tuition, many children do little more than enroll in school, if even that. Though school may become nominally free, in many communities in South Asia and elsewhere teachers or officials must be bribed. Expensive uniforms must be bought. School schedules may interfere with children's work on farms, shepherding, fishing, or other activities. Once children are healthy enough to learn in school, how can schools better reach the poor and serve their needs?

A GOOD BEGINNING:
PRATHAM'S ACCELERATED AND
COMPUTER-ASSISTED PRIMARY LEARNING IN INDIA

Pratham comes from a Sanskrit word meaning "first," "primary," or "beginning." Now it is also the name of an innovative Indian NGO, founded in 1994. The name reflects the group's focus on basic education, and is a good example of a strategy to address the illiteracy trap.

Pratham's own beginnings were in the slums of Mumbai (formerly known as Bombay). A concerned citizen group decided to address the problems of low enrollment and poor school quality by actively involving people who could assist the government in achieving universal primary education. Its motto is "ensure that every child is in school . . . and learning well." A rigorous, randomized evaluation recently found two of its programs to be highly cost-effective. Pratham was a recipient of the 2000 Global Development Network Award as one of three "most innovative development projects."

The United Nations International Children's Fund (UNICEF) donated initial funding and support for Pratham's first three years of operation. Pratham is now independent and receives funds from many sources, led by India's private ICICI Bank, along with local governments, Indian corporations, and local citizens. Pratham has also received international support from NGOs such as Save the Children UK and from corporate sponsors, mostly based in the UK and India. Pratham also has affiliates in donor countries, such as the UK and United States, where it receives support from the Indian diaspora community. Among other support programs, Pratham USA (www.prathamusa.org) runs a Read for Pratham program, which is similar to the well-known Heifer Read-to-Feed children's sponsored reading program.

Today, Pratham works in 13 states across India, increasingly in rural as well as urban areas. From an initial program working with two thousand children, Pratham has grown to work with some 220,000 children in 20 cities and 10 rural areas in India; the organization claims to have reached over one million children in its first ten years.

Pratham's current approach is an "accelerated learning method," in which a child is given a major boost to be able to start reading and doing basic arithmetic in just three weeks. This initial "bridge" to school is often enough to boost self-esteem and confidence in his or her ability to succeed in school. Children are then strongly counseled to go to school and they and their parents are then encouraged to keep up attendance. Cost per enrolled pupil is kept to a minimum with the short jump-start courses, community involvement, spending no resources on "immovable assets," such as building construction or infrastructure, and a cost-cutting organizational culture.

Pratham emphasizes that they take a "total geographical approach," whether a city or urban or regional area as a whole, promoting its work in "complete coverage." It also emphasizes a strategy of working closely with government, along with corporations and the citizen sector. Government is relied upon to make school facilities available for the program. Young women who are themselves from the areas targeted for the program do most of the teaching. Enrolled children identified as at-risk are specially tutored, mainly by young women called *balsakis,* or children's friends, who have managed to finish secondary school but live in the slums. The cost is only about $5 per child per year. Abhijit Banerjee, Shawn Cole, Esther Duflo, and Leigh Linden studied the program in a randomized experiment; the early results suggest that the program is 12 to 16 times more cost-effective than hiring new teachers.

After establishing a network linking slum volunteers with corporate, civic, and government leadership, additional interventions are then added as needed for a comprehensive attack on other poverty problems. Health education has been widely introduced, at unusually low cost due to Pratham's lean structure. Recently, computer education has been established, with "computer-assisted learning" centers established in both Mumbai and Delhi.

To see what difference computer education could make to a slum community, an experimental program was introduced into dilapidated slum areas in the city of Vadodara, also known as Baroda, in Gujarat State, about 235 miles from Mumbai. Like many other such areas in India, most children are enrolled on the school's books but often attend school sporadically at best. Abhijit Banerjee, Esther Duflo, and Leigh Linden designed the study to measure the impact of Pratham's computer-assisted learning strategy. Four computers were donated to each primary school. Students in fourth grade played educational games designed to reinforce their mathematics skills learned in previous grades. One attractive feature of the program is that students can progress through mastering of competencies at their own pace. Results are still preliminary, but after one year the evidence showed a substantial improvement in test scores for all participants, girls as well as boys, and, encouragingly, somewhat more so for those near the bottom of the distribution. Most of the impact on tests was found in the second half of the year, suggesting that persistent application of the program was important. The cost-effectiveness of the program is very high. Although it costs somewhat more than traditional methods, the increase in test score performance per dollar spent seems to be much higher for the computer-assisted learning approach.

PATHWAYS OUT OF POVERTY:
PROGRESA IN SOUTHERN MEXICO

Some government programs are also working, such as the Mexican Program on Education, Health and Nutrition, usually known by its Spanish acronym, Progresa, though officially renamed the Oportunidades program. Progresa combats child labor, by ensuring that parents can feed their children and keep them in school, by providing them with financial incentives to do so.

Progresa builds on the growing understanding that health, nutrition, and education are complements in the struggle to end poverty. The program features the promotion of an integrated package to promote the education, health, and nutrition status of poor families. It provides cash transfers to poor families, family clinic visits, in-kind nutritional supplements, and other health benefits for pregnant and lactating women and their children under the age of five. Some of these benefits are conditional on children's regular school attendance.

In effect, low-income parents are paid to send their children to school, one of the recent strategies most widely believed by the donor and development community to be effective in sustainably reducing poverty. This compensates parents for lost income or the lost value of work at home. Such payments work to increase school enrollments, attendance, progress through grades, other schooling outcomes, and nutrition.

From its inception in August 1997, the Progresa program has grown to cover over four million households, or some 21 million people—around one fifth of the population—in nearly 74,000 localities. In 2002, the program distributed 857 million doses of nutrition supplements and covered 2.4 million medical check-ups. Over 4.5 million "scholarships" were provided to schoolchildren.

Progresa affects child nutrition through four program components, called pathways: cash transfers, which may be used in part for improved nutrition; nutritional supplements given to all participating children under two, pregnant and breastfeeding mothers, and those children between ages two and five who show signs of malnutrition; growth monitoring, which provides feedback to parents; and other preventive measures including required participation in regular meetings where vital health knowledge about hygiene and nutrition is taught.

Participating families receive school program payments every other month. In addition, families receive grants for school supplies and food subsidies, on the proviso that they get regular public health care for the children, including medical checkups and immunizations. Payments are generally provided through the mother, because evidence shows that mothers use more of their available funds in support of the children's well-being than do fathers. The payments are supplied via a bankcard, directly from the federal government and not through intermediaries, reducing chances of corruption; mothers are taught how and where to cash in their payments.

Program payments are conditional on children in grades three through nine attending school regularly. In developing countries such as Mexico, children are often enrolled in school but do not attend for long. These payments increase as the child increases in grade level. This gives an incentive to keep children in school longer, and helps the children continue into higher grades. In third grade parents receive a little over $10 per month. Girls in ninth grade receive over $35 per month. This is close to two-thirds of the income the children would receive as laborers. The overall result is to break the tradeoff that parents face between higher consumption for the family today, and the higher future consumption possible when the child has completed school. Families of girls also receive slightly higher payments than boys, partly because girls are more likely to drop out, while the social benefits of keeping girls in school are high.

The program is also more effective than standard alternatives. For example, evidence shows that Progresa has a larger impact on enrollment and performance per dollar spent than building new school buildings.

The cost of even the much-expanded Progresa program in 2002 was some 18 billion pesos, about $2 billion, fairly modest, even in Mexico's economy. This represented about one fifth of one percent of gross national income. Progresa is also organizationally efficient, with operational expenses of only about 6 percent of total outlays.

However, Progresa is not famous for its modest cost but because it works. It has been subject to one of the most rigorous, randomized trials of any public poverty program in the world. Washington-based International Food Policy Research Institute (IFPRI) has been actively engaged in studying the program. Their evaluations of Progresa indicate that its integrated approach has been highly successful, with large improvements in the well-being of participants. Nutrition has improved, school attendance is up significantly, and the dropout rate has also declined substantially, especially in the so-called transition grades six through nine, when children either get launched toward completing high school or drop out in middle school. The research showed that Progresa increased by some 20 percent the number of children who stay in school rather than drop out just before high school. Child labor has decreased by about 15 percent.

The lessons of Progresa are spreading throughout the region. Some of the best features of Progresa are also found in the Bolsa-Escola program in Brazil and the Scholarships program in Costa Rica. But middle-income Latin American countries with at least modestly competent governments are one thing. Can progress in education for the poor be made in a low-income country like Bangladesh, which Transparency International rates as the most corrupt in the world? It can, when a competent and dedicated NGO reaches sufficient scale.

SPREADING THE WORD:
BRAC'S NONFORMAL PRIMARY EDUCATION SOLUTION

In Bangladesh, just 25 years ago attending school was an unimaginable luxury for most of the poor. Even in 1990, less than half of all children in the country completed primary school. By 2003, about two-thirds were completing primary school. One of the major driving forces in this transformation has been the work of a remarkable organization called BRAC.

An NGO formerly known as the Bangladesh Rural Advancement Committee, BRAC is a stunningly successful nonprofit organization whose mission is poverty reduction. The visionary leader Fazle Hasan Abed founded BRAC in the early 1970s, to aid displaced persons in the aftermath of civil war and famine. Mr. Abed has won many honors and awards for his work, including the Gates Prize, awarded in June 2004. The organization's leaders soon understood that the problems of the rural poor were chronic and structural, and they turned their attention to long-term development and poverty alleviation efforts. BRAC operates primarily in rural areas of Bangladesh, in an environment of pervasive poverty, in which government has low capacity and high corruption. In contrast, BRAC has grown steadily, attracting funds for its reputation for competence, dedication, innovativeness, and accountability.

With whole regions of the country caught in complex poverty traps, BRAC has had to innovate continuously to bring needed services to the poor. Through helping the poor to identify their own needs and priorities, BRAC has developed high-impact and widely emulated program innovations in education, nutrition, health, credit, legal rights, advocacy, and other fields. BRAC programs such as "Microcredit-plus," which integrates village health and business education and other training with microfinance, have been widely replicated in other countries, demonstrating their general value. But none operate at BRAC's extraordinary scale. By some measures BRAC is now the largest NGO in the world, and BRAC's activities constitute more than the one percent of the GDP of Bangladesh. BRAC has successfully made the transition to being a large and complex organization, with some four million grassroots members (one woman per household), participating in BRAC's basic units, the Village Organization (VO). There are some 115,000 of these VOs, each including about 35 to 50 women from a village or neighborhood.

Although Transparency International's rating of Bangladesh as the world's most corrupt government may be an exaggeration, the rating does reflect genuine problems. In this environment, BRAC has helped fill the vacuum left by government, taking on many of the functions of good governance—including emergency relief, public health, export assistance, legal aid, and advocating for the poor. The influence of BRAC has been so great that a well-known saying in Bangladesh is "we have two governments," meaning the government, and BRAC. Despite its size, BRAC remains very flexible. When catastrophic flooding hit the country in August 2004, BRAC temporarily reoriented virtually its entire organization to relief activities.

Today BRAC works in 64,000 of the country's 80,000 villages through a system of 14 training centers and over 1,500 field offices, with a budget of about $175 million. In addition, BRAC is more than 80 percent self-financed, with donor contributions to its budget just 18 percent in 2003; and this figure has been under 22 percent for several years. A major source of its revenue is a network of productive enterprises that it has established, with twin aims of poverty reduction and net income generation for its poverty programs (these are described later, in the BRAC Enterprises sidebar). BRAC has over 60,000 employees, making it the country's second-largest employer. Some 34,000 of them serve as primary teachers in BRAC's widely emulated Nonformal Primary Education Program (NFPE).

BRAC began its highly innovative village nonformal primary schools in 1984, in response to the needs and requests of the village women with which it works. A major reason that parents do not send their children to school is that their work at home and on the small family farm plot is needed to help the family survive. A second reason is the intimidation and alienation that uneducated parents and their children feel in traditional school settings. A third is harassment of girls.

The program structure was developed to respond to schooling problems identified by mothers taking part in other BRAC programs. BRAC schools teach the children of poor, often landless, families. Over two-thirds of the students are girls. First, the school operates for only a few hours a day so the children can help at home and on the farm. Parents decide whether classes will be held in morning or evening, depending on the nature of a village's needs. Little homework is assigned, as homework requirements were identified as a major stumbling block to keeping children in school. Yet BRAC works to make up for shorter school hours with a higher quality education. One can see this quality in the smaller class size, the engaging teaching styles, and the obvious care shown for the pupils. In these ways, BRAC is addressing features found in child labor traps.

The NFPE has grown steadily. Today there are about 34,000 schools and about the same number of teachers—a few hundred less, as some teachers run two schools that meet at different hours. Over 1.1 million pupils are currently enrolled, and over 2.6 million students have graduated since the NFPE programs began.

The program has evolved over the years as the needs of the rural poor change. At first the program lasted three years, usually for children between ages 8 and 10. This was a year or two later than students start public school; the reason for this, BRAC officials explain, is to identify students who are likely never to start public school or to drop out almost immediately. The greatest emphasis was on literacy and numeracy, health and hygiene, basic science, and social studies. The program was designed in part to establish a foundation from which students could enter into the fourth grade of the public school system. There is also a system of basic education for somewhat older children, aged about 11 to 14.

WHEN EDUCATION REFORM
IS LESS THAN MEETS THE EYE

Uganda has been a viewed as a star pupil of agencies such as the IMF, the World Bank, and USAID for following liberalization guidelines. But liberalization has done little to reduce corruption, and in fact has sometimes expanded opportunities for it. And some much-ballyhooed reforms have done little for the poorest of the poor.

Uganda introduced a universal primary education program (UPE) in 1997, which abolished school fees and was supposed to bring school closer to the rural students who were unable to attend. In fact, significant progress has been made and enrollment has increased. But the reality is that there is a long way to go for the poorest of the poor.

The IMF has a short film, "Uganda—A Different Drummer," which can be downloaded from its website. From the IMF we now learn how wonderful it is that students no longer have to pay school fees—without ever mentioning that the IMF and the World Bank pushed impoverished countries to impose primary school textbook and other fees (along with health and other user charges) in the 1980s, in the name of "cost recovery," and, in practice, to facilitate debt repayments. The film shows happy children, most of them in new uniforms and good shoes. One of the themes of the UPE program was to no longer require uniforms, because the poor could not afford them. Very few, if any, children without uniforms can be found in the happy IMF video. From the poor we learn that pupils who do not wear a uniform, because their parents cannot afford one, are taunted by their peers. In fact, parents and children report that pupils without a uniform are also commonly treated badly by their teachers. These children often stop going to school. Although Uganda's poverty reduction strategey is supposed to be a showcase for the IMF and World Bank, contary to the film, poverty has been *rising* in Uganda in recent years.

There is also a government policy of rewarding districts with good educational performance with more resources. This provides some good incentives, but they need to go hand in hand with a good safety net. Rewarding the best school districts can amplify low performance traps for the poorer regions, such as Naka-songola, that cannot afford required local, complementary expenditures (such as construction of local schools). Without sufficient resources a community cannot raise enrollments enough to get further resources. Using current enrollments as a measure for success benefits urban and better-off areas where it is much easier to get kids on the rolls and to attend. There is something wrong with efficiency incentives aimed at local well-off politicians that end up punishing impoverished children.

The UPE program was part of the poverty eradication action plan, or PEAP, and grew out of meetings within the Poverty Reduction Strategy Paper (PRSP) framework of the World Bank and IMF. Uganda was the first country to qualify for debt relief under the World Bank-IMF initiative. It has been growing more rapidly than most Sub-Saharan countries. But visit the more remote rural areas where many of those in extreme poverty live, and different images emerge than those in the flourishing school of the IMF film. Teacher truancy is a big problem. Children are also often out of school; they are dressed in near-rags and wear no shoes. Under the UPE, parents must pay for "optional" uniforms, plus fees on each child after their fourth. While there is a need for incentives for having fewer children, surely there are fertility incentives that don't work at the expense of a child born into extreme poverty for whom education may be the only chance at a decent life.

In 1998, the schools expanded to a four-year program covering the five-year primary curriculum in less time. This redesign was in response to the large number of BRAC graduates interested in continuing their education to secondary level. BRAC says that today more than 90 percent of its graduates continue in the formal system.

I visited a typical school in the Sylhet region of northeast Bangladesh. It was a modest one-room structure, bamboo framed, with tin sheets for walls and roof and a burlap floor. (In many other BRAC schools the walls are made entirely of bamboo with a thatched roof.) While I was there, there was a cloudburst downpour, and the school stayed entirely dry and the children stayed focused on their lessons—even though later, outside, we had to step around rushing rivulets flowing through the school grounds. Inside, decorations hung from the roof. Lessons and papers were posted on the tin walls. The children sat around the periphery of the room. In addition to lessons, in which all were expected to actively participate in recitations, traditional dances were also practiced, along with other more engaging activities. The class size was about 30 children, which I was told is typical, and this compares favorably with the very large public school classes.

Teachers are usually (about 97 percent) village women, who are trained and supervised by a professional staff. They are required to have had nine years of education, less than required by public schools but sufficient for the materials being taught, with supervision. This keeps costs low and employs women who have attained somewhat more education than most other village women.

We will encounter other innovative and encouraging BRAC programs later in the book. Along with other NGOs such as Grameen and ASA, BRAC is one of the reasons for the remarkable progress in Bangladesh, which has been transforming from symbol of famine to symbol of hope.

BRAC's NFPE program is the most famous of its kind. But BRAC is widely hailed as one of the most effective NGOs in the world. Is there something unique about BRAC, or about Bangladesh, that makes this possible? Or can similar results in providing accessible primary education for the poorest of the poor be achieved in other parts of the world struggling with poverty traps?

GIVING CHILDREN A CHANCE: SAVE THE CHILDREN'S NONFORMAL PRIMARY SCHOOLS IN UGANDA

Nakasongola district in Uganda has many problems, including a high child mortality rate, a low school enrollment rate, and a high dropout rate. Girls are often sold into marriage at an early age in exchange for a bride price. Public schools follow a national curriculum that can be quite irrelevant to the lives of these children, who come from impoverished farmer, fisher, or pastoralist families. Moreover, if a whole community of fishers and herders must move with the seasons, then it seems their primary school ought to move with them. But the public system assumes that every child has a fixed address in a single school district where they live year round.

Save the Children (Save) brought their Child-Centered Alternative for Non-Formal Community-Based Education (CHANCE) program to Nakasongola because it was one of the regions most in need. Could an organization like Save really make a difference, even in an environment like this? I went to Nakasongola to find out.

Save is a highly rated NGO. For example, it receives a grade of A- from the American Institute of Philanthropy (AIP) and a four-star (highest) rating from Charity Navigator. Education—particularly the nonformal education CHANCE program—was regularly cited in interviews as among the most innovative and cost-effective of Save programs. Education officials at Save nominated the Uganda program as one of their most effective in Africa, a judgment that was supported by independent observers (Save's village education programs in Mali and Malawi also receive accolades). Uganda government officials also view the program as the most successful nonformal education experience. Because the program operates in one of the most backward areas, positive results were difficult to demonstrate, so the program had to overcome larger obstacles than NGO programs in more "mainstream" regions. Yet enrollment, retention, and exam scores are higher than local government schools, achieved at a lower cost. The CHANCE program is focused on nonformal schools, and also supports reproductive and other health training, children's health activities, and adult literacy. Some communities are endeavoring to build a health clinic on their school grounds.

The Save guesthouse in Nakasongola consists of small rooms around a central courtyard where many of the staff live and eat together. The main staple in Uganda is a tasty mush of green bananas boiled into a chewy paste. They also serve delicious stews. Sleeping areas are little more than curtain-covered cubbies. Toilets are literally holes in the floor. All this is actually nicer than most people have, but the staff is not being spoiled with luxuries.

I had an opportunity to take a three-hour trip north of the Save guesthouse, along deeply rutted dirt roads, some of which had just reopened after the rainy season, to see some of the hinterland communities they are serving. (Some schools still farther away remained inaccessible even in a Land Rover because of road conditions.) Teachers travel locally to their schools and to staff meetings by bicycle, sometimes a two-hour trip.

I met with a family in their mud hut. Poverty in the African bush is like camping in the backcountry forever, with no money, no goods, and nowhere to go. People grow corn, cassava, and bean plants, which they hope produce some beans before bean rot sets in. In one village I visited, I was shown a lone coffee plant that was dying of a coffee blight.

The CHANCE schools were greatly needed. Those communities face extreme poverty, both in its income (most living on less than $1 per day) and its broader sense. I visited three of the schools, meeting with teachers, students, and parents, and watching classes in session. The children assemble in mud huts built by the communities, or under a tree for shade, a blackboard leaning up against it.

In the Save schools, it is fairly rare to find a child wearing shoes. This is not because it is quite warm there, but because the children do not own any shoes. (One quick way to gauge the poverty of an area is to look at people's feet.) Lack of shoes can be hazardous in some of the work the children have to do and areas in which they have to walk. The clothes the kids wear to school are usually the one outfit saved for school. Visit the kids at home and they are almost always dressed in near-rags.

In the CHANCE schools, classes meet at times of the day and seasons of the year when the community members say is most convenient.

For example, in fishing communities, when the children are away fishing at the islands on Lake Kyoga, "school vacation" is declared. Parents decide if they want school in the early morning or the late afternoon. This may differ depending on the types of chores the children typically do in a village, or whether it is rainy or dry season. In one of the schools I visited, classes are held in the morning during dry season but in the early afternoon during rainy season, when children help to plant crops. In Mali, another country where Save the Children works, the schools are in session in the hottest part of the day when the animals are sleeping, so the children don't need to tend them then.

CHANCE schools do not use uniforms, avoiding the awkward contrast between those who can and cannot afford them. Lessons are put in a community context, working with local materials and learning from maps constructed from sticks, stones, and natural dyes. Although by law the CHANCE schools must follow the same basic curriculum as government schools, it is taught in the context of local social problems. Teachers stay with a class through the six grades of primary school, and the students' ages may vary. Students are taken in only in years when a community is ready to start a new class; they begin with grade one, and work their way forward. The program addresses what would otherwise be insurmountable child labor and illiteracy traps.

The teachers were greatly praised by the parents. But villagers are struggling to pay the teachers' salaries, some of whom were leaving—"running away" as the villagers expressed it to me—because they were not being paid. I chipped in $100, which was enough to pay for five teachers for six weeks, three at one school and two at another, and provide a good cushion for any exigencies. Another foreign visitor did the same, which gave them three months. At each school, parents were literally dancing with joy. Despite their extreme poverty, communities are coming together, trying as hard as they can to pay for additional teachers under the program umbrella, so that their children can have a brighter future. Often they cannot quite get there. I am regularly struck by how much good can be done with so little money when we identify and support worthy programs.

It is obvious that the kids love their schools. When I went to classes, the kids were always told they could ask me questions, a cultural tradition when a traveler visits from afar. Rather than news of the outside world, they asked me questions about what they were studying. "What country lies to the west of Uganda?" Fortunately, I had been spending a lot of time staring at my map of Uganda, mostly trying to figure out where I was: the answer was Congo. (The child seemed somewhat disappointed that I knew the answer.) Next question: "what is the skeleton?" That one I really struggled with, and the kids did not look very impressed with my answer.

Figure 4.1   Open classroom: Save the Children informal primary school.

My turn: I asked the kids what they wanted to do when they grew up. Many boys said "driver." Kids aspire to be a driver in Africa the way American kids dream of being a pilot. Later in my stay, I met a man for whom driving was the major family occupation, with a father, uncles, brothers, and cousins all drivers by trade. But many boys as well as girls said they wanted to be a teacher. I was later told that it is possible that some will realize this dream, but it requires more education than most will be able to achieve, though some may become teachers in the Save schools, where fewer years of education is required. But the main point is that the children will have the basics of literacy and numeracy, and exposure to the wider world that will serve as a basis for opportunities.

The schools will need support for some time. Recently the program has had to face a decision on whether to turn some of the well-functioning CHANCE schools to public sector management, and how quickly to do so. The decision was made to quickly get some of the schools in the program off the Save budget and onto the regular government budget. This was done in part to satisfy pressure from donors, to show that funding would not be needed indefinitely, to demonstrate that the program would be sustainable with local resources, and to free up resources to start additional schools.

However, all parties agreed that this had been done too quickly and without adequate preparation. Government teachers were not prepared for the expectations of students and parents. Students arriving late were given corporal punishment, even though these students typically were late because they had to help parents with chores in the early mornings. (Corporal punishment is banned in Save schools, but is traditional in public schools.) Students were ridiculed for not wearing "optional" uniforms, and the curriculum material was taught in a conventional manner without regard for local conditions and the experience of the students. As a result, many students dropped out, test scores declined, the rate of grade repeating increased, and satisfaction decreased.

In some of these schools parents are trying to take control within the CHANCE style schooling system once again, paying community teachers to teach in the Save style with such honoraria as they can afford to pay, under the basic training and guidance of CHANCE staff. The future of the program is uncertain, given the limited ability of the villagers to pay teachers and the difficulty in getting the government to operate using the nonformal system. Save officials say they hope to find additional funding to maintain and expand the program. The determination of villagers who have been exposed to the CHANCE system to somehow find the means to continue it was impressive.

CREDIT FOR POVERTY REDUCTION, AND INSURING OPPORTUNITY

I have interviewed women microentrepreneurs in the Middle East, Sub-Saharan Africa, South Asia, and Latin America. In each region, I was told of strikingly similar experiences with trying to make their tiny businesses work—each with their own special story, but all reflecting some of the same underlying themes. More than any other concern, I was told of problems caused by the lack of working capital. The lack of finance meant inventories too small to make many matches with consumer needs, such as clothes in sizes that fit or costume jewelry in enough variety to attract attention and make a sale. It meant the inability to buy wholesale in bulk, such as the woman who could have made much more money if she could buy a package of twelve sheets and resell them individually as compared with buying three individual sheets and reselling these door to door. It meant that buying low-cost but productive capital goods such as a simple sewing machine remained out of reach.

These hard-working women are caught in working capital poverty traps. They were not getting the credit for how hard they were working to support their families. Now, with microfinance programs, they have a chance to get it.

MAKING CREDIT INSTITUTIONS *PEOPLE*-WORTHY: THE GRAMEEN BANK OF BANGLADESH

Muhammad Yunus conceived the pioneering Grameen Bank in the mid-1970s, when he was a Chittagong University economics professor. Dr. Yunus had become convinced from his research that the lack of access to credit on the part of the poor was a binding constraint on their economic progress, a conclusion that has been confirmed by later studies from around the developing world. Professor Yunus wanted to demonstrate that it was possible to lend to the poor without collateral, and to determine the best system for doing so. To this end he created Grameen as a private, nonprofit, development "action and research project." Today, Grameen has over three million borrowers among the poor, and, what is most heartening, the recently poor.

Yunus said in an interview in Bangladesh, "all human beings are born entrepreneurs. Some get the opportunity to find this out, but some never get this opportunity. A small loan can be a ticket to exploration of personal ability. All human beings have a skill—the survival skill. The fact that they are alive proves this. Just support this skill and see how they will choose to use it." Implicitly, he was identifying working capital traps, which can be a binding constraint on the poor even when other keys to capability are in place.

Yunus began the operation in 1976 after convincing the Bangladesh agricultural development bank to provide initial loan money, the first loans guaranteed personally by Yunus. A series of expansions convinced the government of Grameen's value, and the Grameen Bank was formally chartered as a financial institution in 1983.

The public-cooperative bank continued to grow rapidly and now has over 2,000 branch offices throughout the country. The branch office, covering 15 to 20 villages, is the basic organizational unit, and is responsible for its profits and losses. Each branch has a number of village or neighborhood centers, comprised of about eight solidarity groups. Each solidarity group has five members, so there are about forty borrowers in each center.

Since its founding, the Grameen Bank has enabled well over two million poor Bangladeshis to start or upgrade their own small businesses. Today some 95 percent of the borrowers are women. Borrowers are generally limited to those who own less than one half acre. Representatives of Grameen branches often go door to door in the villages they cover to inform people, who are generally illiterate and very reticent about dealing with banks, about Grameen's services.

Before opening a new branch, the new branch manager is assigned to prepare a socioeconomic report covering the economy, geography, demographics, transportation and communications infrastructure, and politics of the area. Among other things, this ensures that a branch manager becomes familiar with the region and its potential borrowers before the branch begins operations.

Grameen, which can be translated as "rural" in Bengali, is incorporated as a publicly supported credit union, with borrowers owning 75 percent of the bank's stock and the government owning the remainder.

Once borrowers reach a certain borrowing level, they are entitled to purchase one share of Grameen stock. The bank sets its own policy with strong borrower input, independent of government control. Grameen's total annualized interest rate on its basic, "working capital" loans has been kept at 16 percent. The current rate of interest on home loans is 8 percent. Grameen has been promoting home ownership, which can empower families and help neighborhood solidarity and upkeep, and states that its home loans are cross-subsidized by its working capital loans. The average annual inflation rate in Bangladesh has been falling over time; it was about 9.6 percent in the 1980s, falling to about 4 percent for the 1990s and closer to 3 percent today; thus the real interest rate appears to have been rising over time. (Something we need to understand better is whether the interest rates really need to remain so high—and how the poor are able to find such profitable projects so as to be able to pay at this rate. At a 2004 conference on microfinance in Bangladesh, these two questions were constantly debated.)

To qualify for uncollateralized loans, potential borrowers form five-member groups. Each member must undergo a two-week training session before any member can secure a loan, and the training sessions are followed up with weekly group meetings with a bank officer. Grameen relies on what could be called the "collateral of peer pressure." Currently borrowers in the solidarity groups do *not* have to cosign or jointly guarantee each other's loans. However, it is clear that strong social pressure is placed on members to repay. In particular, after the groups of five prospective borrowers are formed, at first, only two members of the group are eligible to receive a loan. The other members qualify for loans only if these first two borrowers adhere to the repayment schedule for principal and interest for a full six weeks, and if all members adhere to Grameen's membership conditions. This clearly generates peer pressure for repayment even without traditional joint liability. Members know the characters of other group members, and generally only join groups with members they believe likely to repay their loans.

There are also additional financial incentives to repay loans in a timely manner. Each individual borrower can increase by 10 percent the amount they can borrow each year if they have repaid loans in a timely manner. For the group, if there is 100 percent attendance at meetings and all loans are repaid, then each borrower can increase her borrowing by an additional 5 percent, that is, can raise their borrowing ceilings at a rate of 15 percent per year. This does provide some incentive for peer pressure. An additional increment is provided when there is a perfect record from each of the eight or so borrowing groups in a center.

Yunus described the current procedures when a member is unable to repay. They are allowed to restructure their loans, repaying at a slower rate, with some limited refinancing as needed. This has reduced defaults to essentially zero, Yunus said. Most borrowers wish to reestablish their credit and resume their rights to borrow increasing sums, so they work hard to get their loans up to date. No doubt peer pressure also remains a major factor.

Group members are trained in such practical matters as bank procedures, the group savings program, the role of the center chief and the chairperson of the 5-member group, even in how to write their signatures. In addition, training has a moral component, stressing the Bank's 16 principles, or "Decisions," to be adhered to by each member. These Decisions were formulated in a national conference of one hundred female center chiefs in 1984. They emphasize mutual assistance and other modern values, including self-discipline and hard work, hygiene, and refusal to participate in backward practices like demanding dowries. Adherence to these principles and attendance at rallies featuring the chanting of the Decisions are not formal requirements for receiving loans, but they are said to have become effective, implicit requirements.

The 16 Decisions cover a wide range of activities. Here are a few: #3: We shall not live in dilapidated houses. We shall repair our houses and work toward constructing new houses as soon as possible. #4: We shall grow vegetables all the year round. We shall eat plenty of them and sell the surplus. #6: We shall plan to keep our families small. #8: We shall always keep our children and the environment clean. #11: We shall not take any dowry in our sons' weddings, neither shall we give any dowry in our daughters' weddings. We shall not practice child marriage. #13: For higher income we shall collectively undertake higher investments. The full list, with their pictorial presentation for villagers, may be found on the Grameen website at www.grameen-info.org/.

The decision approach is very powerful, and has set a pattern that has been replicated or built upon by other successful NGOs, including BRAC, which features "18 promises."

Dr. Yunus recently said that the credit-worthiness of the poor is now established beyond doubt, and the real "question is whether banks and credit institutions are people-worthy."

I met with a number of Grameen bank borrowers. Rozina bought a sewing machine so she can do sewing work in her small home. She also brings it to the market to sew clothes brought to her on the spot. Anwara rears five cows and makes puffed rice, which villagers come to her home to buy. Amela also makes puffed rice, and works with her husband selling cloth and dresses (called *sharis*). Uzala raises poultry in her yard, from day old to 45 days, and then sells them. She proudly reported that she had reached a stock of 500 chickens. Ostonari, a Hindu widow, also sells puffed rice, and works with her son, who is a fish seller. Aysha operates a grocery store out of her home, and with her husband and son have a "mobile grocery shop" that they take to the market.

In one striking project a group of three women had rented low-lying land and built a fishpond. A feeding frenzy ensued as one of their sons threw fishfood onto the water. They use high yielding fish varieties that grow very quickly to full size. Fish are a major part of the Bangladeshi diet, and not a small number of Grameen borrowers are setting up fish farms. Grameen did not "teach a woman to fish to feed her for a lifetime"—with no fish in the village, they identified three mothers who had been caught in poverty traps but were determined to feed their children and who had their own vision about how to do it. Grameen provided them with credit, marketing contacts, and solidarity. The women built the fishpond, fed their children, and earned enough income so they could keep them in school. Progress against poverty is not a myth. Scenes analogous to this one can be seen all over Bangladesh. Helping people to help themselves can really work, if the helpers meet the poor on their own terms and let the poor set the agenda.

Grameen has proven flexible and responsive to the borrowing needs of its members. For example, the Grameen housing program can lend up to 30,000 takas (about $500) as home loans. The program won a 1998 World Habitat Award. To date there have been more than a half million Grameen-financed houses built or rebuilt, adding iron roofs, cement pillars, and sanitary latrines. I visited some homes built with Grameen housing loans. They have mud walls but these are thick and, properly maintained, can last many years. The houses are substantial in size, and seem well constructed, with an electric fan overhead and usually other basic appliances in electrified villages. Grameen has also started offering higher education loans for its members. An increasing number of peasants are proudly witnessing as the first members of their families to ever go to college graduate in fields such as computer science and accounting. It is a remarkable transformation.

BANKING ON THE VILLAGE: FINCA IN UGANDA

The Foundation for International Community Assistance (FINCA) is another leading NGO provider of microfinance. Founded in 1984, it is more explicit than most microfinance institutions (MFIs) that its focus is poverty reduction through credit, rather than partially competing aims such as catalyzing the development of a national financial system and other social goals.

FINCA International is recognized as the pioneer of the "village banking" approach to microfinance, which involves cosigning of loans across larger numbers of borrowers (an entire local branch of 30 or more) rather than the "solidarity group" approach (around 5 members within a branch), pioneered by the Grameen Bank in Bangladesh. According to FINCA, its village banking approach is now used by more than 80 other organizations worldwide. FINCA operates in over 20 countries in Latin America, Asia, and Eastern Europe, along with Africa.

FINCA Uganda is governed by a local board of directors, which is appointed by FINCA International. They have a reputation in Uganda as the only one among many microcredit organizations that takes its services out into the field where the people live. Their stated mission is to empower poor women and alleviate poverty through microfinance.

I spent a couple days with FINCA-Uganda, meeting with top management, front-line staff, and borrowers. FINCA came up as one of the two most cited microfinance programs (along with Grameen) in my interviews with program evaluation directors; and FINCA itself identified their Uganda group as one of their two best (the other was in central Asia).

One of the FINCA borrower groups I talked with was based in the village of Kawempe; they were holding a meeting in a small church. One borrower assembled small packages of beans, maize, roasted groundnuts, and other goods for sale at the market. Another milled rice powder and millet, for porridge and soya powder for tea. Others operated such ventures as eucalyptus sales, a motorcycle spare parts shop, tailoring with a small sewing machine, packaging and selling herbal medicines, and selling lumber and construction poles to building sites. Some said conditions were extremely hard and getting harder. Many felt they had been unable to meet their savings targets. A number were having difficulties making enough money from their businesses to repay their loans, having to work harder to do so. One even told me she was on the verge of dropping out because of difficulties. Despite their problems, most said they felt better off for the FINCA loans.

Another excellent organization somewhat similar to FINCA International is ACCION, which receives high ratings, including an A from the AIP; ACCION was one of the pioneers of microfinance—actually predating BRAC and Grameen as well as FINCA in its programs. ACCION has consciously sought to lend to the less impoverished of the poor, in order to ensure financial sustainability and hope for spillover benefits to the poor and help build the financial sector. In contrast, FINCA has sought to lend to poorer borrowers, if not the poorest of the poor. Each strategy has advantages and this kind of diversity and competition is good for development and poverty alleviation. ACCION has been at the center of the movement to commercialize NGO microfinance organizations, a trend also encouraged by USAID and sweeping the microfinance community around the world. The trend holds promise but also presents pitfalls.

While I visited FINCA Uganda, the organization was in the throes of adapting to commercialization. Staff with whom I spoke identified the recent decision to commercialize their operations as FINCA Uganda's most important decision in recent years. The topic was consuming much of the attention of staff members.

Commercialization is worth a closer examination, both to point out an important microfinance trend and for what it reveals about the influence of big donors, for good or ill, on NGOs running poverty programs. Commercialization involves becoming a regulated, formal financial intermediary, which gives them the legal right to take deposits and make investments as well as offer loans to members. The decision-making process was complex. Initially, key donors, including USAID, and its British and German equivalents, Department for International Development (DFID) and Gesellschaft für Technische Zusammenarbeit (GTZ), lobbied the Ugandan government to change MFI law to facilitate and encourage commercialization. The MFIs, including FINCA International, also supported and lobbied for this legal reform. The staff members I spoke with told me that FINCA supported the reform because they felt they would benefit from having these additional institutional options, if and when they decided they were ready to use them. Foremost was the ability to directly accept deposits, as a source of funding, but, more importantly, as a way of attracting and retaining clients who had wanted this savings feature and were attracted to competitors who did so (legally or not). They also wanted to stay engaged so that they could lobby for favorable provisions in the law. Still, FINCA staff told me that they were unsure whether they would benefit from commercializing at that time, and expected only that they might commercialize at a relatively distant point in the future.

Despite its potential benefits, commercialization was a wrenching decision for the organization. The considerable ambivalence toward commercialization in FINCA and the strong support for it from its major funder, USAID, appears to reflect the influence that major donors have on key decisions. The influence of the beneficiaries was also important: the poor themselves strongly wanted to be able to save with, as well as borrow from, the MFIs to which they belonged; and commercialization was a vehicle to deliver this feature. Moreover, some competitors were already engaging in semi-illegal activities restricted to regulated MFIs such as accepting savings deposits. FINCA supported the rule changes partly to ensure a more rational set of regulations that would potentially put them on an even footing with competitors.

The change in the law changed the rules of the game, and thus the competitive environment. Soon after the law was passed, FINCA realized that its peer or competitor institutions were likely to commercialize, so that FINCA would also have to do so to remain competitive. Ultimately the issue was framed as one of survival in the face of potentially fatal competition. Even so, the (internationally appointed) board was cautious about making this change. There was concern that the regulatory requirements and financial competition might push them away from their focus on poverty alleviation. The open question was whether FINCA will be able both to succeed in their current drive to commercialize their banking operations, while also maintaining their impressive focus on the very poor. But by late 2004, FINCA founder John Hatch told me that commercialization has so far proved a success: new members are lining up to deposit their savings in their own FINCA bank accounts and to participate in FINCA programs.

Despite its apparent impact, microfinance is not a panacea for poverty; microcredit usually has to work in conjunction with other efforts. An increasing number of NGOs are working to do this. Several of the programs of BRAC work in conjunction with microfinance, through what they call "microfinance-plus-plus." Freedom from Hunger (FFH) has been one of the pioneers, creating the Credit with Education program, which adds health and nutrition education to its business training. FFH pioneered the program in Ghana, where it received good evaluation reports, and won a Pro-Poor Innovation Challenge Award, sponsored by the Consultative Group to Assist the Poor. Business education is the most common service packaged with microfinance, by FINCA and other MFIs. But other key capabilities are now being combined with credit, including health education and healthcare. Project Hope has taken this trend one step further with its village health banks.

INTEGRATING CREDIT WITH HEALTH: PROJECT HOPE, ECUADOR

The international NGO Project Hope has also developed an integrated strategy to link microcredit with health and education programs. Historically, Hope has focused on provision of improved public health and other health services for developing countries. They are still perhaps best known for their traveling hospital ship, though it has not been in service for many years. Recently, Hope has experimented with combining its health programs with microcredit.

Project Hope's village banking and income generation project began in 1993. Hope developed the project in part on the premise that their past maternal and child health programs were often limited in providing *sustained* improvements in health and nutrition because of constraints due to poverty. As Project Hope put it, "poor families many times cannot afford the nutritious foods, medicines, health services, or environmental conditions they need for protecting their health." As a result, HOPE sought to improve the health status of low-income mothers, and their infants and young children, by creating village health banks combining loans and popular economic education with maternal and child health promotion. Project Hope health banks have been implemented in Ecuador, Honduras, the Dominican Republic, Malawi, and Guatemala.

Health banks provide health promotion activities focusing on maternal and child health, in addition to providing credit and basic business skills to low-income women for use in productive activities. These activities seek to provide individuals with access to basic health services and knowledge, which may include basic hygiene, maternal health, family planning, and women's preventative health care, in addition to child survival interventions, including acute respiratory infections, Expanded Program on Immunization, control of diarrheal diseases, breast-feeding, and nutrition. The health interventions take the form of fifteen minute health lectures and other activities at each biweekly meeting of the bank, led by each bank's health officer, which all bank members are required to attend.

Banks proceed according to 16-week "loan cycles," the period between the issuance of the loans and their final repayment. Each cycle features a different health theme. Health messages for each cycle are printed in simple language on the reverse of each borrower's account booklet (most participants have at least basic literacy skills). In addition, each bank designates a member as its health officer, whose responsibility it is to monitor immunizations of children and women, record births and deaths, weigh children under two on a quarterly basis, and refer members to local health services for care. The business and health education components worked to instill behaviors conducive to sustained improvements in the health status and income of the family. Improved health is also intended to improve efficiency on the job and to decrease time lost from work due to taking care of sick children.

I was asked by Project Hope to join a team that would evaluate this program. At my suggestion, Hope carried out a randomized experiment to determine the impact of the health banks. In Ecuador and Honduras, Hope established both village health banks and standard microcredit banks, which provide credit and basic business information, without any health promotion activities. Project Hope then assigned these two types of banks randomly across villages. We collected data to understand any differences that emerged. If Hope's theory was correct, the health banks might lead not only to better health, but also to higher income—because people were healthy enough to take good advantage of the credit. It might even lead to better bank performance if people who are more productive default less.

The evidence supported Hope's view that health practices do not improve automatically with higher wealth. Evidence also suggested that this integrated strategy can be effective in raising health and business skills, as well as family income, among participants—but not always and not necessarily more so than with a credit-only approach. In Latin America, diarrhea is one of the most important indicators of problems with child health. In the urban slums of Honduras, results show that health bank participation is robustly associated with a later reduction in child diarrhea but credit-only bank participation does not have this effect. This difference held after accounting for other ways in which participants might have differed from each other. Curiously, however, in rural and small-town Ecuador, results suggest a larger impact of credit-only banks.

In both countries, health bank participation significantly raised subsequent health care over credit-only participation, and reduced the tendency to switch from breast-feeding to bottle-feeding as income rises. But effects on expenditures were ambiguous; at least in the short run the microentrepreneurs may have been investing more money in their businesses rather than increasing family expenditures. Finally, the results showed no clear link between the health tie-ins and bank performance, which might at least indicate that the program's health dimension at least partly paid for itself through better bank performance. Project Hope was so impressed with the program's health impact, however, that they stopped the experiment and added the health components to the standard village banks after less than two years. As a result a full comparison over a longer time period could not be completed.

Experiences of organizations such as Grameen and Project Hope show that an integrated approach can have positive impact on poverty. But can a more minimalist approach also reach and assist the poor? The experience of the Association for Social Advancement (ASA) in Bangladesh suggests the answer may be "yes."

THE MODEL T OF MICROFINANCE:
THE ASA ALTERNATIVE

Not long before he was kidnapped and viciously murdered in Pakistan in January 2002, the accomplished *Wall Street Journal* reporter Daniel Pearl co-wrote a story about microfinance in Bangladesh, published on November 27, 2001. The primary point of his article was a critique of the Grameen Bank. His article raised a number of concerns that I pursued during my visits to Grameen. Officials at Grameen argue that the major criticisms have been largely rectified. However, at the end of his article, Mr.

Pearl offered an intriguing comment that caught my attention: "[H]arder-headed microlenders are stealing the spotlight. . . . One rising star is the Association for Social Advancement," led by ASA founder and managing director Shafiqual Haque Choudhury. ASA has two meanings, because *asa* (pronounced ah-shah) means "hope" in Bengali.

The Association for Social Advancement (ASA) is usually included in lists of major MFIs in Bangladesh, but it gets much less attention than BRAC or Grameen. However, the June 2002 *Finance for the Poor* newsletter of the Asian Development Bank called Choudhury "the Henry Ford of microfinance in Asia." Just as standardization of the car, even though sharply reducing choice for the consumer, was able to drive the cost of cars down to the point where the typical consumer could afford one, so had ASA, the article implied, similarly driven down costs to the point where sustainability was possible.

I was intrigued to meet this Henry Ford of microfinance, and he was kind enough to spend a couple hours meeting with me in his office in Dhaka. Choudhury founded ASA in 1978, and has worked full-time in the organization since 1983. He began by trying to pressure government to take steps to establish basic human services and human rights. Becoming discouraged with this effort, Choudhury decided to try to find a way to provide the poor with what they needed until the government would fulfill its obligations. He and his organization took an integrated development approach until 1990. But Choudhury concluded that, "after years of trying to do everything, we were not doing one thing well." He went on to say that, "When I asked the poor: 'What is the one thing you most need,' they would say income generation—either a job or some other vehicle to increase their income." Thus in 1990 Choudhury and his organization decided to make microcredit their major focus.

"At that time," Choudhury told me, "the Grameen Bank was subsidized. But ASA made a do or die decision, to be completely self-sustaining."

We would alleviate poverty by being financially sustainable; we would accept no grants within five years. We tried to decrease costs however possible, from the branch to the head office. We would find simple ways to identify borrowers; records were kept to the minimum needed. Our loan selection criterion was simple: We would just select the poor. We asked very simple questions. If the borrower made less then one dollar a day they could borrow from us. We set up groups of 20. It was close to the village bank concept; initially, we had group guarantees, but it created more problems than it solved. Grameen did this for 20 years, but we abandoned it in two and a half years. We did not want to punish the whole group for one member's default. So we did individual borrowing with weekly repayments—in a house or wherever they wanted.

As it happened, most ASA borrowers wanted to keep the social gatherings for repayment even though there is no joint liability. ASA accepts savings, but from members only. They re-lend these savings to other members; and depositors can withdraw their funds when they need them. "This is a difference of ASA," Choudhury said: "We allow savings withdrawals, and do not lend to the group. ASA specializes: We are not 'minimalists,' we are specialists; that's why we have such low costs. Our growth is spectacular, because we have only one product. We are like a loan factory."

Currently ASA has 2.3 million borrowers. They charge a flat 16 percent interest. "This is the same as BRAC and Grameen, but our financial ratios look better. We have 99.35 percent repayment. We have only 60 to 70 people in the head office, but 8000 employees and 12,000 branches. Our cost per dollar lent is very low, .37 percent. The plan is to turn profits back over to operations." ASA also offers members a simple form of life insurance: "If you die you get six times the amount that you deposit."

In a period when commercialization is considered the only way to proceed, ASA is not formal or owned by anyone. Choudhury said, "We are still an NGO. It takes time with government to be formal. If we are informal, we have less government regulation and supervision."

Choudhury noted that the organization is also an example of simplicity when it comes to hiring staff. "When we recruit new people we ask only three questions: What is poverty? Who are the poor? And how do you identify them? The question is whether they are listening, and [whether] they can answer with intelligence and strength, not whether they are correct. We do not allow people to use their names, to show that no favoritism is used. We only use an assigned number, and we post the numbers of the people who are offered a job." Out of 20 interviewed at a time, they select 3 or 4.

Our meeting came to an end. The Henry Ford of microfinance had promised to be with his young daughter for an event. But I was sure we would be hearing from him in the years ahead.

INSURANCE AGAINST POVERTY

The poor typically face greater risks than the nonpoor—indeed catastrophic and life-threatening risks—but are generally unable to insure against them. Many of the world's poorest people are farmers. All farmers experience variability in crop yields, but poor farmers using traditional agricultural methods face high personal and business risks. The poor manage to reduce the risks they face only at the expense of lower average yields. Some governments offer limited crop insurance, but it covers only part of the farmland, and is limited in scope. Crop insurance suffers from moral hazard—with crop insurance farmers may not feel the need to work as hard—and adverse selection: Those who know they face declining yields are more likely to sign up for insurance. But the underlying problem is less crop failure than uncertainty about the weather. Someone with fire insurance might become more careless with matches, but no one can create bad weather to collect on weather insurance. Despite this fact, farmers have been unable to get weather insurance.

Recently, the idea of insuring farmers against poor rainfall has received increasing attention. In a 2003 pilot program, smallholder farmers in the state of Andhra Pradesh in India were able to buy rainfall insurance that protects them against extreme droughts. Rainfall during periods considered critical for plant growth receives a higher weight in the insurance formula. With support from the World Bank, insurer ICICI Lombard, an Indian-Canadian joint venture, developed the insurance policies for the pilot. BASIX/KSB, an Indian MFI, sold around 250 policies to peanut and castor bean farmers. One of the top-five global reinsurance companies then reinsured this portfolio. Payouts are very rapid by Indian standards. Interviewed farmers said that they understood the details of the insurance policy, and that the payout system, which depends on when the rain falls and not just on how much total rain is received, makes sense to them, based on their farming experience. The program may help to free farmers from seemingly inescapable risk traps.

Microinsurance of various kinds is provided by a number of the microfinance organizations featured earlier in this section and elsewhere in the book. ASA and BRAC both have developed life insurance packages for its members. In the BRAC plan, an annual fee of $1.25 provides half of the health costs for an entire family for a variety of services. Grameen Bank's cooperative health insurance plan for rural Bangladesh works in a similar way. At least 30,000 households have taken part. Although the service has not seemed to reach the very poorest families, it was a great boon to many people who nonetheless are poor by any standard other than the ultrapoor of Bangladesh.

Some Grameen "replication" efforts such as the Philippines-based Center for Agriculture and Rural Development operate loan redemption insurance along with life insurance. In Uganda, FINCA provides both life and disability insurance through a partnership with American International Group (AIG). In addition, the Self-Employed Women's Association of India, or SEWA, also offers health insurance, life insurance, and property insurance to over 30,000 members. Alternativa Solidaria, an NGO in impoverished and troubled Chiapas, Mexico, has been developing life insurance for indigenous peoples in a joint venture with Zurich Insurance.

Still another form of insurance is provided by the Food for Work Program, which operates in Bangladesh with the support of USAID, NGOs such as CARE and World Vision, and other international donors. Those who need food can work for the day in exchange for basic foods for themselves and their children. With the program, parents may not have to send their children to work in times of hardship. Knowing this safety net is present makes it possible for the poor to take more business risks. It is a politically sustainable safety net for the poorest, because it offers a hand up rather than a hand out; and the strong work requirement means only the poor participate. In an added bonus, the participants work to build infrastructure such as farm roads, irrigation canals, tree plantings for erosion control, and flood protection, which also benefit their communities. While private contractors might be more efficient, without the program in most cases these public works would probably not be built at all. Similar programs have been introduced in other developing countries, including India and Argentina.

But even basic health, education, credit, and insurance are of limited help if you lack access to markets and face barriers to the accumulation of assets.

BOTTOM-UP
MARKET DEVELOPMENT

ASSETS AND ACCESS FOR THE POOR

Even as national and global markets have developed and grown, the poor have often remained disconnected from them, lacking opportunities to benefit. Microfinance helps, but the poor must build family assets and gain better access to markets. Innovative programs in rural South Asia are showing the way.

FRONTIERS OF POVERTY REDUCTION:
BRAC'S TARGETING THE ULTRAPOOR PROGRAM

Life is truly lived at the edge for those at the bottom in remote, rural Bangladesh. Often divorced women, their children, and infirm men, they are tellingly called the "hated poor." They number in the many millions in a country like Bangladesh. These "hated poor" receive very little even in alms. They make a few cents a day in exchange for long hours of labor as housemaids, farm day laborers, or beggars. Rape and other abuse of housemaids is common. Working all day in a rich man's house yields about 14 takas, the cost of two cups of rice. Their children eat this rice, along with any foraged vegetables, plus a fish that the children may be able to catch a couple times a week. These poorest of the poor cannot join microfinance programs in part because the required savings are beyond their reach, in part because they have been unable to start any enterprise, however meager. Isolated from even the mainstream poor community, microcredit merely adds to their unproductive debt, because of the quicksand of poverty and social exclusion in which they live. Many were born into the prison of wretched poverty, never to escape. Even the best poverty programs have tended to overlook those trapped in the daily desperation of living on less than half a dollar a day—the women trying to earn enough rice for herself and her children to survive one more day.

However, BRAC has long been dedicated to serving the poorest of the poor. BRAC offers a microfinance program, which began in 1974. In addition, understanding that the poorest were often not ready for microcredit, BRAC ran the highly regarded program Income Generation for Vulnerable Group Development (IGVGD). The idea was to feed people until they have the strength for education and microenterprise development. In this way, an undernutrition trap can be sustainably escaped. Or as you could put it: "teach a woman to fish, but give her fish until she learns how." Thus, IGVGD serves as a remedial program for the extremely poor, preparing them to graduate into mainstream programs for the moderately poor. BRAC has received international acclaim for these efforts on behalf of the poor.

BRAC has always been its own toughest critic. BRAC founder Fazle Hasan Abed said, "We have been successful at reaching the moderately poor." By this he meant those earning between perhaps 50 cents and $1 per day, poorer than most participants in poverty programs almost anywhere. "But, despite our efforts, we have not succeeded in reaching the ultrapoor." In extreme famines, such as Bangladesh suffered in 1974, the world comes to help feed people who stagger into food centers. But while relief programs sometimes reach the poorest, development programs generally do not.

Despite its reputation as an effective, poverty-focused NGO, BRAC was not quite reaching its goal. In 2002, BRAC decided to take a chance, and design an entirely new program to reach the ultrapoor. The effort reminded me of Tiger Woods, who at the peak of his game decided he had to reinvent his swing. He was hitting the ball a bit too far.

Rather than simply modify existing programs, BRAC developed a new approach, "Challenging the Frontiers of Poverty Reduction: Targeting the Ultra Poor." Targeting the Ultra Poor (TUP) is a broad-based and multidimensional attack on poverty through specific targeting of the ultrapoor not reached by conventional service delivery programs. The focus is on developing human capital (health, education, and training) and "social capital" (that is, village support networks and sponsorship of community leaders) for the poor, especially women; and on confronting the forces that repress and obstruct (or "disempower") the poor and constrain their livelihoods.

The TUP program theme is "pushing down and pushing out." It pushes down, to those with lower incomes, and it pushes out, by moving beyond the bounds of conventional programs to focus on the constraints that keep the ultrapoor so downtrodden that they cannot function. Behind this theme lies an important discovery. The ultrapoor face qualitatively different deprivations of opportunities and basic security, as compared with those who are just above this desperate state. Differences include the lack of able-bodied men in the household, social exclusion, and other vulnerabilities to exploitation.

Targeting the poor involves a multi-step procedure. You cannot do anything for the ultrapoor if you cannot find them, or distinguish them from the moderately poor. To be eligible for TUP, families have to meet three criteria: the household is not borrowing from an NGO credit program, nor a current recipient of a special poverty benefits card (the IGVGD program discussed earlier), and there should be at least one adult woman capable of utilizing the asset transferred to her. If no one is capable of doing any income-earning work, relief, rather than development, is called for. The household could not initially own more than a tenth of an acre of land. In addition, at least two of five additional criteria have to be met: the household is female-headed or contains women who were divorced, widowed, or abandoned; women work outside the household; the main male income earner is physically unable to work regularly; school-aged children had to work; and the household had negligible assets beyond the house they live in.

To find the poorest of such women, several strategies were used. One is called "Participatory Wealth Ranking." A meeting is held in which a village map is drawn on the ground with each household labeled. The villagers agree on a wealth ranking among the households, to identify those who are the poorest of the poor. People are much more knowledgeable or open about being relatively poorer or richer than others than in other countries, perhaps because people live in such close contact with each other. For example, walking around villages where the poor live I found I could often see through the straw walls to the contents of peoples' houses—just walking between huts on a village path, not voyeuristically going up to the cracks and peering through. Those who can afford tin plate walls or roofs are less poor than those with straw walls or thatched roofs. Those who are known to have a steady, formal job are categorized as among the well off. In rural Bangladesh, the "labor aristocracy" is composed of those who have *a* job.

There is an incentive for people to rank themselves as poor enough to receive assistance; but the multiple checks done on family status means their ability to get away with this is sharply limited. The participant identification strategies are not perfect. Better off people may find ways to convince BRAC people that they should be counted among the poor. Conversely, those in the most extreme poverty may not come forward at all; and people may forget their small huts when drawing village maps. Indeed, the more socially excluded among the poor may be less likely to be picked—even though their social exclusion is a fundamental cause of their poverty.

To supplement community meetings, BRAC staff members walk through the village, looking for any hut that gives the appearance of extreme poverty. They then try to bring potentially overlooked ultrapoor people to the attention of the community meetings.

Village leaders are actively involved in all stages of the process, generally people who are relatively well educated such as the schoolteacher, but usually not employers of the poor. These leaders are also clearly ineligible for TUP assistance, and their impartiality and knowledge tends to be respected, so they can help to mediate disagreements about who should be included as among the poorest. This can also reduce the ability of the powerful to strong-arm the weak into stating that certain cronies of the powerful are actually among the poorest and should get benefits. These village leaders then form a TUP support committee that monitors progress and intervenes to prevent personal crises that can overwhelm participants and otherwise lead them to drop out of the program. This feature is based on BRAC's observation that without achieving reliable social support in village organization and governance—"socio-political assets"—the ultrapoor often cannot break the cycle of poverty.

TUP was launched in pilot form in 2002 in three deeply impoverished districts, with 5,000 participants each in 2002 and 2003; a further 5,000 are planned for 2005, with an additional 55,000 in the subsequent two years. If results are favorable, BRAC plans a substantial expansion of the program.

I visited several villages in which the TUP program had already been implemented. In Danga Para, Chowdhury Para, and Barogharia villages in northwest Bangladesh, houses were typically made of bamboo and straw, sometimes tin, and jute rope. The ultrapoor were living in little more than one-room straw shacks. Typically the only possessions inside were a couple of beat-up cooking pans and plates, rolled up straw mats for sleeping, a few clothes and minor items for the children. Cooking was done over a small fire on the floor, with smoke escaping through a hole in the roof. Program participants might have a small straw annex recently built to house their new microenterprise. Most of the women said they had "lost" their husbands, which included abandonment.

I met TUP participants Jeleca and Obzalun, who were tending vegetable plots, helping each other out. Each had rented two-tenths of an acre: a tiny step up, yet for these women the step of a lifetime. Margina was raising chickens in cages in a small coop added to her house; the chicks were supplied by BRAC. Regia was raising two cows and a calf. Jakeda was raising nine goats; she told me that she planned to sell four of them before Ramadan, to buy a cow and things needed by her family. Solay had a tray, carried on her head, from which she sold miscellaneous items such as ornaments and sweets. In other villages some participants had a small pushcart. Alia was one of eight women who had started a small tree nursery on a rented plot, each renting a tenth of an acre. They were growing mango, jackfruit, olive, mahogany, teak, and medicinal herbs. She and her colleagues said the fruit trees seemed to be working out best so far, and they might specialize more in fruit in the future. The work was viewed as a part of BRAC's broader "social forestry" program. Before the program, they were "working in rich men's houses." The women were clearly proud of their accomplishments, beyond anything they had achieved in their lives up to that point.

The TUP program has helped to overcome information traps by showing women alternative means of livelihood. Several are suggested to participants in the early stages of preparation. Ultimately, about half of the income-generating projects were selected by the participants, and about half by BRAC staff. Although each woman was supposed to choose a project on her own, some seemed to feel that staff had given them more than advice—essentially telling them what project to select. This may be because of the pressure staff felt to establish the program in one village and move on to another, or because of what the staff thought would be easiest. Staff suggestions were made on the basis of such things as market conditions, ventilation in the house, and suitability of the land. In some villages, most of the women were engaged in a common activity, such as raising chickens and selling eggs, or keeping a milk cow. A big increase in supply may lower local prices, without a distribution system to a wider market. On the other hand, if a critical mass is reached in village specializations, a distribution system may become economically viable. It remains to be seen whether oversupply problems will emerge and how BRAC will respond to them.

The TUP program is also innovative in directly transferring physical assets. Few poverty programs include asset transfers; they offer various types of loans, or in kind goods and services such as food, health care, development of community organizations, education for children, and training for adults. However, TUP shares the strategy used by Heifer for so long—providing farm animals and training. But TUP differs from Heifer in that it finds a way to transfer assets, even some farm animals, to families with *no land* other than a little patch around their tiny hut. The active involvement of the local village elite at all stages through community support committees is another innovation. Finally, BRAC chooses activities for which there is demand; if there is no local demand but an active market or at least potential demand on a larger regional or national scale, BRAC helps participants to find a way to connect to the market, and to ensure that needed inputs are there. This is one of the purposes of the BRAC enterprises.

CREATING MARKETS THE POOR NEED WHILE FUNDING POVERTY ALLEVIATION: BRAC ENTERPRISES

Many poverty traps are caused or reinforced by missing markets. Thus, BRAC's enterprises are intended both to create markets whose absence may hold back the poor, and to provide employment for the poor who would otherwise have meager if any alternative sources of income. All of the key BRAC enterprises are operated at a net profit, at least after a start-up period; and these profits are plowed back in to other programs.

BRAC's founder, Fazle Hasan Abed, told me:

> The logic of BRAC's enterprise program is to generate job creation in the villages. Each enterprise that we have created has been founded to meet a specific purpose for poverty reduction. For example, we discovered that village people can often make excellent craft items, but the problem was how to market these more broadly; thus we started the Aarong shops. We worked in many villages where women who had a cow could not sell all of the milk for more than a paltry sum, thus we created the dairy.

Dr. Abed also said that availability of reliable inputs for rural people was a chronic problem, and many of BRAC's enterprises had been created to meet this need. An example he offered was the need for making quality day-old chicks available for raising activities in the villages, and BRAC felt it had to step in to supply these. But then, the constraint became adequate quantities of poultry feed. Although maize was optimal for this purpose, it was rarely grown in Bangladesh. Thus BRAC introduced a maize-growing industry. To incentivize farmers, BRAC guaranteed a floor price to farmers to start production; the market is now self-sustaining without this floor. As part of this effort, BRAC established a seed multiplication center in a joint venture with an Australian firm.

Most visibly, BRAC operates "Aarong" shops in five cities, which provide marketing outlets for rural artisans. These are small department stores, employing a significant number of people, and selling the products of thousands of rural artisans. The stores feature beautifully crafted clothes, footwear, and household items. Although Aarong will continue to buy mainly from individual artisans, it now also buys from its own small-scale factories.

BRAC has just opened a labor-intensive shoe factory in one of the most poverty-stricken regions of the country, in the extreme northwest district of Nilphamari. This enterprise employs 30 women in the TUP program, previously employed in day labor or as housemaids at about 14 takas per day (about 25 cents), or begging for 5 to 10 takas per day. Most had no husband, or a disabled or elderly husband, but most had children, many of them very young. When I visited, participants were at work alongside their trainers, proud of their new skills. Training is being conducted through JOBS (Job Opportunities through Basic Services), a USAID-funded employment generation program. While BRAC currently owns this shoe fac-

Figure 6.1 Targeting the Ultrapoor: BRAC program participants at their shoemaking co-op.
Photo: Author

tory, they intend to turn it over to the workers within three years. Workers who show ability are taking on marketing and management roles. Several workers were previously unable even to write their own names; now, workers are learning basic literacy and numeracy, and some are learning basic accounting. The enterprise is seeking to market shoes through additional outlets.

I visited two other new BRAC factories in the impoverished Nilphamari area, one a chalk factory providing basic employment to about 25 girls who have recently completed the BRAC nonformal primary education program. The girls seemed very young: when I asked I was told they were all "about 15 years old." This is not abhorrent child labor in the ILO sense. The girls are over 14, the ILO cutoff age for unacceptable child labor; and their alternatives in life would be early marriage, highly exploitive work as housemaids, or both. Although the girls receive just 20 takas per day, about 33 cents at current exchange rates, this is almost 50 percent more than the 14 takas they could earn as housemaids. Demand is still low, but the plant can increase output without hiring additional workers if demand increases, enabling them to raise wages. For example, there is now several minutes' idle time waiting for the chalk compound to solidify, during which the girls could be filling additional molds if the demand were there. Currently, the chalk is only sold to BRAC's nonformal primary schools, but efforts are underway to market the product to the public schools and other potential buyers.

While BRAC strives to turn a profit on its enterprises to fund its programs, the goal is to raise wages above the poverty line, when possible. Work at another BRAC factory producing sanitary napkins was also labor intensive by design but the working conditions seemed very good. Elsewhere, other BRAC enterprises include a seed processing center employing about one hundred workers, three poultry feed mills, many nurseries supplying fruit and other trees and plants, a printing plant, a cold storage facility, six poultry hatcheries, fifteen sericulture units, a bull station, and twelve fish and prawn hatcheries. Not content with the proverbial "teaching the people to fish," BRAC is building fisheries and restocking the ponds.

The modern BRAC dairy processes milk from BRAC village organization members, who may own between one and three cows, often financed through BRAC's microcredit program. The dairy, north of Dhaka, employs 132 workers. The plant was built with considerable excess capacity to accommodate future growth of BRAC member dairy output, and indeed production is growing steadily. Again as part of an explicit BRAC strategy, as many of the workers as possible are graduates of the BRAC nonformal primary program, which is aimed at families too poor to send their children to public schools.

Although BRAC enterprises provide at least a few jobs with better wages and working conditions, so far the number of jobs remains very small in relation to the enormous needs. But the example of showing what successful enterprises might look like may be one of BRAC's most valuable contributions.

Other new ventures include an office tower, a cold storage and vegetable export company, an Internet Service Provider (ISP), an information technology education unit, a commercial bank, a housing company, and the rapidly expanding BRAC University. It has to be acknowledged that the connection to poverty of some of these activities is rather indirect, by promoting growth and development. Careful monitoring and evaluation, as well as accountancy, is essential as BRAC goes forward. Are these the best activities? And if there are any implicit cross-subsidies, in what directions are they all flowing?

Moreover, as BRAC and Aarong commercial ventures continue to grow and diversify, even if it were a private enterprise, questions would be raised about whether such a diversified company could keep its focus. In large part because of its extraordinarily talented management, BRAC has been able to run enterprises profitably in an economy that has suffered from the lack of trained managers. But it may also hold special advantages that local companies lack, including favorable tax status, better ability to avoid paying bribes because of its special standing in the community, and opportunities for cross-subsidization. Although BRAC management states that the purpose of the enterprises is poverty alleviation, BRAC should preemptively allay concerns that funds intended for poverty alleviation might build the commercial enterprises, rather than the other way around. Along with poverty, the lack of transparency is a key problem facing Bangladesh; and NGOs such as BRAC and Grameen can help by setting an example. BRAC's publicly available audited accounts are unusually careful and thorough for the developing world, but could be further augmented to provide a definitive picture on the extent of any cross-subsidization, and of the sources and uses of funds. It should also be clarified whether BRAC's best managers are being distracted from improving the poverty programs in order to oversee commercial ventures.

But the bottom line for now is simple: NGOs around the world have been told by donors to show that they can "scale-up" and "become self-sustaining." BRAC, along with Grameen, are among the very few which have taken up this challenge.

PUBLIC SERVICE: THE SELF-EMPLOYED WOMEN'S ASSOCIATION IN INDIA

Throughout the developing world, women carry the burden of a large share of the work both inside and outside the home. But women often lack the skills and other resources they need to work productively. More than 90 percent of all women workers in India work in the informal sector, commonly under conditions of great hardship for meager pay. But public policymakers and private investors alike have largely ignored them. The Self-Employed Women's Association (SEWA) has worked to improve the lives of India's hardworking but impoverished women with innovative and effective strategies.

SEWA, which also means "service" in Hindi, was founded in 1972 in the state of Gujarat by Elaben Bhatt as an organization of and for poor, self-employed women workers. The organization is formally registered as a trade union for "uncounted, undercounted and invisible" women workers. The ultimate goal is to empower women, for, as Ela Bhatt expressed it, "so long as the poor remain powerless, poverty will stay." One of the most frequently cited NGOs in my interviews with poverty program evaluators about their choices of high-impact poverty programs, SEWA has enjoyed international acclaim, winning many honors and awards.

By 2004, SEWA had grown to about one half-million members. SEWA organizes women workers to achieve four types of security: of work, income, food, and social security. As a minimum goal SEWA seeks basic health care, childcare, and shelter, and for its members to become "autonomous and self-reliant, individually and collectively, both economically and in terms of their decision-making ability." A key part of SEWA's efforts is to help members find better access to the markets that they need to make their small businesses successful. In addition to representing workers, SEWA provides affordable services that these women typically can find nowhere else, including health care, childcare, savings and credit, insurance, housing loans and services, legal aid, and training. The SEWA staff like to say that they provide these services "at the doorsteps of the workers." SEWA operates about sixty healthcare facilities. In addition, SEWA has worked to help members secure access to government services for which they should be eligible. These activities are helping to overcome regional skill traps that have prevented even modest rises in incomes.

SEWA's leaders define their efforts in moving terms:

> The struggle is against the many constraints and limitations imposed on women by society and the economy, while development activities strengthen women's bargaining power and offer them new alternatives. Practically, the strategy is carried out through the joint action of the union and cooperatives. Gandhian thinking is the guiding force for SEWA's poor, self-employed members in organizing for social change. We follow the principles of *satya* [truth], *ahimsa* [non-violence], *sarvadharma* [integrating all faiths, all people] and *khadi* [propagation of local employment and self reliance]. . . . Through their own movement women become strong and visible.

SEWA has helped members develop services such as midwifery and day care provision into stable income sources. Prior to SEWA, some of these services were all but unavailable or unaffordable. Thus SEWA works to improve the lives of poor women by simultaneously creating missing but needed markets, and then helping members to take advantage of the income-earning opportunities that these new markets provide. SEWA has also helped nascent service providers in areas such as microfinance, healthcare, and childcare to form into self-supporting cooperatives. Successful childcare co-ops have been formed in Ahmedabad, Kheda, Sarbarkantha, and other cities, and three midwives' co-ops have also been created. In many of these educational and economic activities, the local group solidarity among the members is important for confidence, group learning, joint problem solving, and mutual insurance.

As a union, SEWA members are organized according to over 125 trade groupings. Representatives are elected from within each trade group, who

MOTHER-CHILD DAY CARE CENTER SERVICES

In addition to having a place to take the children so she can work, sometimes a mother needs basic education and support services. In response, an innovative, locally designed and managed educational program for mother and child is taking root in Uganda, the Mother-Child Day Care Center Services (Mother-Child). Initially the program was an extension of the National Association of Women's Organizations in Uganda, whose leaders responded to needs they saw in the community, which would go beyond their traditional lobbying and umbrella activities to directly provide services through an independent NGO. Several of its leaders became active directors and employees in the new program, which evolved organically. First providing day care services, the founders found themselves answering questions about a wide range of issues from their clients, and helping to solve problems in matters such as childrearing, marriage, family nutrition, healthcare, job skills, and workplace relationships. As staff did their best to keep up with these needs, the idea of formalizing and enriching this process to base a wide range of services and programs around the day care centers took shape. Today, the day care centers draw the mothers in, who then gain access to other services. As Mother-Child officials express it, over time the centers "evolved into sanctuaries where local women and children could learn, teach, and relax."

Mother-Child has won outside recognition and competitive prize grants, including a World Bank Development Marketplace competition award in 2000 and a special United Nations Educational, Scientific and Cultural Organization (UNESCO) grant. In addition, Mother-Child generates resources for its programs by charging small fees on a sliding scale from the mothers for childcare services, some training fees, renting out its hall for events, and engaging in income-generating activities, such as poultry and pig farming and production of locally popular fruits and vegetables.

The experience suggests that highly useful ideas for poverty alleviation can be developed in a decentralized way. Rather than relying on an elite to develop programs, people working in the field can create useful innovations by reflecting their clients' problems, trying out new programs, and learning from their mistakes. Experiences such as Mother-Child suggest that prizes for innovative poverty activities can motivate people to try out their ideas, and draw attention to ideas that prove effective.

then form the Council of Representatives, from which are drawn 25 of the 30 members of the Executive Committee, with representation across occupational types. The other five positions are held by top executives.

In building individual self-confidence, improving healthcare, providing training, creating markets, and lobbying for needed policy changes, SEWA is addressing the impediments that poor women face in India as they seek to gain market access and build assets.

COOPERATION AT WORK:
KDB IN KERALA, INDIA

Cooperatives also have an important role to play in poverty alleviation and economic development. When there are no jobs, and buyers hold all the bargaining power in your craft, sometimes workers can create their own enterprises. Kerala Dinesh Beedi (KDB) is a largely self-organized worker co-op network in Kerala, India. For decades, Kerala state on the subtropical coast of southwestern India has been heralded as a model for how the welfare of the poor can improved even when economic growth is slow. The state has high literacy, life expectancy, and other welfare conditions for its low level of income. The policies have been pursued in no small part because of the well-organized union sector and community organizing. A vibrant cooperative movement emerged partly as a result in Kerala (prominently including, but not limited to, the KDB co-op network), standing in sharp contrast to the often inefficient and stagnant state-sponsored co-ops in other parts of India. The KDB experience shows that autonomous initiatives of the poor can be successful at creating jobs and reducing poverty.

Beedis are small cigarettes known in India as "the poor man's smoke." The beedi workers' union went through decades of struggle with exploitative employers. Finally, in 1969, a few hundred desperate workers seeking a contract but faced with a lockout decided to form a labor cooperative. From these shaky beginnings emerged a decentralized, self-managed system of labor co-ops with over 33,000 employees. The presence of the KDB, directly and through its strengthening of the union, seems to have forced many local firms to increase pay and make at least modest improvements in working conditions, though beedi rolling is still a repetitive, boring, dirty, and uncomfortable task, even in the co-ops. Although evidence suggests that, despite some internal opportunities, members' upward mobility is modest, the children of members attend co-op–sponsored daycare, are better educated, and escape from child labor. Thus the families of KDB members may experience greater upward mobility over the longer term.

KDB is quite democratic. Workers elect the day-to-day management of the local co-ops from among their own ranks. These elected directors in turn elect the 22 member general body, representing KDB's 22 constituent societies, that has policymaking authority. There are also general annual meetings at which workers may exercise a direct voice. Finally, all KDB members are also members of the sponsoring trade union; and workers elect local union representatives who play a day-to-day watchdog role.

Partly a victim of its own success, KDB today has problems in its internal structure along with its struggles with difficult external conditions. Internally, the co-ops rely heavily on moral rather than financial incentives. This approach worked remarkably well in the historical context of the long struggle with employers and to establish the co-op as a part of that struggle. The first generation of workers was strongly motivated, but egalitarianism is now under threat. There is an expected daily quota, but little bonus for production above it, compared with the piece rate system that prevails elsewhere in the industry. Though work conditions are better, incomes are now only modestly higher than what productive workers can earn outside. In the past, workers often produced considerably over their quotas, but this began to wane. There was some tendency for less productive workers to find their way into the co-ops, and a further problem of less incentive to maintain diligent work once in. Moreover, salaries of managers and other skilled office workers have been kept to a six-to-one range of workers' salaries. This was less of a problem in the past when management was committed to the movement's social ideals, but is increasingly problematic, given alternative opportunities. There is skill involved in learning how to roll quickly, but workers' education is put to little use on the job. An appealing co-op tradition has been to have someone read aloud while others work. But there seems to have been minimal efforts to upgrade skill use in the co-ops, even in its new activities. All this having been said, recent reports by Gaurang Mitu Gulati and his colleagues are much more encouraging. Efforts to expand, enter new markets, and use new technologies have been redoubled. The co-op network seems to have overcome many of its problems, with a renewed commitment to cooperative goals.

Externally, KDB must survive in an environment in which competitors pay bribes and engage in other unethical practices to gain advantage in a climate of extensive government intervention. Moreover, as incomes rise, consumers tend to smoke better quality tobacco products. However, KDB is now able to charge more for its beedis because they have a reputation for consistent quality. Such consistent quality is something that a cooperative, with mutual monitoring as well as support across the workers, is more likely than a conventional firm to be able to achieve.

It is ironic that a product injurious to health would provide a pathway out of poverty. The best outcome would be for KDB to transfer its commitment to its workers to other products—thereby also overcoming the problem of declining demand over time. Indeed, there have been serious attempts to diversify into the production of other intermediate technology products, particularly foods such as pickles, juices, and coconut milk. Their quality is said to be very high, but these products are aimed at the middle class, who are not familiar with KDB's reputation for quality. Another reason for the limited success to date is the reluctance to spend on marketing and advertising; this is something that KDB will have to overcome.

In a strong sign that KDB is focusing on diversification and upgrading, KDB has set up a small information technology park, and is attempting to train some of the beedi rollers to work on computers. If successful, this would be a dramatic leapfrogging indeed, all the more impressive as the workers themselves run the program. This development shows that the poor understand the importance of gaining access to new technologies.

ENTITLEMENT TO NEW TECHNOLOGIES AND THE CAPABILITY TO BENEFIT FROM THEM

JOB ONE—
PROVIDING THE TOOLS TO CREATE STABLE JOBS:
THE SMALL ENTERPRISE ASSISTANCE FUND

The poor say the most important thing to them is finding a job with a steady income. Residents of the shantytown *favelas* of Rio de Janeiro were asked what factors were most important to them for a successful life. The largest number of respondents (69 percent) said a job with a good salary.

While small and medium enterprises (SME) play a major role in developed countries such as the United States and Germany, they are almost wholly missing in many transition countries, where most private enterprise was not permitted under communism. In many developing countries there are countless microenterprises, but few develop to the point where they could be considered bona fide SMEs. While not major corporations, there are many reasons why SMEs have an important role to play in market development and poverty alleviation. They have a high potential to both absorb and disseminate new technologies and more efficient production techniques. Much of the new employment generated in many economies results from SME expansion. SMEs become part of the formal sector—small but officially registered and tax-paying enterprises. And SMEs provide more stable income for employees than microenterprises. Workers often fold a marginal microenterprise when they can find a job in a stable small business. Indeed a steady job can be the most important asset for escaping a poverty trap.

But without access to technology, training, and equity capital, small businesses that might otherwise expand face limitations. Officials at CARE, an international NGO focused on poverty alleviation, recognized the potential of SMEs, but observed that such firms frequently never get off the ground even when led by highly enterprising people. To address this problem, CARE created the Small Enterprise Assistance Fund (SEAF), which it later spun off as an independent nonprofit investment group. While SEAF itself is a nonprofit organization, it invests in SMEs through for-profit investment funds. It has funds operating mainly in transition countries of Eastern Europe, but also in Peru, Bolivia, and China. SEAF raises capital for its funds from both official international financial institutions such as the World Bank and its affiliates and related institutions and private sector investors, most of which seek to have a positive social impact along with a good rate of return. These investors include New York Life, the Ford Foundation, and Calvert Funds, a socially responsible investment group.

SEAF funds usually take an equity stake in SMEs, with investments typically ranging between $200,000 and $1.5 million. Thus, SEAF acts as a venture capitalist for SMEs in developing countries. SEAF also provides some quasi-equity financial instruments and subordinated debt. More importantly, like venture capitalists, SEAF staff work closely with the enterprises they invest in, arranging for training in new technologies, helping to institute improved financial controls, and assisting with research on products and markets. Both international and national SEAF staff visit the firms to provide advice and training. SEAF also makes use of local, publicly funded business support programs and volunteer technical advisors. Ultimately, SEAF wishes to sell off, or "exit," from its investments—it does not wish to be a permanent owner in any of the firms it works with. The return gained from selling off its shares then goes to pay SEAF's own investors, and to generate funds for new investments. They seek to earn commercial rates on these exits, though that is difficult to achieve.

In Peru, some firms receiving SEAF investments, such as Victoria Kids specialty clothier, have taken pains to conform to high standards for occupational safety and health. Victoria Kids and the semi-industrial stonework producer South West Marbles and Stones A.C. (SWMS) have learned to tap into indigenous Peruvian handicraft skills, packaging these in a semi-industrial process with design and local materials in a way that would be very difficult for ever-worrisome competitors from China to emulate. Such skills may not require extensive periods of training for workers with some talent—perhaps no more than a few days for mosaic arrangement, simple flower painting, crocheting, embroidery, and so on. However, only some workers have the combination of artistic talent and patient temperament to achieve proficiency and reliability at these tasks. In the informal sector, they may be paid very little for their talents. Part of the value added of such SME entrepreneurs is to identify talented workers. By making a world market available for these skilled artisans, income to the community can be increased. Some producers find it in their interests to pay somewhat more than minimum wages—around a 25 percent premium. There are five related reasons: to attract and retain more motivated and trainable workers; to provide a greater incentive to work hard based on the greater costs to the worker of being fired; to help ensure a return on investments in training by retaining trained personnel; to increase flexibility, particularly by encouraging workers to make themselves available for overtime work in the event of rush orders; and to prevent labor strife. Such screening may result in a reputation for the country as a whole as a center for high artisanship work. Thus, an organization such as SEAF can help firms to become efficient, to complement craft skills with technology, and to open up export markets so they can expand.

SEAF reports that many of its firms have had a positive impact on well-being in their communities. Many of these firms' employees live there, and many of their suppliers also live and operate there. Regular business operations sometimes generate development activity that benefits the wider community. For example, in Poland a modernized pig-breeding firm called PPZP dug a well for more reliable and clean water for its own use. But the region as a whole also lacked a safe water supply; so PPZP extended a piping system to the surrounding communities, providing them with potable water. Another company, grocery chain Artima in Romania, improved roads near its stores and installed lighting along roads for safety, which benefited the whole community. In other cases, companies donate to community charities and public causes. In Bolivia, for example, Jolyka, a manufacturer of ecologically certified Amazon hardwood flooring, has established a foundation to assist small farmers in their efforts to produce forest wood and certify that ecologically supportive standards have been adhered to. In Romania, the distributor Telezimex sponsored a payroll deduction program to assist the community schools program, winning a prize for "corporate citizenship." The community development efforts enhance the firms' reputations while improving the overall business environment.

Although growth by itself is generally helpful for the poor, finding and supporting entrepreneurs who have social as well as financial goals plays an important role in making an extended and leveraged impact on poverty. There are plenty of top-flight entrepreneurs who are also socially concerned. SEAF has found that the key is to find entrepreneurs who are willing to put up some of their own money toward programs to assist families of their employees and the broader community. This can be matched by some outside funds that go directly to these efforts rather than to the entrepreneur. In SEAF's experience, it is more effective to first identify and invest in such concerned entrepreneurs, than to first invest based only on other criteria and then try to influence them to behave in a socially responsible manner.

Entrepreneurs who want to have an impact on poverty can follow some guidelines, including targeted hiring of the poor—especially underemployed mothers with children, female heads of household, and nonformal primary education graduates.

A WORTHWHILE ENDEAVOR

Another NGO with a mission broadly similar to SEAF but taking a somewhat different approach and working in different countries is Endeavor, which works with entrepreneurs in five Latin American countries—Brazil, Mexico, Chile, Argentina, and Uruguay. In 2004, Endeavor expanded to work in the country of South Africa. Thus, so far the group works in middle-income countries, but ones with high inequality and a significant number of poor people. Endeavor also seeks to close the gap between microfinance and the investment sources for large private or state-owned firms in developing countries by providing support for SME startups and expansion. One of the objectives is to help develop a cluster of dynamic local role models for other potential local entrepreneurs to emulate. Endeavor does not invest financially, but focuses on screening the most promising entrepreneurs, and then provides them with mentoring and training, and opportunities to network with potential investors and business partners, as well as with other Endeavor entrepreneurs. For-profit venture capital firms may generally find it too costly to identify promising candidate entrepreneurs in the low-information environments of developing countries. But when the broader benefits for development and poverty-reduction of stimulating a more dynamic economy are added to the financial return on investment, these screening activities are often socially very valuable. Initially, local Endeavor employees and volunteers nominate candidates to the pool of potential "Endeavor Entrepreneurs." Endeavor then relies on local and international volunteer business specialists through its "Venture Corps" programs, to help screen the best candidates from among these poten-

neurs are selected from among this more limited group by an international selection board; to be selected, an entrepreneur is interviewed in-depth by the board and must receive its unanimous backing. Endeavor selects entrepreneurs who are at what it calls a "tipping point at which Endeavor can help the entrepreneur reach new levels." Criteria for selection include entrepreneurial initiative, role model potential, development impact, degree of business innovation, the entrepreneur's "ethical fiber," and potential to work well with Endeavor and benefit from what it has to offer. This screening process is close in its overall design to the "social entrepreneur" fellowship selection methods used by the pioneering Ashoka network, described later in the book.

Endeavor's new program in South Africa selected its first entrepreneurs in December 2004. One of them, Stephan Roux, operates the Milkworx high-nutrition ice cream production company and is generating employment for thousands of participants. Endeavor official Diego Panama explains that "Milkworx sells its Cream Star brand to wholesale outlets or depots where the bulk products are then purchased by street vendor retailers, who store the ice cream in ice boxes attached to their bicycles and make 50% profit on sales to end consumers. Milkworx currently supplies a network of more than 5000 self-employed individuals." Another entrepreneur, Natalie Killassy, "began a sewing company, producing safety equipment and protective clothing for mining and other hazardous industries. Stitch Wise's products protect mineworkers" from the types of accidents that had previously disabled many of its 128 employees, who are 80 percent black and 40 percent paraplegic. I spent a day at each of these companies and found the employees motivated and the CEOs dedicated both to business and reducing poverty; they are eager to take the next steps with help as needed from Endeavor.

THE GRAMEEN PHONE LADIES

Until recently in Bangladesh, telephones were an unimaginable luxury for most people. Even if you were in an urban area that had been wired, landlines cost hundreds of dollars—plus the need to pay huge bribes to get the phone at all, which put a phone beyond even members of the middle class. Lack of phones meant most business had to be conducted in person. Valuable time was used up just going to the town or city to talk with someone. The poor, meanwhile, were simply cut off from the world.

In 1993, I heard Muhammad Yunus give a talk about his plans for the next phase of the Grameen Bank. In a strikingly original plan, a Grameen

Telecom subsidiary would be established, with the participation of Norwegian and Japanese telecommunications companies. The business plan would be a simple one: "to provide the poorest woman in each village with a cellular phone." Most of these villages are still without a landline phone system. "Now you may wonder," said Dr. Yunus, "what would the poorest woman in such a Bangladesh village want with a cellular phone? Well, everyone in the village who wants to make a call will have to come to her!"

Grameen established three technology and energy companies, with a double mission of economic development and poverty reduction. Grameen Telecom was established in Bangladesh as a joint venture with a Norwegian investor, and other parties have also become partners. Grameen Communications is a nonprofit information technology (IT) company founded in 1997 that develops software products and services and provides Internet services, hardware and networking services, and IT education. Grameen Cybernet Limited is the leading ISP in Bangladesh, a position it has held since it began in 1996. Each of these firms is expected to be at least self-sufficient, and each has a poverty reduction mission, such as employment generation, type of products sold, such as small-scale renewable energy and telecommunications at the village level, or microenterprises made possible. An example that achieves all three is the Grameen phone ladies program, which won the 2004 Delvelopment Gateway Award.

Ten years later, I met with two of the Grameen phone ladies in their homes. While I was visiting one of them, a village man came by to use the phone, conducting some business. The phone lady told me proudly that a mother had come to call her son, who is working in the Middle East as a laborer—the most distant call using her phone yet, she reported. Overall, nearly half of all calls are to family and friends on nonbusiness purposes. This is valued by the customers, who pay for the calls, but also helpful for keeping the villagers' social networks intact in the face of wrenching changes and the loss of ambitious people to out-migration. The phone service helps to ensure that remittances to the villages are received as intended. About 10 percent of calls are health-related, directly improving the well-being of the poor and indirectly improving their productivity and saving valuable time. Nearly half of the calls are related to family income generation.

The phone ladies I met were just two of the more than 25,000 Grameen phone ladies in nearly as many villages around the country. Grameen estimates that each phone lady makes phone usage possible for more than a thousand fellow villagers, more than a quarter of the rural population overall. Remember, most of these villages have no telephone lines at all, so pay phones were not an option. Revenue per phone lady is about $140 per month, which nets out at about $60 per month after expenses. This is double the country's monthly per capita income.

The women I met with were certainly not middle class, but they were clearly far from being the poorest women in the village, even before they became phone ladies.

I asked Professor Yunus about this. He told me, "when we put this in place on the ground, we found that to make it work the woman had to be able to do accounts. It is very difficult to teach this to the poorest woman in the village, who is illiterate, must work all the time, has not learned to think in an entrepreneurial way. You at least have to have an educated person in the family. We decided to leave it up to our Centers to decide who should become the phone lady."

I also asked him about the advertising signs everywhere depicting middle-class people using the cell phones. He replied that "we are now serving 34,000 villages with over one million subscribers; 32,000 of these are our phone ladies. That might not sound like a lot, but if you look at it by airtime, 17 percent is on the phones managed by the phone ladies. This is phone use by the poor."

Despite a published list of rates, reports are that there is some price discrimination going on—some of it socially beneficial. A lower price may be charged to the very poor if it is all they can afford. The practice of some phone ladies is apparently that bad news may be phoned for free, but a premium is charged for good news.

The phone lady system makes good use of the knowledge of the poor and of their organizations, in this case the local Grameen Bank organization. Grameen was able to help identify which women in each village would likely be the best for the phone lady role. The phone ladies were usually Grameen members of some standing, who had previously demonstrated that they were able and willing to build up microenterprises, were capable of basic bookkeeping, and who were generally known and had a good location. Women seem to trust using a phone operated by another woman—especially putting trust in them to answer the phone and contact them right away when a return call comes through—though men seem perfectly happy to use the phone ladies' mobiles as well. As the market grows, new competitors can be expected to enter the market, driving down prices, which should be good for the villagers as a whole.

The phone ladies program creatively helps villagers to overcome information traps by providing the rural poor with a viable alternative source of income and simultaneously increases the flow of information into and out of the village.

In fact, as the number of villages with phone ladies has steadily grown, demand for phone use in each village has grown with it. This is partly because the more villages that have a phone, the more villages there are that could potentially be called. We in the West have experienced similar processes of network growth in recent years, as services like fax, email, and instant messaging (IM) took off once a sufficient number of people had signed up.

TECHNOLOGY WITH A SUBTEXT: MUSIC VIDEOS SUBTITLING IN VILLAGE TELEVISION IN INDIA

Many educators deride television as a medium for the couch-potato illiterate. But in India, an educator is turning rural TV into a wildly popular medium for participatory literacy training.

In India today, even many remote villages have a community center television, receiving signals by satellite. Villagers watch indigenous language music videos produced by India's Bombay-based answer to Hollywood—aka "Bollywood." But access to a technology like television is not the same as the capability to benefit from it. Some 290 million adult Indians are completely illiterate; and another 300 million are considered semi-literate. But popular songs are learned by heart. Recognizing this, Brij Kothari, a professor of literacy at the Indian Institute of Management in Ahmedabad, created a system called Same Language Subtitling. The system uses color to highlight subtitles word by word as the songs play—akin to "follow the bouncing ball."

The Same Language Subtitling system can build on the basics learned in periodic village literacy campaigns, or reinforce rudimentary skills learned in many villagers' three or four years of schooling. Unlike traditional literacy programs, which can be embarrassing to the adult learner, time consuming, and tiring, this approach lets people learn a little at a time while having fun, according to their own schedules and timing. Even when just one member of the household improves their reading skills, the whole household benefits—just from having someone who can read a government form, a medicine prescription, or a job announcement, for example.

The Same Language Subtitling project won a World Bank Development Marketplace Award for $250,000, which enabled Professor Kothari and his Center for Educational Innovation to greatly scale up the program, in partnership with Indian television. The program has high impact for low cost. Viewing of the already popular programs went up by 18 percent after Same Language Subtitling was introduced. The idea is spreading to other parts of India, where the press has widely celebrated the program, and from there, it is to be hoped, to other regions such as Sub-Saharan Africa, where it is also needed.

PEAS IN A POD—
BETTER PRODUCTS AND BETTER MARKETING:
TECHNOSERVE AND PARTNERS IN TANZANIA

TechnoServe's Pigeon Peas Program in north central Tanzania is working to improve the prospects of smallholder farmers, by helping them to add value to their hard work.

TechnoServe is a Connecticut-based private voluntary organization governed by a volunteer U.S.-based board of directors, with affiliates in several Latin American and African countries. TechnoServe is a top-rated NGO, with a grade of A from the American Institute of Philanthropy. TechnoServe's focus is on market development and improved products and technology, factors that go together like "peas in a pod." In agriculture this involves moving farmers away from subsistence and toward commercialization, while developing higher value-added activities so more income can be retained by the producers.

The Pigeon Peas Program, launched in Babati district in Tanzania, is one of TechnoServe's highly praised programs. It is also an unusual example of successful partnering across diverse NGOs. The technical and marketing groups have worked together remarkably well with community development organizations.

Production of pigeon peas, the fundamental lentil legume used in toor dal, had been grown in the area for several decades, but the farmers had not much benefited. Even farms with progressive land management had problems increasing productivity and incomes. Beans of all varieties, both in-demand "Babati white" and less desirable types, were harvested and thrown together in piles. These were shelled and sold by the bag in mixed varieties. Later, middlemen sorted the mixed beans, at big markups.

By getting the farmers to specialize in the higher-paying varieties, and to do any remaining sorting themselves prior to sale, the program was able to retain a much higher share of value added for the farmers. This was particularly important for the European market, in which the Babati white variety is in strong demand. While this approach may seem obvious to outsiders, it required substantial education of farmers to get them to change their practices. TechnoServe publicized the prices received for each product at each step in the production and distribution chain, so the process would be transparent. TechnoServe estimates that 70,000 to 100,000 families could see substantial income increases from higher bean prices and processing jobs that would be created in the project.

The Pigeon Pea Program also introduced more disease-resistant varieties of products, working with several research partners, notably the International Crops Research Institute for the Semi-Arid Tropics (ICRISAT), an affiliate of the UN Consultative Group on International Agricultural Research (winner of the King Baudouin International Development Prize), and the government-affiliated Selian Agricultural Research Institute. The program worked to provide farmers with needed credit, inputs, and marketing assistance, along with training. In addition, simple processing of the peas to produce toor dal and similar products was introduced. This processing can be done with just two stones and water, requiring only basic training and set-up procedures. In its work with farmers, TechnoServe-Tanzania partnered with Catholic Relief Services, Lutheran World Relief, and other NGOs.

Like many poverty programs receiving U.S. support, the Pigeon Pea Program was partly funded by monetization, in which surplus agricultural products are given by the U.S. Department of Agriculture to NGOs and sold overseas. This is a two-edged sword. It provides funding for many valuable projects that could not otherwise be undertaken and increases food availability. But it also undercuts the local price, lowering payments to farmers and reducing incentives for farmers to expand local production. Many NGOs conclude that the benefits outweigh the costs.

As a final component of the program, a loan guarantee arrangement and minimum price guarantee was introduced, funded by monetization. After four years of operation, the capital of this $200,000 fund is still intact, suggesting that the program can be financially sustainable in the long run.

The programs made good progress towards the goal of helping these impoverished farmers retain more valued added. But some lessons have to be learned the hard way. Once underway, management of the program was turned over relatively quickly to beneficiaries and stakeholders, on the assumption that the program was already self-sustaining. The results of this decision were not favorable.

Project sponsors expected that, once outside buyers had seen what producers in the region could do, the market would sustain the program. However, both decision makers and farmers considered the early withdrawal of TechnoServe from the direct management of the program to have been a mistake. Sales of higher value - added pigeon pea products promoted under the program fell drastically during the year following withdrawal, from 15 containers (300 metric tons) to just 6 containers. The decision has now been reversed; TechnoServe is again working actively with these farmers to get the program back on track. And TechnoServe is actively working to bring new private sector actors into the picture, rather than rely only on NGOs and traditional private actors.

TechnoServe found that farmer groups seeking to export their produce require a full package of credit, market linkage, and business management assistance for at least four years before "graduating" from the assistance program. Without active steps to capture value added, export of pigeon peas to lucrative niche markets in Europe or India does not necessarily create good quality employment opportunities in the rural areas where the products are grown.

There are three lessons from this experience. First, an agricultural product development program has to be supported for a longer period of time—at least five years—to take root. Second, higher value–added stages of production must be developed, such as exporting toor dal rather than raw peas. Third, the program showed that "the job is easier when you deliver the whole package," as a staff member told me. The package includes the supply chain, credit, inputs, markets, and technological progress.

Two key influences drove the decision to end active management assistance for the program at an early date. In Africa, USAID contractors are placed under a great deal of pressure to declare programs organizationally and financially "sustainable" and no longer in need of funding. Local NGO officials, conversely, stated that their decision was mostly driven by their wish to shift their attention to new programs. In any case, the decision was clearly embraced by local staff, which in turn was later able to reverse its decision when results proved less desirable than expected. One reason this reversal was possible was the diversity of funding sources the program received. Donors also did not want to squander a model program. TechnoServe had several partners working in collegial joint ventures who shared perceptions of the issues. All these factors put TechnoServe's managers in a good bargaining position. Withdrawing support before gains are truly financially sustainable leads to a waste of resources. If we are serious about showing that poverty and development programs are sustainable, we have to stick with them until they have taken full root, and thus become an example and a beacon for those around them.

William Massawe, a Tanzanian TechnoServe staff member who worked on the project, told me: "It is very frustrating work, to convince people to try new things, but when it works it is very rewarding. I feel that I am helping to make a better future for my country."

Figure 8.1   Kenya women's crafts co-op: Practicing for a dance performance at the workshop.
Photo: Author

SUSTAINING THE ENVIRONMENT FOR ENDING POVERTY

The ongoing destruction of the environment of the poorest countries—both from actions within the country and without—is emerging as possibly the single greatest threat to ending global poverty. The question is whether the poor will gain the capabilities to preserve their life-sustaining and livelihood-providing environments before those environments are largely destroyed. Groups working with the poor cannot stop global warming, but they are finding creative solutions to some vexing problems, from programs to buy timber rights from logging companies and pay indigenous communities to guard the forests rather than cut them, to community participation in managing game parks. Here are just a few of the creative efforts underway.

CROSS-POLLINATION: HONEY CARE AND AFRICA NOW IN KENYA

Can the environment and economic development mix? What about a private business and an NGO? They have all been cross-pollinating with an innovative strategy to bring beekeeping to some of the poorest farmers in Kenya—jointly providing higher incomes and a better environment.

I visited Africa Now-Kisumu, Kenya, an NGO with international headquarters in the United Kingdom, which is sponsoring a "Honey Care" program to teach self-help groups, many of them women's groups, how to keep bees. Honey Care, which is a for-profit, socially conscious Kenyan company operated by activist businessmen, is a winner of the UN's Equator Prize. Africa Now Kenya developed community honey production as the major focus of western Kenya operations in a joint venture with Honey

Care. The Africa Now Kisumu program won a World Bank development marketplace award for its work in the program, succeeding in a deeply impoverished part of the country where beekeeping was rare, despite an unusually good environment for it and a ready market for honey. The honey raises incomes—as much as doubles them, though from only around $140 to $280 per year—and also benefits the environment through pollination.

Africa Now works with local community-based organizations (CBOs) that show interest and capacity during Africa Now program demonstration meetings. The expansion of capacities of the nascent CBOs is one of the program goals. One of the umbrella groups Africa Now works with—an association of 64 village women's self-help and cooperative groups—has constructed an extraordinary building of offices and shops standing like a castle in the small town of Funyula. I met with the council of the umbrella group. Several of us ate lunch together at one of the restaurants renting ground floor space in their building. Then we went off to the field for two days of visiting the villagers beginning beekeeping at the grassroots level.

The program provides modern-design "Langstroth" centrifugal-collection beehives, which have several advantages over hives traditionally used in East Africa; with centrifugal removal the honeycomb is not destroyed in harvesting, so it can be more quickly refilled.

One of the roles of Africa Now is to negotiate with Honey Care on behalf of Africa Now participants. Although socially minded, Honey Care is a business. Smallholder farmers may feel intimidated, and perhaps would not get as good terms if they had to negotiate individually. For example the product price was first offered at 80 shillings, but was negotiated upwards to 100 shillings. By having the CBOs collect the honey, substantial costs are saved on middlemen, raising the price received by the growers. The CBOs also serve implicitly as a guarantor of quality, though this is largely ensured by the technology.

Africa Now provides these hives on a lease-to-own basis as a form of microcredit, using a revolving loan fund. After the honey is collected, half the proceeds go to the farmer, and half go to pay down the cost of the hive, until the farmer fully pays off the cost of the hive. Leasing provides its own collateral, and enables borrowers to try a product such as an innovative beehive, to find out for themselves how productive it can be in their own environment. This reduces the risk for the poor farmers just entering the honey market, because their payments are strictly based on what they can produce. And, because the technology requires special equipment to harvest the honey, the productivity is entirely verifiable by the lender, in this case Africa Now.

The importance of pioneering this strategy is seen from the fact that, in the United States, leasing in one form or another has been estimated to comprise some 30 percent of private sector capital formation. It has an important role for small businesses that lease buildings, vehicles, and capital equipment. Leasing also plays a role for households; it has been used in the United States and developed countries for decades, for goods such household appliances and musical instruments for children. More recently, the market for auto leasing has expanded steadily.

Of course, leasing has its limits. For example, as we have seen, the critical need for microenterprises—and for many SMEs—is for working capital, and, well, you can't lease working capital. But for both microenterprises and SMEs in low-income areas such as East Africa, leasing lends itself as a vital part of the mix of getting market development underway.

Africa Now is planning to establish a new program to help farmers learn to produce sunflower oil. This would provide more pollen for the bees, while developing a new source of income and nutrition. Use of the low-technology oil press systems have been spreading rapidly throughout rural Africa, with a major role played by NGOs such as U.S.-based EnterpriseWorks, formerly known as Appropriate Technology International, and Africare.

While participants in the Africa Now communities remain poor, there have been visible reductions in their degree of deprivation. Their specialization in beekeeping points the way out of subsistence traps. That this is being accomplished in a way that actually improves the environment is a cause for double celebration.

SUSTAINING THE FOREST LIFE: THE SULEDO FOREST COMMUNITY, TANZANIA

The Suledo Forest Community won the United Nations Development Program's Equator Prize for environmentally sustainable development, recognizing programs that alleviate poverty while preserving the environment to meet the needs of future as well as present generations. Suledo is a network of autonomous community-based organizations (CBOs) managing the forests of nine villages with a combined population of about 54,000. Traditionally the area has been the home of Masai herders, whose 40,000 cattle graze between the trees in the ecologically rich miombo forest. Their traditional grazing practices were environmentally sustainable, as was the limited timber harvesting. More recently, other tribes with new lifestyles moved into the region. The Masai also began to farm part of the land. The government of Tanzania had zoned the remote area as "unreserved forests" on public land, and collected license fees from the harvesting of valuable tree species, such as mpingo, related to ebony and used for making flutes, and the now nearly vanished sandalwood.

In recent decades, with encroachments by government and by outside private property owners, village control had broken down. "Investors" from Dar es Salaam were essentially stealing the villagers' land. With assistance from the Swedish International Development Agency and its land management program (LAMP), community organizations under the Suledo umbrella are restoring traditional village management of common property resources, but with a modern organization and focus; decision making bodies are elected rather than controlled by chief or other village rulers; and it has a modern scientific foundation for environmental decision-making.

Prior to development of the program, the forest was managed by corrupt local officials, who either poached, took bribes from poachers to look the other way, or provided timber licenses whether they were warranted or not. Even when trees were removed "legally," only 20 percent of the revenue was returned to the district, and of that only 20 percent to the villages, that is, just four percent of revenues from even legal tree removals were received at the village level. Much of the valuable tree species in the forest were removed. While the Masai had sustainably utilized the forest for millennia, government was simply exploiting it for short-term gains, without reinvestment or sustainable management. At the same time, invading farmer settlers threatened the Masai and government forest revenues alike.

Things came to a head in 1993, when the government decreed that the forest would now be classified as a government reserve. This would have made forest grazing illegal, eliminating the means of support for the Masai villagers. Despite strong opposition, the forest administration went ahead with the plan. In 1994, the government surveyed and marked off land in which activities such as forest grazing would be illegal, while government took an inventory of trees that could be cut for timber. The villagers lived inside these boundaries. The government department that made the boundary decisions may not even have been aware of their existence. Either way, their livelihoods and indeed their entire way of life were now illegal.

At this point the villagers, through their Village Environmental Management Committees set up with funding and advice from the Swedes, decided to take the direct control of their natural resource management away from government. The communities organized to protect the environment, first in Sunya, then spreading to the other villages. Under pressure, the government agreed to an alternative, community-based management of the land, first as a pilot program in three areas, then, when results proved very positive, expanded to the current boundaries. The central government had to override the interests of the specialist national and local government departments, particularly forestry. Attempts are now being made to establish similar programs in other parts of the country. With the new system, the villagers have only to describe their claim to land, and the basis for the claim, and they receive a public land certificate. Although the land technically remains in government ownership, villagers are awarded permanent use rights, conveying all rights except for outright sale of the land.

The decision-making bodies at the village level are all democratically elected from among all village adults. Environmental Management Committees at both village and sub-village levels are elected from the village assembly, and include women as well as male herders and, more recently, representatives of other ethnic groups involved in activities such as beekeeping. Under the program, highly participatory methods are used, including activities such as village-based land use mapping. Simple methods that all the villagers can understand and take ownership of are used. The results are then established as official village by-laws, which gives them the force of law. In this way, 167,000 hectares have been included under the forest management program. Each village forest reserve is assigned to one of three land use zones: agricultural expansion, grazing (which is about 80 percent of the land), or totally protected. The grazing area has subzoning to ensure sustainability. Boundaries are marked with bright yellow paint. Young men who would otherwise be unemployed or have an uncertain status at their stage of life have been engaged in forest patrols, providing many young people with a socially useful purpose. The patrols report transgressions that can then lead to fines. Despite this, settlers and even larger ranchers continued to come into the area. The legal system took some time to work, requiring coordination between the village organizations and the Tanzanian government, but enforcement is steadily becoming more successful. There is still some corruption, allegedly even at the village level, but it is getting increasingly under control. The program addressed collective action and common property mismanagement traps with facilitation by outside advisers but made sustainable through community organizational development and training.

All of this took several years to become well established beyond the first burst of enthusiasm. Outside technical assistance was vital. The notion that NGOs or foreign advisors can come in with a little aid and soon everything will be financially sustainable is mistaken. After only a few years, however, reviewers have noted substantial positive effects on poverty reduction and biodiversity. Program officials said that microclimate effects are substantial: Rains significantly increased after protection activities, though the link is hard to prove. Fire remains a problem, but progress is being made. Village Environmental Management Committees are meeting regularly in all nine villages. At the encouragement of the Swedes, the committees have an impressive gender and ethnic balance. Women members of the village's environment committee speak with pride about how participation is transforming their lives in the village. Observers say the main problems such as poaching have now been solved in seven of the nine villages. In turn, the success of the program is having an impact on Tanzanian development policies elsewhere in the country. In the meantime the environment is being preserved for future generations to enjoy and to provide livelihoods.

It took over ten hours, mostly on deeply rutted dirt roads, to reach the district capital, the small town of Kibaya. The program villages were about three hours from town. I had the opportunity to attend one village's celebration of winning the Equator Prize. About 60 Masai in their striking costumes, men in red and women in purple, greeted Swedish program head "Mama" Harriet Rehn and her visitors. A choir serenaded us for half an hour, with songs that included references to the work of Mama Harriet as well as to the programs and to the forests they were protecting, with its beautiful animals and trees. We were also treated to some wonderful performances of traditional dance. They had bestowed me with a gift of a hen. A live chicken was clucking contentedly in my arms while I listened to the entertainment. I suddenly realized that I had no change of clothes within hours of driving time should the chicken decide to leave me with anything untoward. At that point I must have started looking rather uncomfortable, and someone took pity on me and took the chicken. "We will make a good stew with this chicken," he said. Later on Harriet told me they had asked her if I would bring the chicken back to America with me. She told them I wanted to, but would have a lot of difficulty with unreasonable customs officials. Then we followed some Masai down a short path where a goat had just been slaughtered and cooked over an open pit fire. This was a largely Christian village, but earlier they had invited anyone who might be Muslim in the group to observe that everything was done in a proper way. Milk and goat meat are major parts of the Masai diet. The goat was cut up in large pieces, then smaller chunks torn off and handed to us.

In another program village, Olkitikiti, few valuable tree species remained in the forest, after the poaching, corrupt government licensing, and other thefts. Rather than grow low-yield maize in the areas designated for farming, some parts could be designated for tree farming of mpingo, the valuable species related to ebony that seems to thrive there. In an area with poorly developed financial institutions and pressing needs to spend any available money today, the trees would provide the people with a kind of community bank account that the children of today's villagers could draw upon in the future to meet whatever new threats their forests might face. I learned that Olkitikiti means "armpit" in the local tribal language. If it had once been the armpit of central Tanzania, it has a much more promising future.

PRESERVING FORESTS AND
LIVELIHOODS IN COSTA RICA

The Foundation for Development of the Central Volcanic Mountain Range, or FUNDECOR, is a pathbreaking Costa Rican NGO whose central goal is to save the country's rainforests and cloudforests. Their strategy is to help increase the incomes of people for whom forested land is their main asset, and who might otherwise deforest the land to sell timber and establish pasture or bean farming. Executive Director Franz Tattenbach, a Costa Rican national, noted that this strategy for decreasing the incentives to clear land means working with those who hold both formal and informal property rights to forest lands, specifically those who live in the forest, often the poor. FUNDECOR works to package together a combination of income sources, including international payments for forest conservation under the global warming treaty and biodiversity agreements, maintaining watersheds for hydropower and urban water supplies, and enhancing and marketing tree products such as fruits and nuts. FUNDECOR also helps to provide certification for ecological harvesting of timber, which reinforces good practice while increasing the value of participants' moderate cutting of selected mature trees. The combined income, reflecting the value of the forests to the nation and the world at large, is generally higher than the farmer could obtain by clearing the land to plant beans or other activities.

FUNDECOR also develops ecological maps identifying the locations of vital species. It works to educate those who live in these regions about the value of their land and about ecologically sustainable means of harvesting trees. Tattenbach explained to me in Costa Rica that FUNDECOR views the growing of trees as a type of savings of the poor. FUNDECOR encourages poor farmers to plant trees by providing advance payments on sustainably harvested timber in lieu of the money they would have received from short-term agriculture. This important innovation in microfinance may help to solve some of the most environmentally damaging forms of credit constraints. FUNDECOR is also developing special securities to make international income from environment treaties more dependable for farmers over the long term. As of the end of 2004, over 500 farmer-families had participated, covering about 50,000 hectares of forest.

Costa Rica has one of the world's most diverse flora and fauna, and FUNDECOR has been promoting eco-tourism, a sector that now provides steady employment for many Costa Ricans who would otherwise have remained poor. In sum, FUNDECOR's programs are a striking example of the potential complementarities between poverty reduction and ecological preservation. In no small part due to FUNDECOR's work, net deforestation in the Central Volcanic Range has now been virtually halted, and the range of the forest is apparently starting to expand. For its work FUNDECOR won the 2000 King Baudouin Foundation International Development Prize. You can find FUNDECOR on the web at http://www.Fundecor.org.

REGENERATION:
GRAM VIKAS RURAL HEALTH AND
ENVIRONMENT PROGRAM, INDIA

Gram Vikas, which means "community development" in Oriya, works with villagers in Orissa—one of the poorest states in India. Its programs span housing, clean water, health care and education, disaster preparedness and relief, community infrastructure such as latrines and drainage systems, communal forestry, community self-governance, and renewable energy, such as the use of biogas stoves.

Student volunteers came to the region to participate in relief work following the 1971 cyclone, and then founded Gram Vikas to work toward poverty alleviation and economic development. Gram Vikas programs focus on the most socially and economically disadvantaged groups, including the indigenous (or tribal) adivasis, and the dalits (untouchables). Today Gram Vikas works with about 20,000 families in some 500 villages in 12 of the most backward districts of Orissa.

Gram Vikas won a 2002 World Habitat Award for its Rural Health and Environment Program (RHEP). This was on top of its 2001 Global Development Network Award for Most Innovative Development Project, also for RHEP. This program is designed to facilitate long-term community self-help, to overcome the "inertia" caused by extreme poverty and the marginalization and deprivation of entire communities.

The first step in the RHEP program is to ensure safe disposal of human and animal wastes, effective drainage systems, and availability of protected drinking water. These basic village services are set up to improve the quality of life and expand economic opportunities. Privies and piped water are supplied to all families in the village. The RHEP works to build on the momentum created by joint community action to generate sustainable community owned and managed development systems. The community contributes over half of the project costs for water and sanitation infrastructure. Once systems are established, the program puts in place community monitoring to ensure effective use over time. Communities create and adjust with experience a system of penalties to be levied against families that violate norms, just as would have been the case under traditional village governance of natural resources. With this strategy, there is a real chance that communities can sustainably overcome common property mismanagement traps.

Then, community income generation projects become the focus, to ensure that health and environmental preservation programs can be maintained over the long run. This is accomplished in part through renewing village common pool resources such as ponds and forest areas, and in part through developing both traditional and new family and community income sources, depending on village opportunities.

The RHEP approach is notable for involving all the families in a village, cutting across social and economic barriers. Equal representation of men and women in village committees is required, and proportionate representation of all sections of the village is sought. In each village, all families contribute to a community fund, with an average of about $25 per family. The richer families sometimes subsidize poorer families to achieve this average. Other community responsibilities are made clear at every stage of the intervention.

In the context of an oppressive social structure that has existed intact for centuries if not millennia, the impact of the Gram Vikas RHEP can be revolutionary. It is one example of the forces behind the gathering transformation underway in rural India.

FOOD SECURITY AND
A GREENER URBAN ENVIRONMENT:
HEIFER IN THE LIMA SLUMS

Heifer International is a unique organization that provides assets, generally in the form of farm animals, to people who need them. Heifer received the President's Award for Voluntary Action in 1986 and the Presidential End Hunger Award in 1990, among other honors.

Peru is one of the poorer countries in Latin America. The level of income inequality in Peru is very great, meaning that the poor in the Andes, in the Amazon, and in the worst slums in Lima are suffering from extreme poverty by international standards. I visited a Heifer program in Lima, an innovative effort to both alleviate poverty and improve the quality of the urban environment.

Lima has experienced decades of explosive growth, the result of a virtual evacuation from the countryside by people desperate to escape poverty and terrorism. In 1940, just 8.6 percent of Peru's population lived in Lima—about 650,000 people. By 1980, massive urban migration left Lima with over 4 million people—some 22 percent of Peru's total—and was believed to be reaching its limits. But Lima today has nearly 8 million people—one-third the population of Peru—and is still growing. Migrants, sometimes children traveling on their own, often arrive almost penniless. Most districts where the poor live were once government lands or unused private lands, typically rocky, desert soils. The lands were settled by homeless and other impoverished people in what are called "land invasions"—though these are often well-planned incursions orchestrated by politicians and businessmen who get a cut of the resulting cash flow.

Huaycon is one of Lima's worst slums; the Heifer project is located in an outlying shantytown of this larger slum. It has a stirring but tragic history of popular organization. One of their community leaders was mysteriously murdered shortly after the area was settled in the early 1980s. Then, in the mid-1980s, Huaycon became one of the focal points of the Shining Path terrorists, who were extremely violent and depraved, and seemed to reserve their greatest cruelty for impoverished people who behaved independently. Though the cancerous Shining Path had gone into remission, the unfortunate settlers of Huaycon remained deprived of many basics of a decent life. Could a poverty program such as Heifer thrive in such a place? I wanted to see for myself.

We fought crazy traffic for about two hours to reach Huaycon, about 22 miles (35 kilometers) east of downtown Lima. (You get habituated to reckless driving in the developing world. As for finding a seat belt in the developing world, good luck with that too.) We got into a minor accident, fortunately just a fender-bender. But finally we arrived, still in one piece.

The people I talked to said housing is probably somewhat worse on average in Huaycon than in the rural areas the people came from—homes that may be centuries old but made of stone. The holes sometimes seen in the walls or roof would be a much bigger problem if it rained in Lima. Overall people are probably less poor in Huaycon than in the rural areas because they can do some kind of work. Although they are probably worse off for a very short time while they get settled, here, one resident told me, "at least there is a chance to get some money."

The Huaycon group supported by Heifer organized themselves in 1994, first as 14 families and then growing to 30. They sought for several years to be successful on their own, but despite their great efforts they couldn't quite make their project a success. They started by raising ducks, but for various reasons this proved unsuccessful. They also struggled to grow fodder, situated on an arid hillside just above a ramshackle collection of informal factories, whose owners did not like having a poor person's settlement looking over them: Clashes had ensued. Some small animals had been stolen. Water for the project, when it was available at all, was expensive. But the people had won a legal right to stay there, and were determined not to give up. Persevering, they took the initiative to find out what humanitarian groups had to offer, and in 1999 they selected Heifer as a group they could trust, which might understand their needs and be able to provide them with training and a capital infusion to reach viability. Heifer had not conducted an urban agriculture project in Peru prior to this request. But visiting with the people, seeing their determination and solidarity in the face of great deprivations, Heifer contributed materials and money for key purchases. One of the things that most impressed me about Heifer is their willingness to be flexible, respond to needs as they emerged, and let the participants control the program.

The participants came up with a way to have water pumped over a hill from a river in the neighboring valley, and built a cement causeway for channeling water from the hilltop receiving point down into several storage tanks that they constructed. I toured their projects growing crops and raising small animals on the terraced, formerly desert but now greening hillside above their settlements. In various shacks participants were raising guinea pigs, rabbits, chickens, and a few ducks, fed by fodder grown along the hillside.

I met with about 25 participants—mostly women, a few men—over crackers and the locally popular Inca Cola at the cement block center they had constructed. They called themselves a "Noah's Ark"—meaning they were refugees from all races, languages, and regions of the country: white, mestizo, indigenous Peruvian, and black. Indeed, as each participant said a few words about themselves, I was struck that almost everyone came from a different part of Peru. This showed how disrupted their lives were, and how they had come to the city without even the social networks that can be taken for granted in other parts of the world that would allow them to settle near relatives, or at least in an enclave with a preponderance of people from their own region of the country. Despite this handicap, they had achieved an amazing degree of self-organization. A woman explained, "when we came here, we came just to survive. We all came with nothing, so we had the same needs. We created our association as a mothers' club, trying to help our children, to get the assistance that we heard was available, to contact a group that gives milk for children. Only with our organization could we make this in the desert, could we do anything at all."

One woman offered a single simple statement: "Women are brave." Several members looked at me as if to judge whether I understood. I'm not sure that I got all of what she was trying to convey, but certainly, none of what they had achieved would have been possible otherwise.

Most participants had arrived as children, frequently alone. One woman's story was typical. She arrived in Lima, unaccompanied, at the age of eight. It sounded at first as if she had been abandoned, but it later became clarified that her parents had died, quite possibly violent deaths at the hands of either terrorists or militia. She lived on the streets in downtown Lima for a few years before finding her way to Huaycon. When she was 15 she married, but she said her life only became worse. Now she had children of her own to care for, with no help from her husband. But she was resolutely determined to give them a better life than she had known. Now, about 30, her children were still in school, and she was making enough money to feed them three modest meals each day.

Another who had come here at age 11 told me, "I didn't know anything about cars. I only knew about animals. So I thought I should try to raise animals. We built terraces on the hill like our families did at home, because that is what we knew about." Another, who had arrived with one adult relative at age 8, told me "it was a desert when we came to this place. We built our houses with anything we could find. We looked for work, we did whatever we could for money. But there is no work, so we had to find a way to get our own money and our own food." Impressively, two women had somehow gotten enough education to become local primary teachers.

All the participants expressed strong and heartfelt gratitude to Heifer—for training, and help with purchasing some of the equipment they needed to make their project a success. Many movingly recounted the difference in their lives before and after Heifer's assistance. But the women themselves had done the most impressive work, organizing themselves and setting the agenda for what they needed. In the process, they were creating something new—a way to earn an income while also improving the quality of their urban environment. Heifer has a policy of encouraging program participants to "pass on the gift" to other people in need, and this community was already making it a point to do so every year, despite their continued struggle.

9

SOCIAL INCLUSION AND HUMAN RIGHTS FOR THE POOR AND VOICELESS

Social exclusion is built from the systematic, possibly unwritten barriers that often prevent classes of poor people from having access to opportunities to develop and use their capabilities, including access to health, education, training, employment, and a voice in their wider communities. Social exclusion—whether through active and deliberate marginalization of some groups among the poor by the rich or by others in the mainstream society, or simply through benign neglect—causes poverty to become reinforced and then perpetuated. Temporary access to income or basic needs does not generally address the deeper problem of social exclusion. Addressing exclusion directly provides better opportunities to ensure that powerlessness traps can be overcome so that poverty reduction can be maintained.

BIDDING POVERTY ADEW:
DREAMS OF A BETTER LIFE FOR GIRLS

In Egypt, the Association for the Development and Enhancement of Women, or ADEW, works to improve the lives of the women and children living in the poorest, female-headed households in Cairo. Many of these women had to make their way to Cairo from poor rural areas to survive after being deserted, divorced, or widowed. The ADEW Girls' Dreams Project began when staff started hearing about problems with clients' adolescent daughters, who are commonly stuck at home taking care of siblings and maintaining the household while the mothers work long hours, or else must work themselves. Their responsibilities can run from early in the morning until late at night. These girls often have no dreams for their future, except to get some rest some day, or to get married.

Now some of these girls are taught skills for self-expression including drawing and music. They are taken to visit a park to spur their imagination, a great treat in the lives of these girls who virtually never leave their slum environment, and for whom the admissions fee to a park is prohibitive. Meanwhile, in a safe environment, they can begin to imagine a better future. Just as without knowing your destination it is unlikely that you arrive there, so without an image of a better future it is unlikely that you will take the steps needed to achieve it.

As we literally crossed the tracks to reach the Cairo slum, we had to walk up and down the crude stone stairway carefully. The stones were surprisingly slippery in dry Egypt, having been polished by uncounted thousands of human feet. My guide, Mona, told me of reports of women slipping and falling, with serious injuries to themselves or the infants they were carrying. We wound our way through dirt alleys, noxious fumes competing with the stench of refuse decaying in the hot sun. There was no sewage in this "random" community; while not illegal dwellings, they were constructed outside legal building codes and other formal requirements. I thought people looked at me only with curiosity, but Mona told me that whenever a foreigner comes to the neighborhood people are fearful this means their houses will be torn down to make room for another foreign investment project. Saladin's twelfth-century fortress could be seen high above in the distance.

We arrived at the class just as it was getting underway. There were fifteen girls in this group, ranging in age from ten to fourteen, all daughters of ADEW clients. The majority had been born in Upper (southern) Egypt, and had migrated here with their mothers some years before. In the girls' first class they shared their thoughts about the future, but had expressed little beyond the possibility of getting married. After the introductory class, the girls received instruction in drawing and music. Then the girls were invited to select a subject, and they chose the environment.

This was the second session drawing about the environment, and their fifth class together overall. Mona told me she found it very significant that they chose this topic, because the girls "live in dirty places, and would like to move to another, cleaner place." Either they remember the rural areas from when they were young, or they may have seen some TV, in which houses with green around them were depicted. I was shown the work they had done the previous class, when they had made some paintings and etchings on glass as well as paper. Though I saw no trees in the neighborhood, almost every picture contained at least one tree. The girls seemed very happy to be in the class. They drew from their imaginations with obvious enthusiasm, staying engaged and focused for the nearly two hours that I was there.

While the girls were drawing I was asked if I had any questions for the group. I asked them what ideas they had about how to improve the environment where they lived. Fadwa said they should clean the streets, bring garbage baskets to throw away the trash and encourage others to do the same, then plant trees. Nadia noted that there were metal factories in and near the apartment buildings, which gave off unhealthy smoke and toxic chemicals. These should be required to move somewhere else, she said. She also echoed the idea of "bringing in trees and huge trash baskets," because she hated the way "people throw their garbage out their windows."

Rowya told me they should make all the buildings the same height, because the higher ones block the air from the lower ones, and because thieves climb up from one roof to the next. Another girl, named Mona like my guide, complained about noise. She wanted a law preventing using loud machines and other noises such as microphones where the people live. She said there were too many people in her area, and that there should be less. She also said we should stop cutting down the trees, and should use water only for what we need, not waste it.

Sabah said it was a problem in the rural area where she lived her first few years that people wash their clothes and dishes in the water people drink from. This brings microbes, she said. Samia noted that street vendors create a bad impression of her country by loudly hawking their wares, and leaving garbage behind and otherwise not cleaning up after themselves.

Ranya said we should improve the drainage in the neighborhood, bringing in pipes. At first I didn't understand: There is almost no rain in Cairo. But she was talking about the lack of sewage pipes. She said the houses were full of unhealthy stagnant waters that don't drain off. She said they get sick because of this. "I want to live in a healthy place," she added. She also said we should stop "losing the green areas by building on them." She had been born in the delta, about 50 miles to the north, where she occasionally went to visit her grandparents; and she appreciates the green that she sees there.

As a result of participating in the Girls Dreams Program, at least five girls have overcome very long odds and returned to school; and nearly 100 girls have joined the literacy program. The Girls Dreams Program also helps girls to develop important life skills such as negotiating with family, employer, and other people in their lives. ADEW won a 2004 Pro-Poor Innovation Challenge Award, which it plans to use to expand the Girls Dreams Project.

We don't know what will happen to these impoverished but optimistic children, who are now planning for a better future. They have already encountered harsh realities of life, and living in the Cairo slums they will face many constraints. But those in the developed world as well as more afflu-ent Egyptians have also known dreams that came to grief. The point is that we have dreams, and we make some of them come true. Life without imag-ining the future is simply unimaginable.

CHILDLINE FOUNDATION—INDIA

Human rights must start with the child. In India, as in many other countries, children trying to live on the street are subject to terrible abuses. Activist Jeroo Billimoria persuaded authorities to set up a 1098 phone number—something like 911 in the United States for children in need. Easy to remem-ber, because, as one child suggested, it is like a countdown of 10, 9, 8, . . . The posters say:

> You can call 1098 if:
> You are a child in trouble and need guidance immediately.
> You want to help another child in distress.
> You are a concerned citizen and want to report an incident of child abuse.
> You are a child and you need to talk to someone.
> You can call even if you don't fall under these categories.

In Bangalore, Childline usually receives 70 to 80 calls per day, about 10 percent of which are complaints from children concerning their employers. Others call to report child abuse or for counseling.

This project is the result of the efforts of thousands of volunteers, but was conceptualized and brought to life by a single person—a former fac-ulty member of the Tata Institute of Social Sciences and social entrepreneur, Jeroo Billimoria. For her work, Jeroo was made an Ashoka fellow. Partly through the publicity, networking, and openings for additional funding that this made possible, the idea has now spread and taken root in many coun-tries, as well as throughout India.

Bill Drayton, founder of Ashoka, described to me what he saw in Jeroo's work, and how it exemplifies social entrepreneurship.

> She saw the need as the number of street children was increasing with the urban collapse of the traditional [rural] extended family. So what then hap-pens when a kid has a problem? The kid can't connect with people who could help him solve his problem. A good entrepreneur figures out steps to solve this. We have the phone system as a way to communicate. [Instead of having] a middle-aged bureaucrat answer the phone, have trained street kids. Then the police have to change their behavior because a child's report-ing their behavior is just a phone away, and excess demand for a service be-

comes visible. At the local level this arrives, and upsets everything. It is like plowing the field before you seed it. You weaken the idea that things do not change—prepare the ground for seeding. A social entrepreneur wants a product so easily understood that lots of local people can make it work. So Jeroo has a product that has spread now globally from a simple seed.

But Jeroo is modest about her accomplishments and recently said that "success will be when every child in the world has access to a service like Childline and knows that someone who cares is just a phone call away." But she would start with the children in India (there are more than a third of a billion of them). To spread her model around India, the Childline India Foundation created a franchise style of organization to facilitate growth and provide quality assurance without forcing new efforts in other cities into a preset bureaucratic mold. Jeroo Billimoria's franchise approach is an innovative way to spread a poverty program, but she said it is really not very different from business franchising. Franchisees must demonstrate financial accountability, have good training capacity, hold regular meetings, and show that they can network with government, the private sector, and other NGOs providing vital services for children, so that they can effectively refer clients. This is a good example of cross-fertilization between the business and NGO worlds.

HUMAN AND LEGAL RIGHTS FOR THE POOR IN CAMBODIA

When many people think of Cambodia, the Killing Fields of the Pol Pot regime come first to mind. The Khmer Rouge and their genocidal reign of terror were ousted from power in 1978, though more than 12 years of brutal civil war followed. After that nightmarish world, almost anything seems an improvement. But for the poor and voiceless, routine human rights violations and a culture of violence have remained a part of daily life, a factor keeping them trapped in poverty. Now courageous social entrepreneurs such as Dr. Kek Galabru are working to empower the poor to uphold their human rights. Galabru, a medical doctor, founded and chairs the Cambodian League for the Promotion and Defense of Human Rights (LICADHO), which promotes, monitors, and educates the public about human rights, particularly for poor women and children. LICADHO also provides victims of human rights abuses with needed medical care, legal aid, and other forms of assistance. Dr.

Galabru emphasizes that the poor are more likely to be prosecuted and convicted for crimes that the rich can get away with. In a throwback to the eighteenth century, the poor may spend years in prison for indebtedness, while their children sink deeper into poverty. Long periods of pretrial detention have similar effects. Access to friends, family, legal assistance, and human rights workers is sharply restricted. Dr. Galabru told me that a growing number of children live in prison. Torture is common, particularly of women, and is used to extort money as well as to extract confessions. Rape is used as a tool of intimidation. Trafficking of women and children is also very common, and rarely prosecuted. Many "adopted" children are actually held in slavery. Land that has been traditionally owned and used by the peasantry is routinely stolen, or "grabbed," by the rich, often with government connivance. Even NGOs are subject to intimidation. But through its work with the UN and other foreign observers, as well as Cambodians, LICADHO has been able to raise awareness, change legislation and enforcement, rescue many enslaved women and children, and create conditions for the escape from poverty. Another NGO working for basic legal rights in Cambodia, as well as China and Vietnam, is International Bridges to Justice. IBJ founder Karen Tse was recently named an Ashoka Global Fellow.

BRAC LEGAL EDUCATION AND GROUP ACTION IN RURAL BANGLADESH

As with many other keys to capability, BRAC has been a leader and innovator in legal rights and empowerment for the poor. In 1986, BRAC began to focus on legal problems faced by the poor, believing that the lack of legal and human rights was a major factor keeping them in poverty traps.

To make up for this lack, BRAC developed a program of human rights and legal education (HRLE) using village legal aid workers, known as HRLE shebikas. These play a role analogous to the shastho shebikas, BRAC's highly regarded village-based health workers. BRAC has conducted almost 100,000 legal literacy courses to date, and well over 2 million low-income women have completed them. I attended sessions in which the HRLE shebikas were themselves being trained, and some in which the shebikas were training others.

In northwest Bangladesh I visited a shebika teacher training session. As is traditional in Bangladesh, learning in both cases was largely by rote, and answers to questions were almost chanted, such as on the legal requirements for Muslim and Hindu weddings. The volunteers had between nine and twelve years of schooling, so they were among the most highly educated in their villages. They receive some pay for their work as land surveyors—a skill learned as part of the training program—but their legal assistance work is on a volunteer basis.

The trainees named the biggest legal problems in the villages: demands for dowry (which is illegal) and torture for failure to pay, lack of women's rights in initiating or dealing with the consequences of divorce, throwing of acid on women as punishment, rape, and trafficking of women and children to India. They also identified polygyny, early marriage, and inhuman punishments. But the volunteers were emphatic that something could be done about these problems in the villages where they worked, and that real progress was being made.

At a village meeting in northeast Bangladesh, I saw BRAC village organization (VO) members receiving training from a HRLE shebika. The VOs receive 22-day legal education classes. They learn about Muslim and Hindu family and inheritance law, and civil, criminal, and land law. It is mandatory that all VO members participate. The class was meeting outdoors, under a tree for shade. The teacher would ask a question, such as the legal age of marriage, and the class as a whole would chant back the answer. Child marriage, though illegal, is still a major problem in rural Bangladesh. What is the punishment for child marriage, they were then asked. One month in jail for the parents and all related to this action, came the chanted answer. Similar questions were asked about laws governing divorce, dowry, and other matters, and the punishments for breaking these laws. The class also talked about criminal laws, and what police must legally consider before making an arrest.

The women also answered questions such as: What are basic needs? ("Food, clothing, health treatment, education, housing, rightful work, rightful rest," they chanted in melodic Bengali.) What are the fundamental rights of the woman? "According to law, all are equal, have the right to cast your own vote, to express your opinion, to live peacefully, to keep the right to privacy, to free movement, and not to be punished cruelly." About distribution of land after death of the father or the mother, the women chanted the Islamic law, "two girls equal one boy."

In the two-hour session, a wide range of legal issues was touched on. Clearly they had covered this ground before, as most of the women chanted the answers almost in unison. In addition to this package, new topics were being added, on laws concerning trafficking of children and women, and acid throwing.

Some two million BRAC members have participated in these sessions since 1986. Many problems have proved solvable through local binding arbitration, once the women gained legal knowledge. Sometimes there was no alternative but to go to the courts, and since 1998 BRAC has run legal aid clinics, in conjunction with a Bangladesh legal aid organization, offering services once a week to BRAC members and nonmembers alike.

BRAC rural legal aid services have been a lifeline for many women. For example, many have faced conflicts over the size of dowries. Families of the husband who do not believe they have been paid adequately have "tortured" the wife until her family finds more dowry money. All too often violence has taken the form of acid thrown on the wife; some women have been killed and others badly burned and disfigured. Some women have been the victims of severe acid attacks after taking leadership roles in community organizations. This has been ascribed to religious fundamentalists who are culturally uneasy with women holding power, but at root much of the issue rests with economic power. The response is to first provide hospital treatment, then to file a legal case. In addition, BRAC helped to establish an Acid Survival Foundation. Three acid attack perpetrators were recently sentenced to death, and observers say this horrific problem is being steadily brought under control.

SPIRIT OF THE LAW:
HUMAN RIGHTS CENTER, CHIAPAS, MEXICO

When one thinks about human rights abuses of indigenous peoples in Latin America, remote areas of the Andes and the jungles of Central America come to mind. In contrast, Mexico has burnished its image as a modernizing society and as a member of the North American Free Trade Agreement (NAFTA). A decade ago this image was tarnished when, on New Year's Day 1994, a dramatic peasant uprising in the Mexican state of Chiapas momentarily captured the world's attention. As many in the press interpreted the events in early 1994, the backward state of peasant agriculture and human rights of indigenous peoples in Mexico suggested that the country was "closer" to its Central American neighbors than its NAFTA partners.

In the meantime, for the poorest of the poor in Chiapas, it feels like two steps forward and at least two backward. The government has greatly expanded social services in the region, and improvements in nutrition, health, and education of children have resulted from the Progresa/Oportunidades program. But some children have failed to benefit. Terrible abuses continue, keeping peasants trapped in poverty. Without basic human rights, true opportunity remains a dream for many.

Improved human rights have been a cornerstone of efforts to reduce poverty of indigenous peoples in Latin America. Chiapas is a very poor and highly unequal state on the Guatemalan border with at least one-third of the population comprised of indigenous Mayan peoples. Nearly three-quarters of the population lives below the national poverty level, with almost one-fifth of the economically active population earning no cash income. Malnourishment among children is widespread, and school attendance has been very low among the poor. Yet with about four percent of Mexico's population, Chiapas exports more coffee than any other state, and is among the top three exporters of corn, bananas, tobacco, and cacao. Leaders of the uprising demanded changes in the agrarian system and national trade policies that, they argued, would benefit impoverished peasants throughout the country. Peasants thought these changes had been agreed to—but they still wait.

The uprising over land inequality and injustice was striking because for decades Mexico had claimed progress in redressing the gross injustices—and inefficiencies—of the agrarian system established by the Spanish conquerors. In Latin America large, paternalistic, inefficient plantations often exist side-by-side with tiny, labor-intensive, impoverished farm plots. Numerous studies have demonstrated that a system of family- or medium-size farms is more efficient than a highly unequal land distribution. Mexico was one of the few countries in Latin America where serious moves toward land reform were attempted, a central legacy of the Mexican Revolution. More than one-half of Mexico's total land and roughly two-thirds of its cropland was redistributed from larger estates to small farmers under the cooperative *ejido* system. In Chiapas, some 54 percent of the land is in the *ejido* sector. But large landowners were typically able to reserve their holdings of the best land, while more marginal lands were slated for the *ejido* sector.

Repression of human rights aggravates these problems. The rich coerce the poor to work, buy, and sell under grossly lopsided contractual arrangements. The indigenous poor have also been systematically denied fair voting rights for decades. Paramilitary forces are believed responsible for hundreds of peasant deaths and "disappearances." Mexican troops active around communities believed sympathetic to the Zapatistas creates an atmosphere of fear and intimidation, and reluctance to confront daily injustices, along with a stream of urban migration. Many ordinary and innocent peasants have been forced to remain in detention camps with their entire families. Journalists and groups such as Enlace Civil have charged that abuses are occurring such as rampant rape and torture by military and police, deliberate poisoning of water sources and spoiling of food, systematic destruction of the natural environment, withholding of government

services from villages that fail to support the government, police participation in the destruction of crops, and preventing villagers from tending
their crops.

In this environment, an NGO has fought for the protection of human
rights. The Fray Bartolomé de Las Casas Human Rights Center (HRC) de-
fines its mission as "assisting and serving the poor and marginalized who
have become victims of structural and historical injustice. While respecting
the will of the people to lead and construct their own future, we aim to enforce the exercise of human rights, through education and defense." Don
Samuel Ruiz Garcia, for nearly forty years the Catholic Bishop of San
Cristóbal de Las Casas, founded the NGO in 1989, and it received recog-
nitions for its work even prior to the headlines of 1994, including the 1993
annual Institute for Policy Studies Letelier-Moffitt Human Rights Award.
Bishop Ruiz received the Martin Ennals Award, the Niwano Peace Prize,
and the UNESCO Simon Bolivar Prize. He was also a three-time nominee
for the Nobel Peace Prize (the maximum number allowed), and millions of
admirers signed petitions in support of his nomination. Bishop Ruiz survived a number of attempts on his life; and HRC has experienced repression, but has managed to stay active.

To promote sustainability of their efforts, HRC helps create and support autonomous community-based human rights organizing committees.
HRC also provides legal defense for victims of human rights violations.
Following an HRC investigation to determine the evidence and facts of the
case, the NGO decides where to press the case—to international, federal,
or state legal authorities. In some complex and specialized cases, HRC
works together with partners.

HRC also works to provide documentation of human rights conditions
and violations throughout Chiapas. They try to keep careful track of the
record of such extreme abuses as "extra-judicial executions" (i.e., assassi-
nations), torture, arbitrary arrests and detentions, "disappearances" (which
generally signify death) and forced community "displacements." HRC
monitors indigenous peoples' inherent right to self-determination, to keep
their traditional lands, and their legal right to self-government. HRC promotes greater knowledge and awareness of indigenous peoples' human
rights and of their existing means of enforcing them, through creative educational strategies including dramas and discussion groups.

Through legal empowerment, the poor can take important steps away
from social exclusion and toward social acceptance and economic opportunity, ultimately to economic and social development of their communities
on their own terms.

FREEING PEOPLE HELD IN DEBT BONDAGE

Another frontier for assisting the ultrapoor is identifying and freeing people held in debt bondage. Nongovernmental organizations (NGOs) have played a central role in identifying debt bondage traps as a widespread problem, raising public awareness of the problems, and lobbying at both international and national levels for legislative reform. Examples include the work of Sankalp with bonded quarry workers in India and the work of several NGOs united under the Kamaiya Freedom Movement Mobilization Committee (FMMC) in Nepal. These NGOs have helped bonded workers achieve alternative sources of income, which may vary from arranging to buy the quarries in which bonded laborers work, to assistance with migrating and entering entirely new types of employment.

COMMUNITY EMPOWERMENT AND DEVELOPMENT

WOMEN'S VOICES MAKE A DIFFERENCE IN THE COMMUNITY: AN EXPERIMENT IN INDIA

In India, the government decreed (via an amendment to the constitution) that at least one- third of village councils would be required to have a female head. In West Bengal this was carried out rigorously. Every third village (in alphabetical order) was assigned to a category in which only women could seek this office. Alphabetical is essentially random, so this resulted in an opportunity to, in effect, observe the results of a social science experiment on poverty policy. Esther Duflo of MIT and Raghab Chattopadhyay of the Indian Institute of Management took advantage of this as a research opportunity.

They found that ensuring that women's voices were heard in this way did make a real difference. For one thing, women are about twice as likely to address a complaint to the village leader when she is also a woman; and the issues they address are different from those of men. Women are more likely to raise the problem of drinking water and the men irrigation. These village councils with female heads made greater investments in the kinds of water, transportation, and energy infrastructure that are directly helpful to women. The women had to walk long distances to collect water; the women-headed councils built infrastructure such as tubewells and drinking facilities to alleviate that problem. They put more emphasis on health expenditures. They also emphasized roads more. Both men and women frequently complained about poor roads, but women also provide much of the labor for public works programs involving road building and repair, and so benefit doubly from roads programs.

Of course, the money had to come from somewhere, and these councils spent less on some areas than those headed by men. According to the report, education is an area of lower spending. This curious result, Esther Duflo told me, does not reflect a low value placed on education, just that, given the tradeoffs they faced, women thought health should come first. Raghab Chattopadhyay, whom I caught up with at his West Bengal home near Calcutta, noted that councils with women chairs tended to spend more on a more informal type of primary education, which have more female teachers and are more accessible to girls. But, he said, the evidence for this was somewhat less robust than for some of the other spending preferences. I hope that follow-up research will clarify this, and identify the impacts on poverty outcomes.

The women decision-makers were not necessarily or even very often poor, but as women they may have better understood the needs of those who make up a large majority of the poor—women and their children. Left unclear is how one could ensure a balance of infrastructure relevant to both genders across all communities. But the most important lesson of the study is to put to rest the notion that it won't really matter in the end for political decisions affecting economic allocation whether men or women have political power. It does matter; and given the pervasive second-class citizenship of women in poor countries, women's voices need to be heard and heeded. The community develops differently when voices are given to those who need community development the most.

EMPOWERMENT IS ELECTRIFYING—
POSSIBILITIES OF RURAL ELECTRIFICATION

Think about the last time you experienced a power failure. All the things you took for granted that you suddenly could no longer do, such as refrigeration or simply turning on a light to read. In the world today, more than two billion people live with a permanent power failure, because the electric grid has never reached their house. Edison invented his long-lasting light bulb in 1879 and then started an electric power distribution company. But 125 years later, a composite NASA picture of the Earth taken at night from space shows the United States, Europe, and Japan very lit up, while Africa is almost totally dark. The night sky is beautiful in rural Africa—Sagittarius and Scorpio shine brightly, a lovely sight. But in their huts, people remain in the dark.

On the other hand, how important is electrification compared to other possible investments, such as supplying safe water or education? One has to be careful in identifying the benefits of electricity. Advocates and USAID reports claim benefits based on the fact that people are richer and more educated in electrified villages than in nonelectrified ones. But villages that are richer are more likely to pay to use electricity, hence attracting electric power companies. Villages that are better educated are more likely to know about the potential benefits of electricity and about how to demand that their village get a high priority for hookup. Richer villages are generally found closer to the capital or other large cities where they have a ready market, and their proximity also makes it easier to extend the grid. Sometimes energy companies are actually contracted to do the poverty impact studies, which is rather a conflict of interest. Much more serious research is needed to identify the actual impact and comparative cost-effectiveness of investments in electrification.

Pending better studies, it is clear that access to electricity makes many things possible. A light bulb can let a child study after dark. Television images can give a young mother the knowledge that things are done differently in other parts of the world, and provide her daughter with a new sense of possibilities. Lighting from houses and along paths makes walking at night safer, especially for women who have to walk some distance to the village latrines, and helps prevent thefts, including the thefts of women's hard-earned assets such as animals and carts. A chance to work after dark can provide additional income. Small-scale industry made possible by electrification can increase job opportunities.

The National Rural Electric Cooperative Association of the United States has been working to extend electrification in the developing world for over 40 years. In Bangladesh, over 100,000 irrigation-pumping stations are possible because of rural electrification. If you live in a remote area, Grameen Shakti (Energy), a nonprofit enterprise, is now bringing solar electricity to rural villages far from the grid, and promoting other forms of renewable energy. This is one more way in which the future of Bangladesh is looking brighter.

RIDING ON THE WINGS:
YOUTH WINGS IN INDIGENOUS VILLAGES
IN MEGHALAYA, INDIA

Poverty and social exclusion are not synonyms. One can be included socially in his or her community, but the whole community may be stuck in a poverty trap. And the form of social inclusion is all-important. Sometimes, social inclusion means the annexation of your community into a more powerful community that surrounds it, on the terms of the majority, in a way that may reinforce poverty traps. What is needed in such cases is not so much social inclusion as social acceptance. The self-help by an indigenous community-based young peoples' organization of a "scheduled tribe" in India illustrates how excluded groups can take the first steps to self-esteem and empowerment.

In 2003 I spent a week in Meghalaya, meaning "abode of the clouds," a mountainous state in northeast India, with some 80 percent of the population comprised of "backward" or "scheduled tribes." I was the guest of Khasi tribal peoples. The state is reminiscent of the West Virginia of decades past, with its subsistence hill agriculture and the good jobs being found in coal mining or government work. In the Khasi areas at least, "scheduled tribes" is a rather resented government term that makes the Khasis seem culturally inferior. Many Khasis also believe they are lumped in with low-caste peoples, in a backhanded way, because they receive special government benefits at a level equivalent to the lowest Hindu castes and untouchables, and in this way are incorporated into the dominant society but with an inferior status. Social *in*clusion is seen as the very heart of their problems. Meghalaya is predominantly Christian, and traditionally matrilineal and matrilocal—children take the last name of the mother, and families live in the mother's village.

But like most other places, traditional social organization is eroding in the face of modern influences, and while modern technology in health for instance has brought benefits, there have been significant social impacts. Traditional matrilineal society is breaking down, and communal lands are being "spontaneously privatized," which often means that some unscrupulous village chiefs are selling the land and keeping the proceeds. Individuals sell their share of land to the rich out of need, but then become part of a growing landless class. Something is needed to restore social cohesion and a sense of individual responsibility to the community and the environment.

In this setting it is encouraging to witness the emergence of the Synjuk Seng Samla Shnong (SSSS), a CBO network, which literally means Federation of Village Youth Wings. These village groups grow out of a traditional young people's component of the durbar, the Khasi social organization. They take care of environmental cleanups, social service, and whatever needs arose in the villages, and today also in urban neighborhoods. In 1992 a loose confederation of these youth associations was formed across the Khasi areas, working for common goals in the fields of income generation, health, and environmental protection, along with cultural and sports activities. Some SSSS efforts include a project for rural solar disinfection of water, and urban river cleanup and solid waste management. Their objective is to convince the entire community that a healthy environment is a basis for successful economic development as well as a healthy life, and that each member has a personal responsibility to protect the environment. Some 600 young people have volunteered in SSSS reforestation activities. But 90,000 youths are unemployed in Meghalaya. The SSSS is working to motivate them, to prepare for employment, and to generate self-employment activities. They have ambitious hopes, but are proceeding step by step. The federation has the opportunity to emerge as the guardian of communitarian values and champion of village self-reliance and hopes for poverty reduction among the marginalized.

A WORLD VISION PROGRAM IN THE ANDES

World Vision has long enjoyed a solid reputation for working with communities, assessing their needs, and designing programs that respond to them. World Vision is a participant in the Better Business Bureau Wise Giving Alliance's National Charity Seal Program and is listed as a four-star charity at Charity Navigator. Although proud of its Christian faith, World Vision programs are open to people of all faiths, including in Islamic countries.

I visited a World Vision community development program in one of the most stubbornly impoverished areas in the Western hemisphere, the Peruvian Andes, in the slums of Huanta and rural areas of Ayacucho province. World Vision works in 13 urban slums and 60 rural communities here, some of them several hours from Huanta by car. This description is illustrative of the work of World Vision with poor communities.

The city of some 100,000 people is situated about 8,000 feet (2,700 meters) above sea level and is not an easy place to get to. The highway to the city is paved only with rocks of all sizes that have fallen from the hills and cliffs, and the road is rutted with deep potholes, making driving there something of an obstacle course. Poor maize plots are tucked into little corners of land at the bottom of steep hills. The previous January, heavy rains had caused nighttime mudslides and the collapse of adobe walls, wiping out three whole families. Other risks abounded. The police and military were out in force, apparently looking for drug traffickers, who are endemic in this part of the country. The area was also one of the strongholds of the Shining Path, one of the most vicious terrorist groups that Latin America has ever known. While claiming to fight the extreme human rights abuses of the wealthy oligarchy against the indigenous Incan population, the Shining Path indiscriminately murdered illiterate and malnourished peasants, creating an army of orphaned street children. Some of them grew up to be participants in the Lima Heifer program described earlier. If community development to alleviate poverty could work here, with powerlessness traps just one of the binds holding back the poor, where could it not work?

The goal of the 15-year project, begun in 1997, was to work with a cohort of children through adolescence. In the beginning, children were lucky to finish third grade. Now, most finish sixth grade. While they often have no access to a nearby secondary school, many high schools are now being established in response to political pressure from the community. A few children can stay with relatives near a school so they are able to continue their educations. World Vision also runs a program to send highly able youths to the university in Ayacucho. Some of these youths have returned to become teachers or work with World Vision, including in the villages they and their families initially fled for Huanta.

World Vision helped set up a mothers' club to share ideas, and provide mutual assistance such as watching each others' children. World Vision also runs a youth club. Children in the small city of Huanta have better prospects than those in outlying rural areas. But many of the adolescents suffer from low self-esteem, anxiety, and depression—the effects of experiencing violence at an early age. Some had witnessed murder and the torching of houses, and many others had been affected by it. While some youth became depressed, others sought violent reprisal against those they thought were responsible. Some have sought social support in gang membership—whose fights and criminal activities only compounds the community's poverty trap by destroying assets, diverting resources to personal and property security, and causing injuries and death. The psychological aspects of poverty and social exclusion deserve more attention; emotional scars can be a major handicap for the poor, and can lead to criminality traps. Building the self-esteem of youth has been a central focus of World Vision's work.

The integrated community development program has several other components. Job training was provided when needed. There was no health clinic in the service areas, only irregular visits by traveling medics; so World Vision expanded health services, providing vaccinations, health education, latrines, and clean water. Infection with parasitic worms was so prevalent among the children that costly testing was dispensed with in favor of treating everyone. As seen earlier in Africa, deworming children makes a critical difference to the success of education.

World Vision is helping to build capacity for the slum neighborhoods to take a greater role in self-governance under decentralization procedures. Even when municipal resources are meager, residents at least have a say in establishing priorities.

A microfinance program was also initiated. As in most parts of the developing world, microcredit was in short supply. In this part of Peru, the problem was compounded because many public records had been burnt as part of a systematic terrorist strategy. The effect was to make it difficult for most poor residents to prove their identity, locking them out of credit and other private and public services. Children also need identity cards to go to school—but if parents cannot pay the fees, children may be denied enrollment. World Vision is working with local governments to address this problem, parallel to the work of the Association for the Development and Enhancement of Women in Egypt.

One advantage of an integrated community development approach is the ability to remain flexible and learn about and then address a range of problems, such as the lack of identity cards. World Vision is seeking to address the great needs of these slums and rural communities in a holistic way. In the meantime a community is rediscovering the hope it had lost.

INTEGRATED SUSTAINABLE COMMUNITY DEVELOPMENT: HOW IT CAN WORK (AFRICARE-UGANDA)

Africare is a remarkable NGO with a reputation for making integrated community development work effectively in remote, impoverished African villages. Africare receives a grade of A from the American Institute of Philanthropy (AIP), the full four stars from Charity Navigator, and was widely cited by peer NGOs as effective. Africare identified its Uganda Food Security Initiative as one of its best programs in Africa. The external evaluations of the program were extremely impressive, and I decided to go to see it for myself.

Just a few miles north of the Rwanda border, and about twenty miles from Uganda's famous "Impenetrable Forest," Africare has been doing grassroots work in backcountry villages. These are impoverished rural areas with no roads, in which the people rely on smallholder subsistence agriculture. It is widely noted that Africare goes where other NGOs do not.

This part of Uganda is very hilly, and very densely populated, with some 400 people per square kilometer, on rugged, steep terrain. It is an ecologically fragile area with considerable soil loss through dangerous landslides and in the slow process of erosion. The area of arable land was shrinking alarmingly. Population growth had meant that land could no longer be given the long rest periods needed with traditional agricultural practices. The problem was exacerbated by deforestation for fuelwood. Cultivation was expanding to dramatically steep hillsides and erosion was accelerating. Areas previously forests or farms were becoming near wastelands.

Poverty was extreme; farms are usually less than one hectare in size and barely provide for subsistence. The villagers lacked improved seeds—they

ENTITLED TO PROGRESS—
BENEFITS OF TITLING FOR SQUATTERS:
PERU AND ECUADOR

An Untitled Story: The lack of secure title hampers and distorts the lives of the poor. Maria and her three children live in a shantytown in the city of Guayaquil, Ecuador. Abandoned by her husband, Maria left the countryside three years ago in hope of a better life for her children. She had to pay much of her meager savings to a slum broker for the right to her plot of land and the existing hovel on that spot, even though she did not gain legal title as a result. Maria does much of her work at home. If she leaves for too long, she is afraid that her tiny hold on real estate will be stolen by another squatter in this untitled world where might can make right. Possession may be 90 percent of the law, but possession is something that can change from day to day. Without a title, she cannot get a mortgage or use her plot as collateral for a business loan.

Throughout the developing world, people in rural areas often lack a title to farmland that is objectively theirs. The poor can benefit from the codification of ownership rights with a public registry. In cities many migrants like Maria settle in "random" or "informal" communities, on unused or government land. They typically pay something for the land. Poor settlers do their best to figure out who is regarded as the most plausible owner in the eyes not necessarily of the official law—the whole settlement may be considered illegal and hence of no concern of government—but of the informal law of the district. But their ownership remains insecure.

Hernando de Soto brought these problems to the public's attention in his book, *The Other Path*. De Soto described tragicomic efforts necessary to obtain title to property, based on the role-playing experiences of his associates. As a result of his efforts, movements for land titling have sprung up around the developing world, especially in the large coastal cities of Latin America. In Peru, the fourteen agencies involved with land titling were consolidated into a single streamlined agency. It was estimated that the time necessary to obtain title to property was cut to less than six weeks; before it required anywhere from three to fifteen years.

Erica Field of Harvard University found that people work at home partly to keep their claim on their plot of land so that they didn't lose it to rival squatters while away at work. Once they obtained secure title, they were more likely to begin working outside the home where they could earn more money.

Unfortunately, the poor are the least likely to be included in titling programs even though they are likely to benefit the most. Jenny Lanjouw of Berkeley and Philip Levy of Yale studied informal and formal claims to property ownership in Ecuador. They found that, to some extent, informally enforced property rights substitute for formal legal rights. Overall, acquiring title raised property values by more than 23 percent on average. But their finding that to a degree informal property rights can substitute effectively for formal property rights suggested that the biggest impact would be found where informal rights were least secure and effective. This meant that titling programs should be targeted at young disorganized communities—precisely where the poorest residents, new migrants from impoverished rural areas are to be found.

There are limits to what can be accomplished with titling programs. Access to reasonably functioning markets is critical; but formal property rights are sometimes neither necessary nor sufficient. In Africa, private, social, or communal ownership of land has made very little difference in the degree to which land is sold. Few loans there are collateralized by land holdings, even when individually titled. Titling, including of urban squatters' properties, is no panacea, but it does seem to loosen one of the binds that tie people into poverty traps.

There are also benefits to giving the poor title to agricultural land in rural areas. Land reform is beyond the scope of the book, but where genuine and carefully implemented land reform has taken place it has reduced poverty and improved efficiency at the same time. For example, land reform in West Bengal has improved the social standing of lower-caste farmers in rural areas while reducing poverty and helping to spur technological progress. One of the unheralded but critically important sources of development success in East Asia has been the region's thoroughgoing land reform. After World War II, radical land reform in Japan, South Korea, and Taiwan were key factors in these economies' subsequent rapid social and economic development. In Latin America the failure to implement such far-reaching land reform is one of the major causes of continued rural poverty, rapid urban migration, settlement of rainforest areas, and continued social conflict. Unfortunately, land reform is difficult to achieve politically and even more difficult to implement on the ground. Peasants, NGOs, and well-meaning governments facing strong resistance from landowners will require more help in their land reform efforts from the World Bank, USAID and other donors.

were only carrying over last season's leftover cereals. The result was blight and low yields. Food shortages plagued the population. Even if a few crops were made available for sale, prices paid by middlemen were much lower than what was available at fairly nearby markets—but there were no roads to get there, only footpaths. Even worse than exploitation by middlemen, often no middlemen could be found at all.

The children have had very high rates of preventable diseases, including protein deficiency, malaria, and parasitic worms and the resulting diarrhea. There is a shockingly high incidence of Kwashiorkor, severe malnutrition in children primarily caused by a protein-poor diet, which leads to growth retardation. Not only was caloric and other nutrient intake low, there was a failure to assimilate nutrients due to disease. Population growth was an extremely high 4 percent per year.

In short, this was a region where extreme poverty and environmental deterioration were endemic. It seemed that if sustainable development can be made to work here, it can work almost anywhere.

I went with a group from Africare to see several villages that they have worked with, and was inspired to see the extraordinary progress in one of most backward and impoverished areas of East Africa, one that could almost be called the Appalachia of Uganda. The people were filled with enthusiasm about the program. As we walked up the hillsides to see the results of the agriculture and land management programs, villagers who were singing and drumming followed us. In most successful village programs, there was a charismatic "natural leader" who took the initiative and kept the program going. In one that I visited, the leader was a minister; and the village association met in his church. The church had mud walls, thatched roof, and mud floors, arched open-air windows and doors to let in light and air, and inside the simplest of short wooden benches. The spirit of the villagers meeting in the church, with their continuously energetic enthusiasm, much more than made up for the humble surroundings.

I asked some hard questions. Why such an elaborate program, aren't you afraid of losing focus? Is this cost-effective?

Given the complex nature of the interrelated problems in the region, an integrated program was needed, so the program combines such elements as: introducing tree species with favorable ecological and commercial properties; new crops; nutrition and health education; healthcare; child growth monitoring and management of disease; better and more efficient stoves; fuel wood use; natural fertilizers; improved land management practices; and last but not least building sustainable and environmentally sensitive roads in this densely populated but almost roadless area, so villagers can sell produce, and reach medical care and schools, using a combination of community labor and equipment purchased for the program. Within this region, program villages were selected at random, with minimal political interference. While not a rigorous randomized trial, village comparisons suggest that the Uganda Food Security Initiative (UFSI) impact has been substantial in most if not all of the program dimensions.

Health, nutrition, land management, and other information are conveyed in multiple ways, including indigenous-style drama, which people willingly pay to see and learn from. The community participates financially as they do in decision-making and tasks. For example, villagers and communities donate land for the road program. Everyone is motivated to be connected to a road: Both figuratively and literally, the road gives the people a way out.

The roads are needed to enable residents to sell their produce, concentrating on higher value-added crops using the most suitable land, rather than extensive subsistence agriculture extending to fragile areas. It gives the incentive and the means to invest in land preservation. By opening up communication with the rest of the country, the best techniques can be learned. With high-value products and higher productivity, less child labor will be needed, decreasing the child labor fertility motive. By making residents aware of opportunities in less environmentally threatened areas, and by raising productivity in the area, eventually there will be some out-migration. Perhaps ironically, with the roads program the population is likely to be smaller in the long run. Finally, the community roads program is promoting measures to prevent soil erosion, selected based on an environmental impact assessment. Trees were planted, and drainage channels dug with attention to erosion control. Regular maintenance resulted in expanded employment opportunities for women.

Africare works with local leaders to initiate projects. All villagers are invited to work together, and a large fraction chooses to participate. The process begins with "participatory visioning," which examines the dynamics of organizational and community change in recent years, opportunities, needs, and potential partners. Then the group negotiates and plans for implementations of projects. In each village I visited, community leaders showed me detailed drawings and diagrammatic representations of the land uses in the village, the problems they had identified, and the plan and timeframe for addressing them. The villagers draw these themselves, with technical assistance from Africare; they were impressive achievements and a basis for the work at the village level. Monitoring indicators are chosen jointly by Africare and the villagers to assess progress. The process is finalized by forming development committees, made up of community members who either volunteer for or are elected as committee members. The committees are given the task of coordinating and providing leadership for the implementation of village action plans.

Figure 10.1   Agricultural and conservation training: Africare's Food
Security Program. Photo: Africare Uganda

Before villagers decide which commercial crops their village will specialize in, farmers visit area markets to get a sense of demand for various
products, and visit villages with similar profiles to get a sense of the way
various products can be grown. The emphasis has been on finding ways to
capture as much of the value-added as possible while growing environmentally sustainable crops. The program has introduced crops, including
apples and similar temperate fruits, previously only imported, but for
which the higher-altitude environment (about 7,500 feet, or 2,500 meters)
is well-suited, despite the equatorial location in which there is no winter.
(You have to prune all the leaves off the apple trees, essentially to trick
them into "thinking" it is winter. The bonus is that the trees give you two
crops of apples each year.) Traditionally, the only cash crop had been the
unprofitable sorghum. Now, one village grows Irish potatoes year-round,
using root-rot resistant seeds, for the Kampala French fries manufacture
market. Production is timed so that a new crop is ready every two weeks.
Rather than import frozen fries from abroad, which Uganda has been doing
despite the high cost of electricity and rarity of freezers, the country can
now get fresh fries made from recently picked potatoes. It helps the poorest farmers, it saves foreign exchange and scarce energy, and it tastes better,
too. Perhaps most importantly, the programs help farmers sustainably escape from subsistence traps.

The participatory approach is yielding unexpected results. One community member, while on an Africare trip to northern Uganda to get a sense
of potential activities, observed fishing on a lake. He decided to start fish

Figure 10.2   Building a better life: At a village kitchen with improved storage, safety, and wood-fuel technology.

farming in an artificial pond. His ponds, beautifully prepared and maintained, are now raising tilapia, a popular fish in the region. The program also integrates indigenous medicinal and other traditional plants into the plans, thereby saving species that might be overlooked.

Africare teaches villagers to raise small animals to increase protein intake. Cows or even goats were too large to manage, and meat presented a storage problem. Africare builds demonstration animal raising centers, to be copied by villagers. Rabbit rearing, though new to the area, has been spreading, and Africare concludes there is a direct connection to the reduced protein deficiency in the villages covered. While not as elegant as the demonstration models, the villagers' rabbit hutches are functional, and people are rightly proud of their efforts. One preteen boy enthusiastically jumped up into a rabbit hutch and gleefully held up a healthy looking rabbit. The spirit of innovation appears to be spreading. Based on their experience with rabbits, villagers on their own initiative began raising chickens. Africare responded to villager priorities by providing needed assistance with poultry disease prevention.

Southwest Uganda is a male-dominated culture. Africare works to ensure women are represented on all committees. Women are directly trained in farming methods. Women project leaders identified the UFSI program as a catalyst for improving the status and power of women in the villages. In the planning stages, men, women, and youth meet separately to decide on priorities, which are then integrated into the overall village plan. This way, women's voices are heard, and the problem that women may be reluctant to speak up in a group of both men and women is avoided.

Southwest Uganda has an overexploited and deteriorating ecosystem, but the USFI program is bringing environmental benefits. Soil erosion is dramatically reduced in program areas. Trees are being planted including useful tree species, such as calliandra and gravellea, which add nutrients and improve soil stability. In addition, the rapidly growing branches of these trees are used for fuel, beanpoles, and construction materials. The beanpoles enabled a switch from bush beans, vulnerable to blight, to the more productive and disease-resistant climbing beans (an excellent source of protein well-suited to the environment). Each village chooses a cash crop appropriate to its terrain and to the skills and preferences of the people.

Farmers are taught land management techniques, to capture water, reduce erosion, and add nutrients to the soils, and proudly show visitors how they have put them into practice. For example, the farmers demonstrated the types of trenches needed in various situations and how to best recapture nutrients from them. There is real hope that villagers are sustainably escaping a farm erosion trap.

In example after example it was shown how virtually everything is recycled in the program: a use is found for every product and waste output of each component of the programs, whether it be rabbit manure for fertilizer, husks for feed, trimming border trees for domestic uses such as fuelwood, banana fiber for potting, refuse for fish farming. You could say they are really thinking outside of the recycling box.

Farmers are learning the importance of environmental sustainability and taking ownership for the environmental quality in their village. This is probably one of the most important prerequisites for sustainable biodiversity. Africare's records show that over 5,337,000 tree seedlings have been raised on community nursery beds since inception of the project. While promoting tree biodiversity, Africare promotes several major categories of trees: for soil fertility replenishment and maintenance; for terrace stabilization and soil erosion control; for wood/timber/biomass production; for fodder; and for medicinal purposes.

I nominated the UFSI program for the Equator Prize. Having previously read the unusually enthusiastic outside evaluator's report, I contacted the chief evaluator, who seconded my nomination. She wrote me: "I would be delighted to second your nomination. I, too, was extremely impressed by the UFSI Program. As someone who has spent some 25 years in development, and—I have to admit—had become a bit cynical of the effectiveness of aid in Africa, I was impressed with how effective and efficient this program was."

To help ensure sustainability, Africare has worked to actively involve national and local government. Africare set up the overall program as a component of the government's poverty eradication action plan. Although initial resources contributed were small, Africare has found ways to include government departments. The hope is that by giving government a stake and share in the credit for success, it will take over the roles that cannot be managed and paid for by the villages alone, making the project financially sustainable after Africare has moved to other villages. Early indications suggest the strategy is working. The government is maintaining the new roads. Having driven on four of them, these four at least continue to be better roads than those found in much of Uganda. The programs were explicitly integrated into the development plans of local government.

The Africare UFSI program has been operating since 1997. Many have already benefited: Africare estimates over 67,000 in agricultural production, 73,000 in nutrition, and 94,000 in natural resource management. The next phase is just starting, and with more resources the program could clearly be scaled up considerably. I visited a village that was trained in an early stage of the project, and has not received Africare assistance for three years. Practices taught in the programs are continuing. Participants were actively engaged in training other villages, both out of a sense of obligation and to develop markets—for example, for the disease-resistant seeds they now produce. Participants continue to contribute, from attending meetings to maintaining roads. The most important reason for expecting sustainability is that the program works. The community associations are generating significant income, so both families and villages will have resources to continue programs and to afford the better nutrition, health, and land management practices they have learned.

It is no wonder that Nelson Mandela said, "I regard Africare as one of America's greatest gifts to Africa."

TEN STRATEGIES FOR INNOVATION IN ENDING GLOBAL POVERTY

Ten characteristics of innovation in NGO poverty programs are apparent from the general patterns of the case studies in the book. This is a typology, a search for common patterns in *innovation;* there is not yet enough evidence to identify these characteristics with *effectiveness,* let alone to be *prescriptive* about how best to innovate. But categorizing innovation channels can be helpful for thinking about new solutions for poverty problems.

1. Listen more. Find a way to listen more, and listen more perceptively and open-mindedly, to the concerns and grievances of the poor. As a result, we become better able to identify constraints on the poor that others have overlooked or for some reason have not addressed. Examples in the book: the Association for the Development and Enhancement of Women (ADEW) in Egypt and World Vision in Peru—who by listening to the concerns of the poor learned about problems caused by their lack of legal documents, and then found a way to help the poor to get them.

2. Let the voices of the poor ring louder. Find a way to make the voices of the poor and excluded ring louder and clearer for the outside world—and policymakers and opinion leaders in particular—to hear. Examples in the book: mandated village council positions for women in West Bengal, which changed the way local resources were allocated and the way people thought of women's roles in the community; BRAC legal education and group action; the Human Rights Center, Chiapas.

3. Involve paraprofessionals. Find a way to get dedicated and motivated but less-trained (and much less costly) paraprofessionals to play a key role. Also scale up the program regionally or nationally, by finding a way to finance hiring large numbers of these paraprofessionals in the villages or slums where they live. Examples in the book: nonformal primary education such as BRAC in Bangladesh and Save the Children in Africa.

4. Use unconventional assets. Identify and then leverage overlooked and unconventional assets of the poor and the social solidarity and networks in their communities. Examples in the book: the Synjuk Seng Samla Shnong (SSSS) in Meghalaya, India; Africare's Food Security Initiative in Uganda; Heifer International's work to enhance the assets already developed by a self-organized community organization in Lima.

5. Protect the environment. To ensure sustainability, protect the environment while raising incomes—do not wait for it to become too late. Examples in the book: Honey Care in Kenya, the Suledo Forrest Community in Tanzania, and Fundecor in Costa Rica.

6. Identify niche products. Find overlooked niche products that are labor intensive and particularly suited for the local market but can find surprisingly large markets abroad. Examples in the book: pigeon peas development in Tanzania supported by TechnoServe and its partners; skilled semi-manufactured products making use of traditional local skills, like stone inlaying and crocheting supported by the Small Enterprise Assistance Fund (SEAF) in Peru; and entrepreneur identification by Endeavor.

7. Increase value-added. Find a way to increase the value-added that goes to hardworking smallholder farmers and microentrepreneurs. These people are working very hard, and if you can identify and relax the key constraints that are keeping them in low productivity work, you can have a magnified impact on poverty reduction. Examples in the book: the Self-Employed Women's Association (SEWA) in India; Mother-Child in Uganda; and microcredit that reaches the poorest, such as the Foundation for International Community Assistance (FINCA), Grameen, and BRAC.

8. Identify constraints keeping children from learning. Find out the key local constraint that prevents children from staying healthy and going to school or leads to their performing poorly there and then attack that problem directly and relentlessly.

Examples in the book: deworming in Kenya; Childline in India; Progresa in Mexico.

9. Kill more birds with one stone. Find a way to do more by solving two or more needs at the same time. Examples in the book: Grameen phone ladies; Gram Vikas Rural Health and Environment Program; South Africa merry-go-round water Playpump.

10. Evaluate the program boldly. Perhaps most importantly, work with experts to find the most rigorous method—often, randomized trials—for objectively evaluating the impact of the work, without regard to organizational risks. In addition to providing useful evaluative findings, other valuable insights into problems of the clients and other participants and strategies for addressing them have emerged from collected information and the ideas of outside experts engaged in evaluation. Rigorous evaluation and innovation go hand in hand. Evaluation is needed to test the impact of innovations, but many innovations emerge in the process of absorbing the lessons of impact evaluations. Examples in the book: Pratham in India and International Christian Support Fund (ICS) in Kenya.

Each of these ten channels for innovation has been successfully used to generate new designs for programs that observers believe hold promise.

Facilitating the ability of the poor to cooperate for mutual assistance is also a typical and overarching characteristic of innovative programs for those in extreme poverty. Sometimes effectiveness in providing escape from poverty is simply a matter of delivering public services that the well-off routinely enjoy, but in many cases it is a matter of building the self-reliance of the poor. Examples include the role of community leaders in the village cultural transformations in Ethiopia, the community organization of The AIDS Support Organization (TASO) in Uganda and Gram Vikas in Orissa, the parents' committees in nonformal primary schools, the realization of individual dreams made possible in the best microfinance solidarity programs, the community leaders' roles and participants' empowerment in programs for the ultrapoor in Bangladesh, the extraordinary solidarity and autonomy of participants in SEWA in India, the self-management of Kerala Dinesh Beedi (KDB) in Kerala, agricultural improvements with attention to sustaining the environment facilitated by improved rural community governance as seen in the TechnoServe, Africa Now and Africare programs, and legal empowerment of the poor as in BRAC and ADEW. Such programs deliver not just services but freedom and empowerment, and they deliver broader means with specific ends, a broader message along with specific information.

Thus, in the most promising poverty programs the means of escape from poverty traps are consistent with the ends. Unless the poor build self-reliance, they remain vulnerable; self-reliance makes progress against poverty sustainable. In the best programs, the poor are not just "recipients," but are fully empowered participants, who are gaining in empowerment even as they gain the other keys to capability.

The programs described in this part of the book show us that while the scale of poverty is immense, and while an end to global poverty is *not inevitable,* it is *possible,* even for those in extreme poverty far from the centers of world growth. Thus there is a compelling ethical reason to become personally involved in helping to solve problems of poverty. There is a great deal that all of us can do.

PART III

WHAT YOU CAN DO TO HELP

From earlier sections of the book, I hope you are convinced that we should help: Poverty is extreme human suffering, which we can prevent, but which will not end without our help. This part of the book has two main messages. The first message is that thousands if not millions of people are already helping in constructive and creative ways. Businesses, communities, organizations, and congregations are doing useful work to help the poor gain the keys to capability and escape from poverty traps. The second message is to let you know how you can also help.

FIRST STEPS

Many of the activities and donation strategies described in this section are crosscutting in nature, and they are organized according to types of strategy; but all help provide keys to capability. Everyone can identify steps they can take to help.

LEARN MORE

Knowledge is powerful. Explore the references at the end of this book and follow the webpage links. Talk to people working for private voluntary organizations on poverty programs. Enroll in a course. Follow the news from developing countries, either by subscribing or reading in the library one of the newspapers with the best coverage, such as the *New York Times* or the *Financial Times*. Follow reliable websites such as BBC or CNN—be wary of lesser known and unvetted sites. Subscribe to newsletters and e-mail listserves from groups you trust most. Our knowledge is growing rapidly and there is always more to learn about the causes and remedies for poverty.

Join a group such as the Society for International Development (SID), and go to events. The Society has 65 chapters and numerous topical networks. If there is no SID chapter and no other comparable group where you live, you can start one. It takes only one person to get things started and to get others to join in.

The World Affairs Council, at http://www.world-affairs.org, is another potential group to get involved with. They have a wider focus but many local activities, including hosting visitors and classroom programs.

GO TO EVENTS

Many large nonprofits have local events over the course of a year. You can find out about these by calling them. You may travel to a city in which a NGO you are interested in is based. If you have some spare time, visit. You can usually arrange an interview; and once there you can learn a lot about the organization. Is it housed in lush offices or do employees work modestly? Are people busy or in busywork? Is good material on program evaluation readily available?

Most of us have no idea how well off we really are. Money is an imperfect measure of welfare in many ways, but it does give you some idea. Go to http://www.globalrichlist.com/index.php. Type in your annual income, and you will see how many people in the world are poorer than you.

PARTICIPATE IN STUDY TOURS

Some groups such as World Vision and Oxfam sponsor poverty program study tours. Participants on these tours generally report a very positive experience. Heifer International in particular gives frequent tours and is quite well organized; you can read about their offerings at: http://www.heifer.org/get_involved/study_tours.htm. You can find Australia-based offerings of Oxfam Community Aid Abroad at http://www.caa.org.au/travel/.

Global Exchange offers "reality tours" of conditions of the poor and efforts to help them improve their lives in many countries, from Afghanistan to Zimbabwe. In Mexico, the Global Exchange works with the Fray Bartolomé de Las Casas Human Rights Center (HRC) in Chiapas, featured earlier in the book. Go to http://www.globalexchange.org/tours/.

Some operators combine history and current efforts to end poverty, such as Legend Tours visits to South African townships where the struggle against apartheid took place.

Such tours are a great way to learn and to have an unforgettable adventure at the same time. And you never know what small bit of information you might impart that turns out to be a major part of the answer to problems they are facing. Remember, they are starting with low productivity, and simple and useful ways of doing things that we take for granted may never have been introduced there. But be mindful that you are a role model—consuming unattainable goods, coming off as wasteful, or being scornful can have unfortunate consequences.

The more adventurous can organize trips on their own. However, in many developing countries social conflicts and other problems can make travel dangerous, especially in certain areas. Before you make your travel plans, check on travel conditions and advisories, such as those provided on-line by the U.S. Department of State, at http://travel.state.gov/travel_warnings.html.

Most NGOs are happy to receive visitors. But if you visit, please remember that you are costing the NGO time and resources. To them, giving you a ride out to a program in a jeep is not like giving someone a lift is to you. Resources are scarce, and the time diverts them from their primary work. Please ask the NGO to make a full accounting of all your visit is costing them, directly and indirectly, and pay what they ask without question. If they make a little profit on your visit, good for them—and good for you.

Some trips are specifically work-focused. This gives you an opportunity to participate in service at the same time as you learn, and to forge bonds with both local people and with fellow tour participants while giving something of yourself.

Some work trips are part of what has come to be known as "alternative spring break." Students work with poor communities for a few days, generally in low to lower-middle income countries in Central America or the Caribbean such as Honduras and the Dominican Republic, but give themselves a couple of days at the beach as well. They come back with feelings of accomplishment; and some students say they learned more during alternative spring breaks than in any other single week in college. These events are not just for college students. And if you have children in college, you could go with them. Valuable projects are also taking place for the less well off in the United States, some sponsored by the same organizations, such as Habitat for Humanity.

SHARE YOUR KNOWLEDGE

One of the most effective ways to share your knowledge is one-on-one. Tell your family and friends what you have been learning and encourage them to learn more and decide for themselves what can be done.

Many people are afraid of public speaking. In fact, it really can be quite scary. One way to overcome this is to start small, in comfortable settings where you know most of the people.

The pulpit is a medium of educating and energizing people. Some denominations have lay talks and others utilize guest speakers. Nearby universities may have experts on poverty and development who would be willing to come out and talk if you invite them. Lay-led talks can be a venue for members to learn more and to share what they have learned.

Write letters to your local newspaper. This can be easier if you get involved with a private voluntary organization, as I talk about shortly. Explain why they should be giving greater coverage to problems of global poverty, and why readers like you would be interested.

Start a blog, and tell your relatives, friends, and colleagues about it. Post what you learn. People may be interested to follow your journey, and you may get interesting and unexpected feedback.

CONTRIBUTE WISELY:
FIND YOUR ISSUE, ASSESS YOUR TALENTS

There is a traditional saying that we should think globally and act locally. But sometimes the most pressing needs are not local. And we are better equipped to think and act wisely when we make both local and global connections. International giving, not necessarily only to addressing problems of extreme poverty, is an important part of a giving portfolio. We have special obligations to our own country, but we are also citizens of the world. As world citizens part of our concern goes to wherever needs are the greatest. And the way we respond to global needs today will affect our well-being at home in the years to come. Citizens in America and other rich countries will be affected by climate changes brought about by the loss of rainforests. Social instability in the poorest regions can eventually spill over to our own security problems. Diseases that spread unchecked in the poor countries can eventually show up in the homes of the rich countries.

How does one even begin to think about where to give? Choose a poverty problem you feel passionately about; maybe it is hunger, environmental protection, or the right to human dignity. Get to know your issue thoroughly. Find out what groups are innovative and effective.

In the case of U.S. NGOs, often called private voluntary nonprofit organizations (PVOs), a basic minimum criterion is whether the NGO meets the Council of Better Business Bureaus (CBBB) Wise Giving Alliance Standards for Charitable Solicitations, described at http://www.give.org/standards/cbbbstds.asp. Charities can apply for the BBB National Charity Seal program. The American Institute of Philanthropy (AIP) offers the Charity Rating Guide & Watchdog Report, with ratings for a large number of poverty and development related charities—to receive the report, send a check for $3.00 (to cover postage and handling) to 3450 Lake Shore Drive, Suite 2802E, P.O. Box 578460, Chicago, IL 60657. The AIP offers more limited information online at http://www.charitywatch.org. A relatively recent system of alternative ratings, which can be useful to consult for comparative purposes, can be found at Charity Navigator at http://www.charitynavigator.org/index.cfm. Idealist.org is new and very interesting online source, which also provides volunteer and career information.

Additional information can be found at GuideStar.org, which provides links to other useful information, such as the tax filings and other documents of many nonprofits. Independent Sector, a coalition of U.S. foundations, nonprofit organizations, and involved corporations is another good source of information on NGOs, at http://www.independentsector.org/. In the United States, a supplementary consideration is membership in InterAction, the association of organizations involved in international development and poverty work; member organizations must commit to several principles of good practice. However, it does cost at least a modest fee to participate in programs such as the BBB National Charity Seal Program and InterAction membership; if an NGO does not join, this may mean they chose to spend their resources in other legitimate ways.

These ratings may have some surprises in store for you. For example, the AIP has given the Citizens Against Government Waste an F rating, based in part on the small percentage of funds raised that go into program services. Larry Jones Ministries Feed the Children received an F, spending just 20 percent of its income on programs.

Several financial magazines such as *Fortune, Worth,* and *Money* also rate charities; their methods of selection vary, but these lists can also be helpful for stimulating ideas for further investigation. It is important to take all ratings systems—whether from *Consumer Reports* on autos or *U.S. News & World Report* on colleges—with a grain of salt. For one thing, when quality is important, measurement is difficult and different people value different attributes. For another, the presence of such rating systems leads people to game the system.

To give an idea of some of the complexities, consider a U.S. religious-affiliated development organization that receives an excellent rating from the AIP. This organization has now moved its U.S. church work under the budget category of program expenses—the same category as for its work with the poor in Africa. I am not saying this is necessarily illegitimate; certainly educating congregations about poverty is worthwhile, though it has indirect and uncertain impact on actual poverty. But officials told me that their reason for doing this was in part to have a higher rating: If work with U.S. churches is part of program, rather than fundraising expenses, then the share of program expenses in the budget appears to be larger. This earns a higher score from AIP and the other rating agencies. My point is not to criticize this organization, whose candor in this matter is admirable. The point is that these numbers can be gamed. Just as you would not choose a college based solely on its *U.S. News* ranking, be sure to supplement ratings information with further exploration of what groups are accomplishing.

On the other side of this coin, in many sectors it is also unreasonable to expect very low overhead levels for serious and effective organizations.

Many donors are unwilling to support overhead expenses, but they may include activities that are vital for effectiveness, including research, evaluation, training, office expenses, and information technology. Overhead expenses, properly allocated, can be vital to reducing waste and in improving the impact of program efforts. But beware of overhead that is unusually high, especially for fundraising and top-heavy administration.

Despite the limitations, these ratings, especially when corroborated across more than one of these ratings services, is one factor to consider in your giving. But the difference between, say, an A and a B rating is not sufficient evidence upon which to base withholding a donation. Ultimately, you must investigate and judge charities for yourself.

BE CAREFUL

Like many others who have had the misfortune of getting onto spamming lists, I received my first email from a purported "non-profitable" organization (they might have meant to say nonprofit), based in Nigeria. In this case the intent to scam was transparent. But I worry that, as these charlatans get better at their scams, the unwary might be fooled. The safest strategy is to never send money to a charity in response to an e-mail. If you get an e-mail from a developing country reporting on work that sounds too good to be true, it probably is. Although it is nice to think that in the information economy direct assistance to worthy charities in the developing world becomes more possible, at this point the risks to doing so are just too high.

STRATEGIZE YOUR GIVING

Before you contribute to any group, do thorough research. Treat this book as only a starting point. Look up the organizations you give to in reports from the ratings systems described earlier, and look for independent research reports on specific programs. Read the organization's materials with a critical eye. Remember to take all these with a grain of salt.

Most substantial NGOs have fairly extensive websites. They and many other sites will encourage you to give on the spot via your credit card. I would suggest being very cautious about this. At the very least do your due diligence first. Reputable groups will send you materials in the mail. Also, talk with people that you know to be long-term donors to poverty programs, or people you trust who are knowledgeable. Supplement your Internet research by using reputable databases available in many libraries, such as Academic Search Premier and Proquest Research Library Plus. In the end, there is still no alternative to doing some of your own work on this. The best answers are always improving, and it is worth spending some time to keep abreast of new developments.

Don't be hesitant to e-mail or call the organizations and ask them pointed questions. It leads to good incentives and occasion for reflection on the part of development professionals; and the donors will learn more, give more, and get more involved.

In large organizations, questions will be directed to PR staff members who may not be fully knowledgeable about your questions, especially if you have specialized interests and questions about specific programs in particular countries; but they can relay these questions when they need to. It may take a couple weeks or so for staff to get back to you, and this is a reasonable timeframe given the demands on everyone's time. Always get a name and way to contact the person directly.

TARGET YOUR DONATIONS

Give to organizations you can support overall, but try to target your giving to good *programs* rather than generic *organizations*. Look for—ask for—serious program evaluations. Make sure they are working actively with local officials. See if locals are also contributing something to the programs—it shows whether people will take ownership and make it as self-supporting as possible. Make sure the program has a culture of accountability and rigorous control mechanisms in place. Specify what program you want to support and why. Which of the key(s) are the organization working toward in general, and what does the specific program contribute to the keys? Can it help address any poverty traps? Stay engaged, stay informed, ask for follow up.

By concentrating your donation on a handful of organizations, you can be more effective. It is not like the stock market, where maximum diversification is best. There is a direct value to you and the organization of giving more to a fewer number of organizations. You might be surprised by how modest your gifts to charity can be for you to be considered a "major donor." In some organizations, this can be as little as $250. As Tracy Gary and Melissa Kohner point out, as a major donor, you will often have special opportunities for interaction with key staff. This can also be an opportunity for the NGO. You may have good ideas that might be overlooked. So make the time worthwhile for the staff, in more ways than just securing future donations. Just by asking good questions, you can stimulate creative thinking, and, just as importantly, remind leaders of the need for thorough program evaluations.

If you have been giving substantially to one organization and, as a result of your research or changing personal priorities, decide to reallocate this support to other NGOs, Gary and Kohner point out that it is a good idea to let them know in advance. This does two things. It lets them plan. And it gives feedback. If it is because of poor percentage of donations going to programs, or the lack of available or serious program evaluations, tell them so. It may encourage them to improve. If there is some threshold that they could reach that might bring you back, tell them.

You may also want to think about your giving in relation to what others are already doing. Perhaps your alma mater is relatively well funded and doesn't need your donation as much as some other worthy cause (as a professor I may hear from my dean about such an observation). If you switch giving from one cause to another, will other donors be able to take up the slack?

Foundations and giving are also interwoven in the fabric of business. In business, charitable contributions are sometimes a perk, like seats to a football game. Donations to charitable organizations known to be favored by clients and business associates are used to grease the wheels of business transactions. If you are in the business world, you can make it known that you follow the work of organizations fighting poverty, and that you currently give to a particular organization that has impressed you. Companies may make donations accordingly. It is a way for them to be noticed by you, but by its nature a charitable donation cannot come with any expected reciprocity. If this is going on anyway, why shouldn't more of these donations go to NGOs fighting poverty?

Finally, follow up on your gifts. Get information on what the organization has been doing. Go to events if you can.

CREATE A PERSONAL GIVING MISSION STATEMENT

In *Seven Habits of Highly Effective People,* Stephen Covey suggests that everyone create a person mission statement about our purpose in life. In a similar way, authors Tracy Gary and Melissa Kohner suggest that to make a real difference in charitable giving, whether to help end poverty or for other worthy goals, "then all of us—donors, novices and experts, new and old—must put more planning into our giving." They recommend that even us small givers put their *mission and vision* onto paper, and referring to it to make sure giving fits with their overall vision. As they put it, "creating a giving plan fosters more enjoyment, ingenuity, and effectiveness in personal philanthropy than automatic, reactive giving."

If you want to contribute to the fight against poverty, it is a good idea to put that commitment onto paper. Write down why the fight against extreme poverty is important to you personally. Then, decide for yourself what fraction of your giving you want to go to fighting poverty, what fraction you want to give to other purposes, such as supporting your place of worship, protecting the environment, and so on. In doing so, consider the connections between the causes you want to support. Ending poverty is connected to environmental protection in impoverished countries, and to solving global environmental problems such as global warming. If protecting the earth's environment is important to you, you may want to focus some of your giving to groups that work for environmental protection and sustainable development in low-income countries.

Then see how this compares with the giving that you actually do. Draw this from your tax forms, checkbook, and credit card statements over a period of a year or two. How much of your giving goes to programs to address extreme poverty? Is it about right?

As Gary and Kohner also point out, you can give your anonymous gift more impact by having it delivered with a message, saying something about you, your values, and or your priorities. You could have the gift state that you are "a donor concerned about poverty" or "I am partly giving to you because of your strong commitment to rigorous program evaluation," or the "very high percentage of funds that go directly into programs in the field." Finally you can target specific programs based on their rigorously demonstrated impact, for example, "I am giving to your accelerating learning program, because I have read the reports about how effective this strategy is in improving the lives and the educational opportunity of children."

Have a clear plan in advance. For example, say you donate a total of 5 percent of your income to charity each year. Of this you want to allocate one-fifth to poverty programs and related forms of development assistance. You know that if you give some of these funds to one organization, then you have that much less to give to others. If you have such a plan in advance, then you won't be unsure what to do when faced with an unexpected request for funds. You can even tell groups that ask you for money which organizations you are giving to, and on what criteria. That can provide them with valuable feedback.

Timing and targeting are important. Watch for special matching opportunities, such as sponsors who will donate two dollars for each one that other individuals donate for a limited time. You would not generally want to alter the set of groups you give to, but you can alter the timing or distribution of your gifts to leverage your impact.

If you can offer a match yourself, there are several good reasons to do so. It calls attention to the problem you want to focus on, gets more people involved, and motivates people to donate more resources than they otherwise might. It is a way to respond to a special sense of obligation in an energizing way. You may choose either to be named in the match—that is great PR—or to offer it anonymously.

A personal giving statement should reflect your broad strategy and would normally not be revised very often. But you can also maintain a more specific plan that reflects your own tactical approach for giving to alleviate poverty. You can do this in a simple way, just as foundations do. It need be no more than such statements as: "Because I read about independent research showing the impact of this program." "Because I care about this issue, and because those injustices are very upsetting to me." "Because I have seen their work firsthand and know what a difference it makes." These are all valid reasons to focus your giving tactics. But in all cases, write this down, and revisit it from time to time. Finally, make sure the organizations and programs you support still pass the test of demonstrating substantial impact for the money spent, and that there are not better alternatives that have emerged or that you may have overlooked.

INVOLVE YOUR CHILDREN— BUILD UNDERSTANDING AND MORAL VALUES

Tell your children about your gifts, and why the need is so great. You can help build generosity and good values in your children this way. If you do this, your children are likely to follow your example when they grow up. Some NGOs have programs especially for children, such as Heifer's Read-to-Feed Program (http://www.readtofeed.org/), which has great resources for children. This program was used in my own church with great success—both in the surprisingly substantial funds raised and in the impact on the one hundred children who took part. Children read books, including but not only those related to poverty, and sponsors contribute to a Heifer fund based on how much they read. Pratham has similar programs operating in the United States and the UK in support of basic education in India.

But even if the group you want to work with does not have a special program for children, after you read the materials of the groups you decide to give to, you can think of ways to explain the work of the programs you give to in ways the children will understand. Make sure your children know how much they have, in comparison to other children who have very little. When she was small, I explained to my daughter that while she had dozens of dolls and stuffed animals, in some places girls were lucky to have one doll made out of discarded rags. Ask your children to imagine a world in which they have no running water, where they, as the children, would have to walk two miles to fetch drinking and cooking water for the family.

FURTHER QUESTIONS

This chapter looks at some of the questions people most commonly ask about having a positive impact on poverty and sustainable development.

LIFESTYLE CHANGES:
WOULD THEY MAKE ANY DIFFERENCE?

The United States consumed 15,184 pounds per person of fossil fuels in 1997, while India consumed only 590 and Bangladesh consumed a mere 147 pounds per capita, less than one percent of U.S. levels. Similarly, while the United States consumed a staggering 615 pounds of paper per person, China consumed just one-tenth as much, while India consumed only about one percent as much per person. The United States and other developed countries consume a similarly disproportionate share of other environmentally sensitive products, such as ocean fish.

A substantial part of developed country consumption is wasteful. It seems clear that the world as a whole cannot consume natural resources at current U.S. levels. Responsible consumption on the part of the developed countries is not just setting a good example; it is an ecological necessity. This does not mean that economies cannot continue to grow indefinitely—they can, if productivity continues to rise while more consumption becomes knowledge-based and more modest in its use of raw materials. It is rather that the patterns of consumption must change. In part because of the impact of global warming on the poor, we must reduce greenhouse gas emissions, and this means more fuel-efficient vehicles. Markets will induce some the needed changes with rising prices, but this effect is not large enough or fast enough, partly because the impact is on the poor in distant countries, or on those who will be born in the future.

I have been asked by some of my students, Should we stop eating meat? Unfortunately, solving hunger is not that easy. As Howard Leathers points out, if we eat less meat, this will trigger a chain of responses in world markets. First, the price of meat will fall, which will lead growers to produce less meat. They in turn will purchase less grain, which will lead to a fall in the price of grain; but that will also lead to less grain being produced, dampening the price fall.

Even if grain prices fall, the impact on the poor may be limited. Somehow food must be transferred to the poor. As we have seen, we already send food, but this is often ineffective or counterproductive, or both. Among other things the food often tends to go to urban areas, while the poor are still predominantly rural. And by lowering urban food prices, it can actually make the rural poor who grow the food worse off. What is most needed is to raise the productivity of poor farmers in developing countries, and give them at least a level playing field on which to compete.

Nevertheless, responsible consumption is part of what we can do. Perhaps the most important reason is that the fight against global poverty depends crucially on protecting the environmental resources on which many of the poor directly depend. One reason to consume modestly is that U.S. standards are broadcast throughout the world and become the aspirations for everyone else.

There are undoubtedly good reasons for eating less meat but in doing only this, a person will not have a measurable effect on poverty. The real question is what to do with the money saved by consuming less wastefully. The money saved by consuming more modestly can help guide us to what we find a reasonable increase in contributions. If targeted well, there could be a real impact.

Should we Buy Consciously?

Most of us do not grow, or even much process, the foods we consume. We do not build the vehicles we drive, make the clothes we wear, construct the house we live in, or create its furnishings. There is nothing wrong with this—it is the result of specialization, and that is perhaps the most important factor that gives us the standard of living that those of us who are not poor have come to take for granted. But beyond that, so many objects have become nothing but utilitarian, and even designer and "artistic" objects convey little real meaning. One way to bring some meaning to at least a few of the things we consume is to buy from the poor, and through people who work with the poor.

A growing number of organizations provide wholesome and ecologically responsible products directly from the poor. In the global scheme of things, these initiatives may be just a few drops in a bucket. But if organized well, they can be a rare opportunity for those drops to land in some of the emptiest and most beat-up buckets in the world.

One of the best-known programs is Ten Thousand Villages, a nonprofit program of the Mennonite Central Committee (MCC), the North American relief and development arm of Mennonite and Brethren churches. The MCC receives an A from the American Institute of Philanthropy (AIP), for having low operating costs and spending most of their income on programs. As the MCC puts it, "Ten Thousand Villages provides vital, fair income to Third World people by marketing their handicrafts and telling their stories in North America. Ten Thousand Villages works with artisans who would otherwise be unemployed or underemployed, providing greater income through trade. This income helps pay for food, education, healthcare and housing." You can buy online or find the location of their festivals and their 180 stores throughout the United States and Canada at their websites, http://www.tenthousandvillages.com/ (or http://www.villages.ca/).

Ten Thousand Villages is a member of the Fair Trade Federation (FTF), which directly links low-income producers with consumer markets and educates consumers about the importance of purchasing fairly traded products which support living wages and safe and healthy conditions for workers in the developing world. You can find out more about the FTF at their website, http://www.fairtradefederation.com/index.html. While a much broader group than MCC, you can find information and in almost all cases websites for each of its members.

Another useful site is Transfair USA, at http://www.transfairusa.org/. Transfair is a U.S. affiliate of the Fairtrade Labeling Organizations International (FLO), based in Germany. FLO and its members won the 2002–03 King Baudouin International Development Prize, "for their pioneering role in giving disadvantaged producers and workers in the developing world the opportunity to participate directly and at fair trade conditions in international trade, through a system of certification, producer support, business facilitation, and consumer education." You can find FLO on the web at www.fairtrade.net.

You can also buy directly from co-ops or NGO programs in developing countries. There are many other worthy groups not listed or members. Many allow you to buy through the web. For example BRAC's Aarong is found at http://www.brac-aarong.com/. Grameen's clothing and accessories store, featuring Grameen Knitwear, can be found on the web at http://www.grameen-info.org/grameen/gknit/index.html. You can also buy from the Self-Employed Women's Association in India (SEWA) at Banascraft http://www.banascraft.org/.

In addition to buying products, you can also give donations to some of the NGOs whose work you most respect in the name of people on your gift list. Some organizations specialize in providing such services, such as Alternative Gifts International (www.altgifts.org). But many if not most of the leading poverty-focused organizations provide or directly send cards of acknowledgement for the family and friends in whose name you donate.

SHOULD YOU TAKE PART
IN CHILD SPONSORSHIP PROGRAMS?

We have all seen the images on TV of beautiful sad-eyed children, sure to tug at the heartstrings. And a large number of Americans respond. These programs received more attention than ever when the film "About Schmidt" came out, in which Jack Nicholson corresponds with a six-year-old Tanzanian boy whom he sponsors.

Does this approach make sense?

The concept of basing a strategy for poverty reduction and economic development around child sponsorship is dubious. Spending money directly on a single child would be administratively very expensive, and would not necessarily have any large or lasting benefits. In practice, much of the funds donated to child sponsorship goes to support the community in which the child lives. Even if you are given a name and a picture, this is in many cases symbolic—most of your donations are typically mixed with those of other sponsors and used to support a community program. This is entirely reasonable, and in many respects a better strategy, provided that it is carried out efficiently and with sound principles, and has a solid impact evaluation plan.

Child sponsorship is not necessarily a strategy of education or even of poverty reduction more generally; it seems to me that it is more a strategy of fundraising. NGO officials often say that, for any given project, they raise more money when they employ a child sponsorship angle than when they advertise on the basis of the program's specific features, such as the merits of a community development project. People seem to identify much more with making an individual, personal connection, particularly with a child.

In 1998, the *Chicago Tribune* ran what has been characterized as an "expose" story about child sponsorship. Reporters posed as ordinary citizens to join various child sponsorship programs, and three years later they followed up to see what happened. They reported some sensational results; in some cases the children whom the reporters had been told they were sponsoring and were doing well had in fact died years ago. Some children were reportedly receiving few or no services.

Clearly some serious problems had been uncovered with some of the plans. But the article also focused on whether donations were actually going to the child that the donors thought they were supporting, or to some pool of children, or to the community the child lives in. It is hardly a scandal to support health and education for *all* the children in a village rather than singling out just one child. It makes more sense for poverty alleviation and community development; it is a more efficient way to deliver services, and in many cases it is simply much fairer. Clearly there should be truth in advertising. In fact the better programs are quite explicit about the fact that the community, rather than the individual identified child, is getting the support.

After this "expose," five leading child sponsorship programs, which are members of InterAction, an umbrella group for U.S.-based international organizations working for relief, development, and poverty alleviation, asked InterAction to help with the adoption of standards for child sponsorship and to serve as an "intermediary" in identifying and securing third-party, accredited certification of their compliance with these standards. The five child sponsorship organizations involved are Plan-USA, Children International, Christian Children's Fund, Save the Children, and World Vision. The audits, which take place at the U.S. headquarters of these five agencies as well as at a random sampling of field operations around the world, were launched in October 2004 and are scheduled to be completed by June 2005. Social Accountability International (SAI), an independent accrediting body, was engaged to help the working group to define evidence of compliance for each standard so that independent audit teams could make objective determinations of compliance. SAI will also accredit the certification process. Such audits should be helpful for those who are considering taking part in a child sponsorship program.

Many people who sponsor a child find it very meaningful. They would not give nearly as much money to support abstract sounding poverty programs otherwise. Many greatly appreciate receiving photos and information about the child they sponsor on a regular basis. If individual sponsorship is important to you, start with the understanding that, in the better sponsorship programs, your assistance is going to programs for the child's community. Investigate reports by reputable charity rating organizations. And to make sure there is some legitimacy to the sponsorship process, verify that the group will let you visit the child they designate. Even if you are not able to visit, this provides some reassurance that everything is above-board. If you visit, it is a good idea to bring a gift not only for the child, but to provide something for the whole village. A year of school fees for all the poorer children, or a few months' teacher salary, is surprisingly inexpensive. Note that many of these groups have similar sounding names. It is important to know the organization you are sponsoring a child with, and to make doubly sure that your money is going to the group you intend. Not all programs are equally effective. Research the programs you are considering through leading charity rating organization such as the Wise Giving Allaince of the Better Business Bureau.

Before you sign up for a program, ask some tough questions. Most importantly, does the program commit to careful impact evaluation? A sound program should be able to give you good and serious answers about how projects are monitored and evaluated, with procedures for incorporating lessons learned. If we believe that every child is to be cherished, we must insist that the all-too-limited resources we have available to help impoverished girls and boys are used in the most effective possible ways.

SHOULD YOU FOCUS ON RELIEF WORK
OR ON DEVELOPMENT?

Before development can get begin, relief may be needed to prepare the ground. Relief work is not the focus of this book. But as a rule, the best-designed relief programs take into consideration their future impact and plan strategies for the relief work to evolve into, or team up with other organizations that are effective at longer-term poverty alleviation and development; or, they find a way to do both activities at the same time. Ideally, synergies between relief and subsequent development can be identified and utilized.

If you wish to make disaster relief of other basic welfare support for the ultrapoor a focus of your giving and volunteering, try to identify groups, such as the International Rescue Committee, which earn very high marks in charity ratings, that simultaneously lay the groundwork for long-term development after the immediate crisis has passed, and can show evidence of effectiveness in both types of work. You can also ask relief groups you might like to support how they are thinking ahead to this transition. Once again, careful impact and cost effectiveness evaluations should be a normal part of operations and available to the public.

SHOULD DEVELOPMENT ASSISTANCE
BE PROVIDED BY MULTIPURPOSE
OR SPECIALIST ORGANIZATIONS?

There is a divide in the poverty program community between multipurpose, often constituency-based, nongovernmental organizations such as Save the Children or Catholic Relief Services, and specialist organizations such as FINCA or TechnoServe. There are advantages and disadvantages to both approaches. Some of the benefits of multipurpose NGOs and poverty programs include:

- Their programs can have complementary effects. For example, programs to improve health can improve the effectiveness of the educational system; and better schools can lead to better health knowledge and outcomes. Indeed, when we speak of investing in a person's health, and investing in a person's education, we are after all talking about the same person. Multipurpose NGOs can bring together in-house expertise to run *programs* that have multiple purposes.

- A multipurpose NGO may be more prepared to address changing needs of the poor and poor communities, with its greater breadth of expertise, and greater incentives to be innovative. If a multipurpose NGO identifies an area where the poor now need additional assistance, it does not need to worry that it will lose funding and attention to a different organization, nor have to incur the expenses of bringing another organization up to speed regarding the community and its special characteristics.

- Further, it is costly for an NGO to get set up in a village, not only in administrative expenses for office space and transportation, but also in getting to know and gain the trust of villagers. Once these costs have been "paid," it may make sense for one NGO to work with villagers to find solutions to several of their problems. There also can be day-to-day administrative savings, on everything from transportation costs to building rentals.

- Multipurpose NGOs have the advantage of serving as a kind of "screening" service for donors, who can identify one or a few trusted NGOs to find solutions on a range of issues and then donate to those groups. Similarly such a multipurpose structure enables an NGO to benefit from its reputation for quality services in the field. Although quality in one field is no guarantee of quality in another, the NGO could bring in outside expertise when it needs it.

Specialist NGOs have much to recommend them as well. A division of labor can greatly improve efficiency. Running multipurpose organizations and poverty programs may add extra layers of bureaucracy, and so raise the costs of running an organization. No organization can have a core competence in many activities: having too many "areas of focus" may mean having no focus at all. In fact, it is not clear that the separate divisions of the multipurpose organizations even do very much communicating with each other, let alone active cooperation in the design and implementation of poverty programs. My interviews with practitioners in such organizations suggested that little communication goes on among the separate units of NGOs at the world headquarters level, although more active communication and even coordination may occur at the individual country or district levels. Despite the fact that health and education may reinforce each other, this does not mean that both health and education have to be supported by the same organization. Thus, if specialist organizations *can* effectively cooperate with each other, they have some significant advantages.

Therefore, the answer depends on circumstances. As a starting point, high-rated specialist organizations may be preferred, if they can find ways to cooperate across disciplines and across organizations when necessary, and reach donors without incurring high fundraising costs. When these conditions are not present, multipurpose NGOs may be more cost-effective.

PROTESTING THE INTERNATIONAL FINANCIAL INSTITUTIONS: DOES IT MAKE SENSE?

From Seattle in 1999 to Cancun in 2003, anti-globalization demonstrations have targeted the International Monetary Fund (IMF), the World Trade Organization (WTO), and World Bank, and have shaken up the established order.

The April 2000 World Bank-IMF demonstrations drew about 20,000 people. When demonstrators chanted "Drop the Debt" outside the IMF, the reaction from many insiders was incredulity. One well-connected international economist told me: "they're not even smoking *good* dope," as if both message and messenger—and the need for any kind of debt reduction—could be dismissed in one devastatingly witty observation. At that moment I knew the demonstrators were going to have a lasting impact, even if by their own reckoning they failed to achieve their goals.

On some issues, I disagreed with the demonstrators—some of the ways they wanted to curtail foreign investment and trade would usually hurt the poor more than help them. Restricting imports from developing countries can hurt their workers, whose alternative jobs would usually be in worse conditions; working with business to improve work conditions is more effective. Sometimes they had an exaggerated view of the World Bank's scale and influence, not realizing that the flows of capital from the private sector now dominates in areas such as financing energy investments. Further, the universal global debt forgiveness, or "Jubilee," proposal that many of them supported, if it included canceling the debt of the *middle* income countries, would leave too few resources for additional aid for new poverty programs.

But I strongly agreed with them about the need to completely cancel the debt of the *poorest* countries.

The demonstrators have had a larger positive impact than they seem to realize, or that the World Bank acknowledges. Unknown to the demonstrators outside, some of the discussions inside the World Bank in April 2000 were precisely on the question of how to reduce debt. But the demonstrations significantly speeded up this process. First, they called attention to the ethical issue of extreme poverty. The moral arguments of the demonstrations were one of the sources of the renewed public discourse about poverty. They reminded both specialists and the general public of the moral imperative of relieving extreme suffering when we have the power to do so. There are other reasons for this renewed commitment. Deepening religious sentiment in America is another source (and indeed some of the demonstrators were there out of religious conviction). But the demonstrators' stand helped change perceptions about the purpose of aid, and recharged it with an ethical dimension that had been largely missing for the previous twenty years in Washington.

Poverty is not simply an economic issue, or a matter for politicians or for health experts. Whatever one thinks of particular positions advocated, the most important part of the demonstrators' message was the moral basis on which it was formed. When that is forgotten, people lose their way. Seeing the moral fervor growing around them focuses the attention of experts at the IMF, the World Bank, and the national governments on problems of poverty.

The demonstrators, partly through their influence on public opinion, have influenced the Group of Seven industrial countries, the IMF, and the World Bank to commit more funds to debt reduction. Drop the Debt and Jubilee advocates are not satisfied with the progress on debt reduction to date but they can give themselves credit for putting the debt problems of low-income countries on the international agenda, which is beginning to be addressed with real money. It is quite clear that much less progress would have been made if protesters only treated poverty as a technical, rather than a moral, issue.

The demonstrations also re-energize the weary. Many people went into development work because of a concern with poverty. But it is difficult to maintain energy and dedication over time, particularly if the rest of the world seems indifferent, or if your bosses appear to be focused on relatively narrow, technical issues. The protests have served to re-energize weary staff at NGOs and remind them that their mission is important and valued. And, if truth be told, though World Bank staff found the demonstrators irritating (which they sometimes were), not a few of them were also energized by the attention to poverty as an issue.

The World Bank could benefit from further reforms. The big idea of the Meltzer Commission and others, of transforming the World Bank into a World Development Agency or a foundation focusing on extreme poverty, deserves much more serious attention than it has received to date. There is a role for objective policy advice, but without strings and without the appearance of hidden agendas and conflicts of interest. A more important role for the foundation would be to make grants, to serve as a clearinghouse for effective poverty strategies, and to function as a source of technical assistance on vital matters such as program evaluation. After identifying potentially effective innovative programs, the foundation could support the documentation, evaluation, and, where appropriate, the scaling up of these local programs. It could arrange and pay for program tours by key developing-country poverty workers within and outside the region, to help diffuse good ideas and inspire local adaptations. It is often inspiring to see what can come out of direct exchanges across government and NGO poverty workers in different regions of the developing world. To accomplish such objectives, further decentralization is probably called for, with many more staff based in developing countries. But while such reforms continue to be rightly debated, we should not lose sight of how much progress and improvement has been made at the World Bank since the excesses of the 1980s, and particularly since the late 1990s.

14

STEPPING UP

GETTING MORE INVOLVED:
BOARD AND WORKING GROUP MEMBERSHIP

Consider contributing your time and services, in addition to financial do
nations. The observations in this section are largely framed in terms of
board membership, but the same principles apply to many types of volunteer activities.

It is easiest to follow and work with organizations based near you, to
learn from them, and to volunteer regularly. Although many U.S.-based organizations are based in Washington and New York, others are spread
throughout the country. For example, in the United States, Heifer is based in
Arkansas, World Neighbors in Oklahoma City, CARE in Atlanta, Catholic
Relief Services in Baltimore, and World Vision headquarters in Washington
state. Many leading organizations have additional offices around the country. Places to look include Guidestar.org and Idealist.org. The best way to
step up your involvement after you get your feet wet is to just say "yes" when
asked to help. Lots of unexpectedly interesting things happen when you say
yes to a volunteer opportunity. Put your special skills to work.

Some organizations such as Amnesty International sponsor active local
chapters that meet to work on joint activities such as writing letters on behalf of a beleaguered champion of the poor. You can speak on behalf of an
organization you support to community groups, churches, schools and
clubs. Sponsoring and publicizing a program within your religious community can be beneficial for all concerned.

If your church or community organization can achieve sufficient scale,
supporting or cosponsoring a project in a particular village in a developing
country is a great way to personalize the effort, build trust, and energize the
whole campaign.

You may consider becoming a participant in a key working group, perhaps for a small NGO based in the region where you live. Do your research until you find a group that you can support for the long term. If you are very comfortable with them, make a generous donation and tell them you would like to get involved at a deeper level. You may let them know you would like to help them raise money as well as give regularly. You can help by speaking on their behalf, listening to their problems, and helping them devise creative solutions as someone with a fresh perspective. After you show that yours is a serious commitment, you may be asked to join an advisory or other group. If they do not ask, there is no rule that says you can't tell them of your interests. Obviously NGOs, especially the larger, prominent ones, like to have celebrities and well-connected business and opinion leaders on their boards, who can help leverage funds, but many board members, particularly of newer and smaller NGOs, are ordinary but dedicated volunteers. If you have "deep pockets," board membership can compliment donations as a way of "giving something back."

Veterans say that, if you do join a board of directors or advisors or a committee, be sure to attend any orientation sessions that are offered. Most sizable NGOs, even smaller nonprofits, have such formal orientations for board members. If not, see if you can get an informal orientation from a person who has been on the board for some time and who can serve as a kind of mentor. As a new board member, it can be difficult to get your bearings. Be proactive in getting your questions answered and finding ways you can become more involved. Read books about how to be a successful board member. Websites such as BoardSource.org have very valuable material. Commit yourself to never missing a meeting excepting a family or medical emergency. Try to understand the subtleties of the issues before the board or confronting the organization. Don't be afraid to make some calls to other board members or staff before the meeting to clarify issues and help you think about them in advance. Always make a generous pledge. Many boards are required to contribute and have a suggested minimum—exceed it if you possibly can.

The proper role for a board in the nonprofit world is a subject of active study and conflicting views. But it is important to keep in mind what a board of an established NGO is *not*: the day-to-day manager of the organization. Failure to resist the temptation to micromanage is the source of many unnecessary board-staff disputes. In one popular theory called policy governance, championed by John Carver and Miriam Carver, the board sets the mission and goals, or the "ends" of the organization, and sets "executive limits" on what management may *not* do to achieve these goals, but otherwise lets management determine and then implement the "means" to achieve them. Then, the top manager, and, where appropriate, perhaps a small number of other key managers, are evaluated by the board for their success in achieving these ends within the limits of acceptable actions set by the board. The board also runs periodic, in-depth reviews of the appropriateness of the various ends of the organization and of the successes and failures in achieving them. In practice, a board may reasonably want to direct executives somewhat more than merely telling them what the mission is and what they *cannot* do. Flexibility is needed to ensure that the broader mission does the governing, not specific policies. And in newer and smaller NGOs, board members may have to contribute volunteer management tasks. While no blueprint should be adopted in its entirety, and every organization is different, models such as policy governance can provide a useful starting point for NGOs seeking an effective, low-conflict approach to successful governance.

Keep in mind that neither staff nor board members suddenly become angels just because they are working to fight against poverty. In fact, some staff seem to believe that they are "entitled" to certain special privileges, such as working on the topics of greatest personal interest to them rather than of greatest importance to the organization, just because they are "sacrificing something" for the cause. This is a dangerous attitude and needs to be addressed—in yourself, your colleagues, and your staff—before it becomes a standard practice in the organization. As a board member you are in an important position of authority. Remember that you joined because you decided this was an organization you admired.

Executive managers of NGOs generally have a high level of professional expertise and years of valuable experience. Don't take what they say on simple faith, but be sure to show that you respect the expertise of the staff. Still, whatever the governance model, sometimes the board is asked to make difficult decisions about matters such as asking senior management to leave, and to deal with other painful conflicts. When these situations arise, make yourself a model of integrity and moderation. Do not be too quick to side with one faction or another.

Look for outcomes that are best for the organization and the causes for which it has been formed. If you are asked to do some tasks that you believe do not play to your strengths—or that you would really dislike doing—there is no problem saying no. In fact it is probably better for the organization if you do. If you are asked to evaluate the organization's success in achieving goals in an activity that you are less interested in and less expert in than others, explain your thinking. It is best to do so while suggesting some other task that would be of equal value to the organization but that you can do competently and enthusiastically. If there is no such task on the horizon, it may be time to move on.

One way or another, for most people there will come a time to move on and do something else. That is the time to step down or ask not to be renominated whether from a board or working group. If you can no longer dedicate yourself to helping the organization, you should let someone else take your place. The last thing you can do to help is to suggest a replacement that you know will be able to take up where you left off—not a friend you want to do a favor, but someone who can make the most positive difference. Again, these comments are just a starting point for thinking about a more active leadership role.

INVESTING WITH POVERTY AND SUSTAINABLE DEVELOPMENT IN MIND

Investing is another sphere where you can make a difference in poverty alleviation. There are legitimate differences of opinion about what investments are "socially responsible." But certainly boycotting companies because their working conditions in developing countries are not up to developed country standards is counter-productive: you want companies to be better than average in the countries that they operate in and not to expose workers to excessive risks. But to punish firms for investing in Africa, for example, is not an outcome that helps end global poverty. In fact, identifying sound and responsible investments in Sub-Saharan Africa and taking some calculated risks to pursue them, whether this is popular with "the herd" or not, is one of the most constructive things that investors can do.

Yet there are some company activities that are so negative to prospects for sustainable development that it is important to refuse to invest in them. Environmental destruction of the poorest countries is looming as probably the single greatest threat to ending global poverty. As a result, companies that unreasonably add to this destruction are hurting more than helping the poor.

An increasing number of companies are adopting codes of corporate responsibility, described below. To some extent, company embracement of these codes reflects the fact that they have been under scrutiny and attack by watchdog groups. But a public commitment to adhere to such codes is a useful signal, particularly if they become part of independent associations monitoring these agreements. Some investment funds only invest in companies that pass minimum standards in these dimensions.

Companies set themselves up for public relations disaster if they embrace a code and then flaunt it. So, other things equal, I would make membership in an externally monitored code of conduct a positive factor in socially responsible investment decisions. Such firms are less likely to be standing in the way of the struggle to end global poverty. They might also prove to be better investments. By joining, a company signals that it is doing well enough to afford decent standards of behavior in poor countries and to support code associations. Scrutiny and expectations will be higher, and the company will have to pay close attention to its environmental and social impact. But at the same time, the company also signals that it is less likely to be sued for environmental or safety performance or receive unfavorable publicity for actions in the developing world. Such firms might actually give a better long-run return, with better public relations, new avenues for branding strategy, less advertising needed to repair a bad image, and fewer costly lawsuits. Useful information on these topics can be found at harrisinteractive.com.

Programs such as Pax World Service (http://www.paxworld.org), an affiliate of Mercy Corps, can help you get started. Other targeted funds such as Calvert attempt to invest responsibly, with a fairly transparent selection process. The Social Investment Forum, a nonprofit organization (http://www.socialinvest.org), provides additional useful information. The faith-based Socially Responsible Investment Coalition provides other resources. Socialfunds.com provides additional information for individual social investing. Analogous programs are available in other countries. In particular, the U.K Social Investment Forum sponsors Just Pensions (http://www.uksif.org/J/Z/Z/jp/home/main/index.shtml), and in Canada, the Social Investment Organization sponsors a useful website, http://www.socialinvestment.ca/. As with all investments, get independent advice, complement it with your own research, and read all prospectuses and other explanatory materials carefully.

PARTNER PARISHES AND FAITH-BASED INITIATIVES

Many faiths offer assistance programs, in which congregations in America or other wealthy countries are matched with counterparts in the developing world. These programs are sometimes called partner parishes; in Catholic communities they are usually called sister parishes, or "twinning." But other faith communities not organized on a parish basis sponsor similar programs. These partnerships engage many people who otherwise would not have participated in poverty assistance. The programs can wonderfully connect people on a personal level. Many programs offer congregation-to-congregation assistance, as needed, with matters such as church repair or divinity school scholarships. But some sponsored programs also work to reduce poverty by creating something of value for the whole village or region. Some projects organized through churches, or developed on the basis of a connection to a church, are offered for whole communities without any strings or expectations. There are thousands of these partner parishes in the United States alone. I have not systematically evaluated the actual impact or cost-effectiveness of church programs, but I will mention two in passing that I happen to be familiar with, to give a range of possibilities.

My brother, Reverend Dr. Christopher Smith, now a pastor in East Lansing, Michigan, was for almost ten years pastor of an American Baptist church in Williamstown, Massachusetts, which along with several other American Baptist congregations around the country partnered with a church in the Dominican Republic. The church was made up of hundreds of Haitian expatriates who were working in the sugarcane fields. Chris told me that they "built first a sanctuary and a parsonage, and then a medical clinic. Each year we sent down a team of volunteers—anywhere from a couple to a handful—to join with others from the other churches on work teams. We also sent money for construction, medicine (that was hand-carried through customs), and clothing. The people who came back from the work tours talked about their exuberance and strong sense of community." He said it was a great exchange—"we just gave money and time, but we got back love."

My own church, the Unitarian Universalist Congregation of Fairfax, has partnered since 1992 with a Unitarian church in Szentgerice, Romania, in the rural Hungarian-speaking region of Transylvania, one of about 170 such partnerships between North American UU congregations and Unitarian congregations in Transylvania. The church has joined with another village church with a Dutch partner to help build a health clinic as well as provided medicines, school supplies, and a school bus for the benefit of the community.

The potential for assistance across faith communities is large. Evangelical churches are providing support for church members in Africa and other developing regions through activities sponsored by World Relief (WR), such as microcredit programs. Catholic Relief Services (CRS) sponsors a Global Solidarity Partnership program in which a growing number of dioceses participate. Both CRS and WR are based in Baltimore.

The number of mosques in the United States, Canada, and the UK is growing steadily. Zakat, or almsgiving, is a Pillar of Islam. There is great potential for alms to be used for poverty programs that go beyond charity and relief and foster development that benefits the poor in Muslim countries such as Bangladesh and Mali. There are probably already partner Mosque programs that I do not know about. There may also be partner temple programs among Buddhist and Hindu religious communities.

Despite the fact that there are probably tens of thousands of faith-based assistance programs originating in North America and Europe, there has been no systematic, comparative evaluation of their poverty benefits, or their sustainability. This is an important part of the future research agenda. Nevertheless, such partnerships represent a forum that can be a source of unexpected opportunities for transmitting keys to capability, from ideas for income generation, to growth of individual self-esteem and community self-confidence to face up to oppressive circumstances.

The Catholic Church has played a role in taking action and advocating on ending poverty. You can find the statement of the U.S. Conference of Catholic Bishops, "A Place at the Table: A Catholic Recommitment to Overcome Poverty and to Respect the Dignity of All God's Children," and other resources for education and action at http://www.usccb.org/sdwp/placeatthetable/index.htm.

Bread for the World is one of the largest and most respected Christian public policy advocacy groups working in the field of poverty alleviation, relief, and development; some 2,500 churches participate. They sponsor a very informative website at http://www.bread.org/. BFW describes itself as a Christian citizen's movement, and is organized both by congregation and by congressional district. BFW members write, call, and visit members of Congress, the president, and other government officials about legistlation that addresses hunger and generate media attention on hunger issues. Its president, David Beckmann, is an ordained Lutheran minister who previously worked for 15 years as a staff member of the World Bank—a parson at the Bank, he called himself—and was assigned there to work as a liaison with NGOs. Other resources for congregations are found at the Jubilee Congregations site, http://www.jubileeusa.org/jubilee.cgi?path=/jubilee_congregations.

One of the fastest growing resource and advocacy groups is the Micah Network, an international organization bringing together more than 200 evangelical Christian relief, development, and justice agencies with many church memberships. You can find them at http://www.micahnetwork.org/home.

Many Muslims are also inspired by their religious faith to become involved in careers and volunteer work to alleviate poverty. Ismail Serageldin, an Egyptian working at the World Bank for many years, including as first head of the environmental sustainability division, wrote that his Muslim faith was the source of his inspiration to work for global stewardship (in his essay in *Friday Morning Reflections at the World Bank*, "The Justly Balanced Society, One Muslim's View.") Serageldin extensively quotes the Koran on humanity's role as "vice-regent on earth." And he notes that in the Hadith the Prophet says, "If one of you sees something that is wrong, then let him set it right; first with his hand; and if he cannot then with his tongue, and if he cannot then with his heart, and that is the weakest of all possible forms of faith." He reads this as a call for action to end poverty.

In Egypt, I was struck by the respect that Christians and Muslims working to end poverty held for each other. For example, Muslims often told me that they were impressed with the work of CEOSS, the Coptic Evangelical Organization for Social Services. Surely, the struggle to end extreme poverty is a cause that can unite all religious and ethical peoples.

PARTNER CLINICS AND HOSPITALS

The sign at the district hospital compound in West Africa said it all. In large letters was the word "mortuary"; below it in smaller letters was "maternity," and below that "pediatrics." The sign served as an unintended commentary on the underfunding of public health, with high maternal mortality along with high death rates among children under five in the poorest countries.

If you work in a hospital or clinic, you can form a partnership with a counterpart in a low-income country, such as in Africa. Already, thousands of doctors, nurses, and other medical personnel have volunteered their vacation time to help the global poor. This idea received wide publicity when Dr. Carter, a character on the U.S. television program "ER," went for a short vacation tour of duty in the Congo and ended up staying for an extended period. This type of work is not as exotic as it sounds. Nor is this usually nearly as dangerous an activity as Dr. Carter found it to be! In most cases there is minimal risk to participants.

This type of valuable pro bono work can be taken to a higher level through formal, ongoing partnerships between hospitals, clinics, and other practices in developed countries and a clinic in one of the poor countries.

Choose your partner carefully. Remember that it is the rural areas where the poorest of the poor are almost always to be found. This poses logistical issues for medical work. Be prepared to bring the equipment you will need.

If you have been going abroad to help with pro bono medical treatments, consider extending your efforts to a formal, ongoing partnership. This can bring more regular and predictable care to those who need it most, while creating a structure that makes it easier for others to participate.

You can also work with NGOs. Project Hope, for example, involves many volunteers and has an active alumni group. Doctors without Borders deservedly won the Nobel Peace Prize for its work in developing, post-conflict regions. The Red Cross/Red Crescent works with poor and vulnerable people.

Public health NGOs and health professionals have already contributed greatly to improving health in developing countries. One of the most encouraging successes in the struggle against global poverty has been the tremendous benefits to the children of the poor from immunization and targeted vitamin supplements. These have made possible a better present and a brighter future. Martha, a Ugandan Save the Children public health nurse, whom I met in the rural community in which she works, told me proudly of the progress she has seen in reducing child mortality, even among semi-nomadic peoples, now that immunization and Vitamin A boosters have reached the remote district in which she works.

While much remains to be done, great progress has already been made in reaching the poor through increasingly effective health interventions.

PARTNER CLUBS

Many clubs have international affiliates, including in Africa and other poor countries. There are many opportunities to establish partner activities with affiliates in developing countries. Your national organization can help.

Some clubs have organization-wide initiatives to help end poverty. Probably the best-known and most successful effort is that of Rotary International's polio eradication campaign. The campaign is proof, if any were needed, that citizen organizations can make all the difference in the struggle to end global poverty.

In 1988, the World Health Organization (WHO) launched its drive to completely eradicate polio. Since then, there has been a 99 percent reduction in the number of polio cases worldwide, and the current goal is complete eradication by 2005. Rotary deserves a substantial share of the credit for its initiative and active and generous work in getting this drive underway, and then for continuing to work along with partner agencies, including the United Nations Children's Fund (UNICEF), the United States Centers for Disease Control and Prevention, and governments around the world, as well as the WHO. Rotary actually began working toward polio eradication in 1979 and launched its "PolioPlus" program in 1985. Their efforts and special research funding catalyzed the international community into action, raising unprecedented sums for the task, and committing key international agencies to the goal. Rotary International assists local Rotary clubs to find out how they can participate actively in the program. You can read about Rotary's efforts for polio eradication at http://www.rotary.org/foundation/polioplus/, and in the Rotary magazine.

Unfortunately, there are a number of other diseases still plaguing the developing world. There are good opportunities to build on the foundation established by the Rotary Club.

ENVIRONMENTAL PARTNERSHIPS: PARTNERING NGOS

Most states and many communities have local chapters of environmental groups, and some of these have active programs with developing regions. An example is the Sierra Club's "Beyond the Borders" program. These efforts enable people to focus on their special concerns, such as in protection of Africa's wildlife, while enabling the impoverished peoples who live alongside these natural riches, so they may benefit from these resources while protecting them for the future. You can get involved by partnering with an environmentally oriented NGO in Africa and other developing areas where people's struggle to escape poverty traps are threatened by environmental catastrophe. The national offices of your club can provide you with ideas on how to get started.

The Climate Action Network is a global association of some 340 NGOs working to promote government and individual action to limit climate change and its impact. It has member organizations both in developed and developing countries. Climate changes and rising sea levels are special threats to the poor. Problems such as global warming have global causes and consequences, and this calls for action that joins citizens in both developed and developing countries. You can read about it at http://www.climatenetwork.org.

Dr. Richard Rice of Conservation International proposes simply paying residents to take care of the land over which they have de facto or de jure control. Dr. Rice told me that the timber rights are very inexpensive to obtain in relation to the colossal world environmental damage that results from deforestation. So rich countries can buy the timber rights, and pay local people to guard and enforce the integrity of the forest. This is an important supplemental strategy because alternative agricultural uses, like ecotourism, are inherently limited in their possible scope. Dick Rice's proposal is not welfare, but genuine employment, generating income in return for a valuable service for which the world receives a clear benefit. Conservation International is beginning to work along these lines, but public support is needed to make this a reality on a larger scale. This is the type of innovative solution that will be needed to address the full scope of the pressing problems of rainforest degradation.

SISTER CITIES

Many towns and cities have "sister cities" around the world. Most of these partners are in developed countries such as France or Italy. However, there is no reason not to set up a sister city in a developing country. In fact, you might be surprised to learn that your own community may already have a sister city relationship. UN-Habitat in Nairobi, Kenya, has a program to make this easier for cities around the world, working with Sister Cities International and other organizations.

Sister Cities International (http://www.sister-cities.org), a U.S. nonprofit organization established in 1967, helps American towns or cities form lasting and rewarding partnerships. Currently, dozens of cities in Africa, Asia, and Latin America are seeking sister cities. They come in all sizes—some have fewer than 5,000 inhabitants, but many have over one million. From Amlame to Zabzugu—chances are you can find a sister city that matches the profile for the activities you have in mind. You can find them on the "cities seeking cities" list at http://www.sister-cities.org/icrc/cityseek/list.

Sister Cities International offers some assistance with translation. However, one good criterion for choosing a city is to establish a link to a place that speaks a language spoken by some people in your community. You might be surprised, for example, to discover the range of African languages that are spoken in your area by immigrants and political refugees. It is worth exploring these options fully before you decide where to partner. You can make these contacts at the same time that you build support for the effort in your community. It is important to involve from the very beginning not just your own group but others such as churches, hospitals, schools, local government, and civic organizations. The staff of Sister Cities International will help you through the process. Sister Cities has an Annual Awards Program that serves as a repository of creative strategies and best practices. This is helpful to look at when developing a sister city relationship or enhancing an existing partnership.

In 2003 alone, sister city assistance projects involved water treatment, business development and cooperation, flood relief, medical aid, agricultural exchanges, building a children's library, and targeted donations according to local needs.

Sometimes special grants are available to help you establish your sister city program with a developing country; again Sister Cities International can help, and they have links to some of the current grant opportunities on their website.

INFORMAL DONOR CLUBS

Just as many individuals form investment clubs, donor clubs or "circles" can play a useful role. A group can divide up the work of researching NGOs, pooling donations for a bigger impact. With a pooled donation of sufficient size many possibilities emerge, such as sponsoring a special project, arranging to visit the project you donate to, communicating directly with the beneficiaries, and even encouraging an NGO to work in a new region. You can choose a strategy for improving the health of the poor where your combined impact will be very clear. For example, your group can sponsor needed vaccines, or affordable medicine.

NATIONAL AND MULTILATERAL POLICY: MAKING YOUR VOICE HEARD IN THE CORRIDORS OF POWER

Ending poverty is not inevitable—it depends in part on government policies and financial support for development efforts. We know there is strong public support for a much greater effort to end global poverty. But the link from public opinion to public action is by no means automatic. Most extreme poverty exists outside of the rich countries, so it is largely invisible to their citizens. Yes, there is hunger in America, but there is a safety net, however minimal, and a network of well-funded charities. Almost all extremely poor people are in developing countries, and have no voice in the countries that supply the aid. But there is much we can do to influence policy in America and the other rich countries.

InterAction, an umbrella group for U.S. private voluntary organizations working on poverty reduction and development, is active in lobbying. Their membership lists are a great place to start to identify groups you might work with on policy, whether health-focused or environment-focused, whether religious-based or secular. Or you can take a stand and work for change through your civic or religious organization. To whatever degree you want to be involved, there is a channel waiting for you.

RESULTS is an international, grassroots advocacy organization working for greater support by government for effective poverty programs. Individuals can become actively involved; see www.results.org. Another important effort across organizations to work toward a greater U.S. commitment to fighting poverty, hunger, and disease in developing countries is the ONE Campaign, found at www.onecampaign.org.

LEARN ABOUT EXISTING AID POLICIES AND THEIR LIMITATIONS

First of all, it is important to learn something about what is, or is not, being done in development policy. Because you will soon be asked the question—and it is intended to be a showstopper—don't we already give enough "foreign aid"? The answer to that question is a resounding "no."

Official U.S. efforts at poverty reduction are grossly underfunded. The United States and other rich countries committed at the Monterrey aid summit to move seriously toward contributing 0.7 percent of their national incomes to development assistance. This represents just 1/143 of national income. But even this international target level would be almost six times more aid than the United States provides today, even with the recent increase. In 2002, U.S. foreign assistance totaled less than $10 billion, about one-tenth of 1 percent of Gross National Income. Only about $3.66 per American went to the least developed countries, where about 675 million people lived in 2002. And much of what is spent never goes to developing countries, let alone near the people living in extreme poverty. Much "aid" is really thinly disguised subsidies for U.S. companies—corporate welfare rather than welfare or workfare for the poor. U.S. aid amounted to approximately $1.54 per person living in the least developed countries. If we include the people in all low-income countries, total U.S. aid comes to about $1.06 per person.

At the 2002 Monterrey aid summit the Bush administration agreed to raise aid by 50 percent over five years. This is a good start and is certainly better than the Clinton administration ever proposed. But with projected growth in gross national income, this will still round off to a tenth of 1 percent. Incredibly, in 2004 Congress was dragging its feet even on this level of increase. President Bush has also agreed to increase funding for HIV/AIDS, but it is still too little, and less effective than it could be because, rather than combining with the Global AIDS fund, the United States is apparently going it alone. The stated goal of the Bush administration to make aid more effective in poverty reduction is also admirable, but according to analysis of the Center for Global Development, the approach of the new U.S. Millennium Challenge Account does not seem to be adequate to this task.

ACTIVELY SUPPORT INTERNATIONAL POVERTY REDUCTION GOALS

Citizens in the United States and other wealthy countries can help by encouraging their governments to actively support the Millennium Development Goals (or MDGs). In September 2000, the 189 member countries of the United Nations adopted the eight MDGs, committing themselves to making substantial progress toward the eradication of poverty and achieving other human development goals by the year 2015. The MDGs acknowledge the multidimensional nature of poverty: an end to poverty requires more than just increasing incomes of the poor. The eight goals are: eradicate extreme poverty and hunger; achieve universal primary education; promote gender equality and empower women; reduce child mortality; improve maternal health; combat HIV/AIDS, malaria and other diseases; ensure environmental sustainability; and develop a global partnership for development. The "targets" for the poverty goal are more modest—to get halfway by 2015 according to two measures: Reduce by half the proportion of people living on less than a dollar a day, and reduce by half the proportion of people who suffer from hunger (in comparison to 1990 levels). "Halving poverty" has come to serve as a touchstone for the MDGs as a whole. Given that as many as half of the poorest are locked in poverty traps, the first targets are in a sense more modest than "halfway." Ending poverty among those who are "sometimes poor"—not caught in poverty traps but vulnerable—will be easier than among those who are chronically caught in poverty traps. But on current trends, we may not even achieve this target—ending poverty among half of the poor—on schedule. According to the

UNDP, in the 1990s, income poverty increased in 37 countries, while hunger increased in 21 countries. Sub-Saharan Africa is not only off-track, but income poverty is actually *increasing* in this, the poorest region in the world. And while South Asia is on track to halve income poverty, on current trends hunger would not be halved in that part of the world until the twenty-*second* century. As we have seen, improvements in health, education, and environment are critical components of the struggle to end global poverty.

To a degree the immediate MDG targets and their timetables are arbitrary. It is not as if all hope for ending poverty will be lost if some of them are not achieved on time. The MDGs should not be the only filter through which to view progress against poverty. But rather than being thought of as ambitious, these targets were selected in part because they seemed to correspond to the experience with the rate of poverty reduction over the last few decades. And the countries and institutions that signed on to the goals made a public commitment to achieve them. Although we are falling behind, these goals are still achievable with adequate backing from the wealthy countries, according to project calculations by the UN Millennium Project.

BECOME AN EFFECTIVE ADVOCATE
FOR ASSISTANCE IN POVERTY REDUCTION

There are many pretexts for not increasing aid, but there are answers to all the criticisms you will hear. To politicians who say voters don't understand or care, they can invest just a little more political capital in explaining why greater aid for the poorest is important for peace, security, and basic humanitarian obligations, and how much we can accomplish with modest expenditures. If certain governments are too corrupt, we can channel more aid through the many effective international and domestic nongovernmental organizations working in even the poorest countries. If a country has needs but can't seem to make good use of aid, then perhaps we need to fund and facilitate the needed organizational capacity, training, and infrastructure.

The inevitable question: "However big or small our aid has been, isn't that money wasted, and hasn't it been proven that foreign aid doesn't work?" The answer is, again, "no"—though there are some nuances.

Another pretext is that there is little evidence that official aid has spurred income growth. Poverty is much more than lack of money; it is inability to achieve and maintain a satisfactory quality of life that people "have reason to value," as Sen put it. This includes education, health, and empowerment. Even in countries where incomes per capita have stagnated, literacy rates, child survival, and the incidence of democratic freedoms— such as the rights of the poor to form organizations and speak out for their own betterment—have greatly increased. These improvements are due in no small measure to various forms of aid, including international support for the best local NGOs. Thus in evaluating aid impact, we should not just look at growth, but also at key social indicators that tell us whether growth is sustainable, and whether solid growth may be expected in the future.

Moreover, foreign aid has rarely been primarily about poverty reduction. Most foreign aid is actually spent on U.S. companies and consultants, along with U.S. government officials. When aid is to be used for needed imports of goods and services, the aid is often "tied," requiring the recipient to buy the product from whatever country is donating the aid, regardless of cost. Much goes to middle-income countries. And much has gone to serve a geopolitical agenda, such as supporting allies in the Cold War and the Middle East conflicts. It is not surprising that aid in this context may not be effective at helping the poor.

But even if official aid is not increased nearly as much as it should be, there is still much that can be done to use official aid more effectively and to engage civil society. Aid can be redirected to countries with the greatest poverty needs. And good programs can be better identified and aid channeled to where its impact is greatest.

I believe that official and NGO aid are complements, not substitutes, and that the best way to ensure more, and better-targeted, official aid is to have a citizenry that is not only well-informed but also personally engaged in complementary, voluntary-sector activities. Only then can a "constituency" for adequately funded and rigorously evaluated foreign aid be assured.

WORK FOR AGRICULTURAL POLICIES THAT DON'T HARM THE POOR

Joining the fight to end wasteful agricultural subsidies is also an important contribution to the fight against poverty. The average cow in Europe receives $2 per day in subsidies. This sum is greater than what nearly half the world's population has to live on. European subsidies for fishing are hurting the poor and damaging the environment. As the *Economist* magazine reported in 2003, in Japan tariffs on rice are as high as 1,000 percent. Sugar subsidies in the United States lead to depressed prices in producing countries. They also cause environmental damage in fragile areas, particularly Florida. The resulting artificially low price of sugar probably helps fuel the obesity epidemic in the United States, which adds to health bills. The *Financial Times* reports that "Since 1990 the [sugar] industry has given more than $20 million to federal politicians," and documents the enormous impact of lobbying on inefficient and costly subsidies for "sweet deals" for "Big Sugar." Subsidies for cotton, tobacco, sugar, and other crops impose significant costs to the U.S. economy. The impact on American consumers aside, such subsidies harm producers in the developing world. Oxfam International has prepared some of the best critiques of the impact of these subsidies and other developed country trade policies on poverty and development, including their reports, *Rigged Rules and Double Standards* and *Cultivating Poverty.*

Currently, all donors contribute a total of about $50 billion on aid globally, but seven times as much—a total of about $350 billion—is wasted on agricultural subsidies. Subsidies are not only far higher than aid but they are growing faster than aid. This helps a small number of people in the rich countries but hurts a very large number in the poorest countries (not to mention hurting most people in the richest countries somewhat).

OECD subsidies to agriculture are approximately equal to the value of Africa's entire output of goods and services. The claim that agricultural subsidies literally kill people in the developing countries gets widely repeated for dramatic emphasis but it is no exaggeration. The problems were greatly amplified by the huge $190 billion agriculture bill that President Bush signed into law in Spring 2002. It is estimated that some $57 billion of this total will be paid directly to farmers. This is supposed to make up for low commodity prices, but previous subsidies are part of the reason for these low prices. Particularly large subsidies will go to crops that are also produced in Africa such as wheat, corn, sorghum, rice, and cotton, thus harming African producers.

The U.S. government spent some $3.9 billion in subsidies to cotton farmers during fiscal year 2001–02; these subsidies largely went to the richest cotton farmers. This was nearly half of the whole U.S. budget for foreign aid in that year.

As the *Economist* magazine reported, "The world's biggest exporter of cotton is America, even though its production costs are far higher than those of African producers such as Mali or Burkina Faso. America's 25,000 cotton farmers receive $4 billion of government subsidies in return for producing $3 billion-worth of cotton. These subsidies push down the world market price, hurting, among others, 11m cotton producers in West Africa."

The *New York Times* examined cotton subsidies and their impact on the poor in Africa. They pointed out that "Americans would be horrified to learn that all the good accomplished by dedicated [Peace Corps] volunteers and millions of dollars in aid is overwhelmed by the havoc wreaked by Washington's bloated cotton subsidies. By cutting generous checks to 25,000 American cotton farmers whose average net worth is nearly $1 million, Washington underwrites massive overproduction. This results in depressed global prices and a harvest of poverty for Burkina Faso's two million cotton farmers. . . . More than half of all cotton grown in this country is now exported, only because taxpayers subsidize its sale at below production costs."

Burkina Faso's President, Blaise Compaore, stated to the *Times* that "America wants us to comprehend the evil posed by violent anti-Western terrorism, and we do. But we want you to equally concern yourself with the terror posed here by hunger and poverty, a form of terrorism your subsidies are aiding and abetting. If we cannot sell our cotton we will die."

From their reporting on the devastating impact of these subsidies in Africa, the *Times* concluded, "It's hard for most Americans, who don't think about farm subsidies at all, to take this problem seriously. It's also hard for farm states, which think of federal aid simply as a way to help hard-working local farmers, to appreciate how intensely, and bitterly, the Africans feel. But most of the developing world believes in the superpower's omniscience. No one in Burkina Faso imagines the impact on their cotton growers was anything but deliberate."

U.S. cotton subsidies are also killing people in countries such as Benin and Mali. Removing cotton and other subsidies immediately would benefit the poor, and help improve America's relationship with the world. These expenditures can be converted to aid for health, education, and environmental protection in Africa, where the subsidies have done so much harm. These kinds of changes will happen only if citizens get involved and demand them.

WORK TOWARD SENSIBLE ENVIRONMENTAL POLICIES THAT HELP THE POOR

Developing countries have the biggest stake in protecting their own environment, but in many cases they don't know how, and they lack the funds. We can help them do this. It will help to make their growth more sustainable. If the improved environment has a positive effect on our own well-being, such as through preserving rainforests or reducing greenhouse gas emissions, then we should be willing to pay something for this out of our own self-interest. The Scandinavian countries recognize this when they help to pay for pollution control in Poland and the Baltic countries. But perhaps the biggest contribution that we in the rich countries could make is to take actions to reduce global warming, which, as we have seen earlier in the book, threatens to negate much of the progress made in the poorer, tropical countries. Because of the scale of global warming, action by national governments and through international treaties are essential to adequately address the problem. Citizens can help to fight poverty by demanding that their government take stronger action on global warming. Politicians must be held accountable. If the government does not like particulars of the Kyoto global warming treaty, then we must insist that alternative actions— not more delaying tactics—be identified that would have the same impact and on the same timetable.

SUPPORT TRADE THAT HELPS THE POOR
WHILE WORKING TO CURTAIL ABUSES

Generally, greater trade in the form of exports from developing countries can be very beneficial to the poor who live in those countries; trade is the single most important reason for the dramatic decreases in poverty in China. It is not the rule but rather the exception when trade hurts the poor. But the poor *can* sometimes be made worse off by trade, if they end up unwillingly or unwittingly in conditions tantamount to slavery. Opportunities for trade can increase the rewards to criminal gangs or criminal governments from trafficking in the poor. The rich may coerce the poor to work for less money or under worse conditions than they would voluntarily agree to, or deliberately alter the alternatives available to the poor to artificially create an apparent "willingness" to work. This may describe the miserable conditions of captive laborers in Burma, for example, or the loss by indigenous peoples of their traditional rights to use commonly held lands, trends that can be given impetus by new opportunities for trade in commodities. The poor are sometimes made worse off when the rich and powerful steal the natural resources that were historically controlled by poor communities, and forcing them—figuratively and sometimes literally—to find new work at whatever wages are available. Noted authors Robin Broad and John Cavanagh document deteriorating conditions of the poor in fishing villages in the Philippines, and connect the worsening poverty of villagers to the commercialization of natural resources on which their way of life depended. Governments may grant foreign companies forestry and mining rights without regard to the people who depend on these lands for their livelihoods and way of life. In sum, greater opportunities for trade can increase the incentives of the rich and powerful to steal from the poor in one way or another, and we must fight against these terrible injustices even as we support more access for low-income countries to developed country markets. Poverty programs that work to empower poor people and their communities and help them to assert their human and legal rights are one of the best responses to these evils. At the same time, we must also make sure that protectionism doesn't masquerade as concern for the poor.

LARGER VOLUNTEERING
COMMITMENTS AND CAREER AVENUES

Most of the groups discussed in this book, and many other worthy organizations besides, have challenging and rewarding opportunities to learn and serve while volunteering. Many have formal internship programs. Although you must pay travel costs and tuition or fees, a growing number of organizations facilitate overseas volunteer activities, such as teaching in local schools for a couple of months. Fees for some programs, such as Global Volunteer Network, are relatively low, but will generally provide you with fewer support services than higher-priced programs. Investigate programs thoroughly before signing up. Idealist.org is a good place to start.

Involvement in internships and volunteer work can be a step to longer-term involvement in development and poverty alleviation.

The Peace Corps

They call it the toughest job you'll ever love. That is not just a Madison Avenue slogan—ask any Peace Corps veteran. Peace Corps volunteers live in a house much like those of the villagers they work with and interact with the poor on their own terms. Each new cohort of volunteers experiences closeness to the lives of the poor, keeping the program vital. There is a camaraderie, or international poverty alleviation fraternity, among former volunteers. The Peace Corps is not only for recent graduates; people of all ages including couples, mid-career professionals, and retired people participate. The Peace Corps has an extensive website, http://www.peacecorps.gov. It includes resources for returning Peace Corps volunteers to take the next stage in their careers. The website also offers information about graduate school programs in the field. Alongside the Peace Corps there are other programs for people with special skills such as retired executive programs. Finally there are also similar programs in other countries such as Voluntary Service Overseas in the United Kingdom and Canada, and the Japanese Overseas Cooperation Volunteers.

A Word for Students on Degree Programs

There are three main types of academic tracks for people who want to make a career focus on development: a degree in development studies or a related interdisciplinary program; a professional degree such as law, medicine, or an MBA; or a degree in an academic discipline such as economics, sociology, or epidemiology. Whichever route you choose, be sure you have some technical skills.

Degrees in development studies, which are offered at a growing number of universities both at the BA and MA levels, will let you spend the most time on the subject matter of development problems and programs. These programs can be quite valuable. But beware of programs, and tracks of study within programs, that do not stress technical skills—for the most part, those skills are what will get you entry-level positions. If you choose such a program, be sure to talk to academic advisors and professors—several, never only one, to make sure you are getting marketable skills.

An effective combination is to take courses as an undergraduate that thoroughly familiarize you with developing countries and that analyze the many issues they confront. Then, specialize at the graduate level in a professional school or a technical discipline. But the most important discipline for international development is still economics. Development has become more multidisciplinary, but the most direct way to begin a career in development and poverty alleviation is to study economics. The major development agencies are still primarily hiring economists with Ph.D.s for their fast-track positions. They also hire financial professionals, MBAs, lawyers, public health experts, and sociologists, among others.

Economics is a highly technical discipline, and by no means for everyone. If you do not like math, you are unlikely to enjoy economics. Education specialists, health professionals, lawyers, business scholars, public policy analysts, anthropologists, sociologists, and geographers, among many others, all play significant roles.

Your program choice should reflect your interests and your career goals. As you think about the keys to capability for the poor, consider where you see yourself wanting to make a difference, consistent with your natural skills. If you know you want to work for the legal rights of the poor, a law degree will serve you well. If you like the idea of helping to develop businesses among the poor, an MBA may be the right choice. If you want to specialize in health, an MD or a public health specialty may be best for you.

Some disciplines have organizations that help aspiring professionals to realize their goals of working in poverty alleviation and related activities. Beyond Grey Pinstripes, (http://www.beyondgreypinstripes.org) is an organization dedicated to preparing MBAs for social and environmental stewardship. The schools "on the cutting edge of incorporating environmental and social impact management" featured by the organization are George Washington, Michigan, North Carolina (Kenan-Flagler), Stanford, Yale, and York (Schulich).

Most major NGOs have a spot on their webpage listing job openings. Read them, and if you find that one suits you, consider applying. At the very least, you will probably learn a lot in the process. At the most, you may transform your life.

Talk to people who work for NGOs. For many applied fields networking is the best strategy for developing a career.

While in school, and once you finish, don't lose touch with your mission. Join or form networks and stay involved. For example, Net Impact, originally organized as Students for Responsible Business in 1993, is "a network of business leaders committed to using the power of business to positively impact social and environmental concerns throughout the world." Net Impact, http://www.net-impact.org/, has developed into a network of nearly 10,000 executives and other professionals. It has more than 90 graduate student chapters based in many U.S. business schools, as well as active professional chapters.

SOCIAL ENTREPRENEURSHIP

Another model whose potential has only begun to be tapped is to directly focus entrepreneurial talents on social goals. Greater recognition of the profession of social entrepreneur would help direct more entrepreneurial talents to solving social problems. Professor Muhammad Yunus, founder of the Grameen Bank, has asked: "Why has our business world failed to offer opportunities to people who want to invest for the benefit of the people? So far they have not done so because neither the opportunity nor the supportive framework exists. We must change this situation."

Ashoka is one of the pioneers of the social entrepreneurship movement, and is highly rated as a charity, receiving the full four stars from Charity Navigator. Ashoka has been working for two decades to create a vision.

Founder and CEO Bill Drayton described to me his vision of Ashoka and social entrepreneurship this way:

> At a first level, we want to help the best social entrepreneurs get started— help them to start ideas and institutions, but also over their whole life cycle. This is a key difference with venture capital, in that there is no exit point. At the second level, we help the field of social entrepreneurship to work together, so that it is more than the sum of the parts. The "Mosaics" approach in Ashoka is a good example. At a third level [we help] take the ideas out and market them externally. [For example,] we work with groups of fellows in Brazil and India, with a strategy to expand learning, engaging youth programs and schools, and building a certain mass of thought leaders in professional organizations, plus press, and the scholarly community, so we can tip the whole system in regionally leading countries. If we can do this in seven to eight countries we can flip the whole system, when you add in spreading at the global level.

This is an exciting and contagious vision. It means there is even more hope for the future than we would otherwise see in the trends. It means that "best practices" are always getting better and adapting to changing circumstances.

Drayton sees four stages in the career of a social entrepreneur. The first is apprenticeship, followed by launch, takeoff, and maturity. Although there are few degree programs in social entrepreneurship, according to David Bornstein, universities are increasingly adding courses on social entrepreneurship to their curriculum. But many students, including many from developing countries who take a course of study in international development, really want to be social entrepreneurs. Similarly, many such students in business schools seem to have similar preferences. Professional education is likely to be important in mastering a field, gaining credibility, and opening doors. Some choices for potential social entrepreneurs will be obvious: law for those wishing to focus on human and legal rights, medicine and public health for those interested in health and development, and so on. But as one consideration, check whether the universities you apply to have courses in social entrepreneurship, or general courses in entrepreneurship that are highly versatile in their subject matter and assignments, and see if you can work these into your course of study.

Bill Drayton and many social entrepreneurs also emphasize the importance of mentoring and apprenticeship in the formation of a social entrepreneur.

If you are a student and would like to be a social entrepreneur but are not sure what field of work is best for you, I think it makes sense to take some time between college and graduate school to work in a variety of jobs and internships that you think might be closest to your interests. When you think you know where your talents and passion converges, you have probably found the area in which you could contribute. If you have already completed your education, identify the innovators in the field whom you think have made the biggest difference and arrange to work alongside them in an "apprenticeship" role for a couple of years. If you develop and hone your own approaches, you can then proceed to create something new.

CLOSER TO HOME:
POVERTY IN AMERICA ON RESERVATIONS,
IN POOR RURAL AREAS, INNER CITIES—
AND, INCREASINGLY, OUT IN THE SUBURBS—
A BRIEF NOTE

In my talks with Americans about ending global poverty, I have been asked a very difficult question. In one form or another the challenge is: "Why are you so focused on poverty thousands of miles away from home, when people are suffering in America, on reservations and rural areas, downtown in the inner city, and even in the suburbs?"

I focus on the poor in developing countries because they are usually much poorer than even the poorest people in America. But I know there are exceptions: the mentally ill homeless person suffering in the dead of winter, children who fall through the cracks in the welfare system, and many more. Rural poverty can be severe in the "black belt," a long crescent of majority-black and sometimes majority-poor counties stretching from Virginia to

Texas, but many Americans do not even know about the plight of the poor in this region. These people are all poor by any reasonable standards.

The number of Americans living in poverty by the Census Bureau's definition increased by 1.3 million, to 35.8 million, in 2003. There were 12.9 million children in poverty, an increase of about 800,000 from 2002—that is 17.6 percent of the under–18 population. Nearly 44.9 million people in 2003 lacked health insurance, or 15.6 percent of the U.S. population. That was up from 43.5 million in 2002. The last thing I would do is to say we should only work on poverty abroad and ignore this decades-old problem of "the other America."

These issues are acute in the United States, but far from nonexistent in other advanced countries despite their more ample welfare systems.

The United States can also do more on policy, providing a better safety net. Welfare needed reform, not removal. When I travel abroad, I have sometimes been told in poor countries that, "you have poverty in America, too; we have seen it on TV." Images from America become an excuse for inaction in places like Guatemala, Pakistan, and Nigeria. We should have enough pride in America to not provide such a lame excuse.

Poverty in America can be a part of our giving portfolio. We can also help by supporting programs for training workers and expanding educational opportunities for those who have lost their jobs or who are threatened by trade. We can make affirmative action work the way it is supposed to work—providing the needed hand up for African Americans, who often get bypassed in affirmative action by people who need it less.

One reason things are not much worse in the United States is that individuals and groups have stepped forward to plug the dike neglected by government. If your church or religious community is not active in domestic poverty, now is a good time to get started. Most regions of the country already have active consortia organizations that work to help the homeless and other people in need. Some programs such as Our Daily Bread in Virginia and Washington encourage donors to deliver groceries with their children. At a low-income housing project my daughter got to see a girl about her own age light up at the sight of the grocery bags, and exclaim, "Yeah, now we get to have cereal!" That makes a lasting impression on our children, itself worth far more than the cost of groceries and the value of our time taking part—let alone the impact you can have on others in need.

A CALL TO CITIZEN ACTION

Bread for the World has put the matter concisely: "The United States exerts more influence in the world than any other nation, yet is one of the least forthcoming of the industrialized countries in its politics and policies toward poor and hungry people within its borders and worldwide. If the world is to end widespread hunger, U.S. politics and policies must change. . . . Getting back on track to end hunger depends largely on what you and other people do to build the needed political commitment . . . the United States gives less in development assistance—as a share of gross domestic product—than any other rich country." Those of us who are Americans face a special challenge in ensuring that our country does its fair share to end global poverty. But that challenge is also a unique opportunity: If the United States leads in this global struggle, the rest of the world will surely follow. And America will lead, if her citizens take up this simple call to action.

CHAPTER 15

WHAT BUSINESSES CAN DO

There is no question that business as a whole would greatly benefit from an end to global poverty. It would mean many more consumers. It would mean faster growth. And it would probably lead to a safer world with fewer costs for security. And a world in which business can shake off the blame it gets—fairly or unfairly—for global poverty.

It first has to be said that business can also help improve the lives of the poor just through their regular market activities. As Adam Smith wrote in 1776, "it is not from the benevolence of the butcher, the brewer, or the baker that we can expect our dinner, but from their regard to their own interest." When companies act in ways that lower costs for the poor, or bring to market new products that improve the health of the poor, they are indirectly and often unknowingly contributing to the struggle to end global poverty. Indeed the activities of business are necessary for ending poverty. But self-interest alone is not *sufficient* to end global poverty. In *The Wealth of Nations*, Adam Smith also recognized a critical role for government in many aspects of economic life. In his *Theory of Moral Sentiments*, Smith stressed the roles of conscience and of "sympathy" for other people in making a good society, considerations reflected in the role of the best NGOs and the citizen sector more broadly. But the business sector also has it in its power to do more for poverty reduction than just carrying out business as usual. And paradoxically, acting as if the bottom line were not the only thing that mattered can help the bottom line more than one might expect.

In many cases, antipoverty efforts can partially pay for themselves. One of the most important ways is in improved company image. Even the modest efforts of companies such as Starbucks have greatly improved their brand image among a large section of consumers in the United States who care about poverty. Poverty action also pays off in some indirect and surprising ways. Greater personal contacts lead to unexpected opportunities—

lines of business such as the playground-pumps described earlier are one example.

Employees appreciate the chance to spend a little time on the world's most pressing problems. Their morale can be higher; they can make contacts and learn valuable skills and ideas they never would have encountered in the course of daily work. The economic and legal case that companies should care only about shareholders is far from cut-and-dried. There is considerable latitude in corporate governance for firms to work for social betterment and to take into account multiple stakeholders. One easy program to establish is to match the contributions that your employees make to NGOs working on poverty. You can particularly emphasize poverty work by double matching such gifts.

Firms play the central role in economic life and, as a result, they can play a direct and indirect role in broader social aims generally and ending poverty in particular. Companies engage with citizens in the market, and will be held accountable to customer demands as expressed by their patronage of a given firm. As USAID has noted, in their commercial pursuits firms can also provide an important demonstration of initiative, entrepreneurship—and social responsibility. By acting to improve conditions for doing business, firms can increase the opportunities for poverty reduction that come through greater growth and employment. Such roles need not be carried out on an individual basis, and in many cases it makes sense to work in consortia, including industry associations and chambers of commerce.

A recent report of the International Business Leaders Forum outlines three spheres in which businesses can contribute to the Millennium Development Goals, or MDGs, introduced earlier in the book. They can work through: (1) their core business activities (e.g., what they choose to make or sell); (2) social investment and philanthropic activities; and (3) engagement in policy dialogue and advocacy activities (both through leadership in promoting one or more NGOs through public platforms, and through participating in collective action and dialogue with government and civil society to set rules, norms, and standards in support of the MDGs).

WORK WITH COMMUNITIES

In developing countries the poor actually pay more for goods and services than the rich and middle class. University of Michigan business professor C. K. Prahalad and World Resources Institute vice-president Allen Hammond recently surveyed prices for a range of goods and services in the Mumbai area and found the poor often paid 5 to 25 *times* what the rich pay. Pralahad argues that this differential means there is money to be made by mainstream businesses by selling to the poor, breaking the monopoly of local interests and entrenched distributors. He offers many intriguing case studies of the positive impact of creative business strategies for selling goods and services to the poor on poverty reduction in his 2004 book, *The Fortune at the Bottom of the Pyramid.*

Business sector groupings can work together to promote socially responsible standards. Rani Parker recently has closely studied the sometimes-contentious relationships between international mining companies and local communities, and now serves as a consultant on maintaining and improving these relationships. She suggests a number of questions that management should keep in mind:

> Who needs to be involved in envisioning the desired relationship between the company and community? How effective, culturally appropriate and relevant is the manner of communication? What are the processes for decision-making and conflict resolution? What is the desired relationship in the long term? What are official and unofficial processes by which community-wide decisions are taken? What are the implied and stated values? What are the roles and influence of local religious, political, and social institutions? Who are the different gender, ethnic, and other groups that constitute the community? What are identity and cultural linkages to land, water, and ways of livelihood? How does the company understand and practice its commitment to social responsibility with respect to its significant communities? To what extent is there a process for ensuring coherence and coordination among departments of the company regarding commitments to communities in its areas of influence? How is information from the community passed on to decision-making bodies in the company? How is effective and appropriate communication maintained between the company and the community?

Asking the right questions can be the first step to an improved relationship.

Some NGO poverty activists have criticized the growing role of business, and partnerships involving businesses, in international forums and initiatives on poverty and development. For example, the World Development Movement believes that this is a form of "thinly disguised privatization of essential services." There is no doubt that some companies and industry groups have played a foot-dragging and ultimately damaging role on some critical global issues, including opposition to policies to slow global warming and support for policies that undermine poor farmers. But this does not automatically make all company partnerships suspect, including those in the environmental field—much good in the way of recycling, for instance, has come of partnerships between businesses and environmental NGOs.

Without a modern private sector societies cannot possibly generate the means to achieve worthy goals like poverty reduction. Corporate leaders are also often genuinely concerned about problems of poverty. There are usually limits to what executives feel they can do about it—limits to what they can spend before being hurt by competition, for example. But even in comparison with just a decade ago companies have become far more enaged in poverty and development issues.

ADOPT A CODE OF CONDUCT

It is no longer enough for a company to claim, "I am just a buyer—I cannot be responsible for what goes on in the factories, fields, and mines of the companies that I buy from." While such responses were commonly heard in the mid-1990s, they are rarely heard today. This change is in large part the result of activism by NGOs and leadership of a few pioneering companies.

One of the most striking changes has been the increasing acceptance of many companies of the role for a Code of Conduct, or voluntary standards principles, not least for the public relations benefits but also for avoiding behavior by zealous or greedy managers and contractors that can lead to costly lawsuits. And sometimes by having to act according to established company conduct policy, cost-saving innovations and other efficiencies suggest themselves that would otherwise be overlooked. Research by Michael Porter and Claas van der Linde of Harvard Business School has shown that, by adhering to environmental standards, companies often develop useful innovations that can actually save more than the standards cost. Similar principles apply to some standards of labor conditions.

Codes of Conduct intended to assist international companies with ethics have multiplied in recent years. For example, the UN's Global Compact, launched in 2000, has gained the participation of hundreds of corporations from around the world. You can read about it at http://www.unglobalcompact.org/Portal/Default.asp. The United Nations does not "police" the code; it is a voluntary action designed to improve transparency and good corporate citizenship, and to build support for UN environmental, labor, and humanitarian goals. A few U.S. companies such as Nike, Gap, and Du Pont are participating. It shows that companies can gain recognition for becoming leaders in the effort to end poverty. It also shows that activists who have brought concerns forward probably do have some impact on corporate behavior.

The Rainforest Alliance (RA), found at http://www.rainforest-alliance.org/, runs a seal of approval program, working with companies that impact rainforests, such as foresters, farmers, and tourism operators, to help ensure that their goods and services meet high standards for environmental sustainability and social responsibility. RA runs a SmartWood forestry practices certification program, and works to improve environmental sustainability in agriculture including bananas, citrus fruits, cocoa, coffee, and cut flowers. Among the companies that work with RA under its seal of approval program are Chiquita Banana, Gibson Guitar, and Vintage Chocolates.

Another example is the Fair Labor Association, found at http://www.fairlabor.org/, a consortium of companies, advocacy groups, and university representatives that has a more formal code of conduct. Some of the companies and divisions taking part in Fair Labor are Adidas-Salomon, Eddie Bauer apparel, and Reebok. This association has been controversial, and NGO critics such as Sweatshop Watch have complained that the association code "allows workers to be paid below poverty wages, allows excessive hours of overtime, [and] does not adequately uphold the right of workers to organize independent unions." To a degree these are subjective views: the line for what constitutes excessive overtime is not a clean one, but one with shades of gray. Some U.S. unions have not participated in these associations, and their concerns are understandable, but surely it is better to participate, at least for the most promising initiatives, than to stand aloof. For companies, membership at least shows a minimum standard that you publicly and organizationally commit to adhere to. Unions do not always oppose sending any work overseas. The issue is one of legitimate rights to participate in decisions that affect workers. Such participation is institutionalized in works councils in Europe, and unions could play a larger role in the United States.

The principles of the Global Compact address human rights, the environment, employment conditions, and other matters that impact on poverty, perhaps indirectly. But few of those in extreme poverty will work for participating firms. None of the principles or related materials of the Global Compact, or other codes such as the Global Sullivan Principles or Goodcorporation (http://www.goodcorporation.com/en/), or Fair Labor Association seem to directly address the question of extreme poverty, and behaviors and initiatives of companies that would help reduce poverty. They do support some measures that would clearly help such as not to participate in or benefit from forced labor. But they leave unanswered a basic question: What can a corporation that is particularly concerned about reducing global poverty and wishes to help with its corporate actions and behavior (i.e., rather than or beyond simply making certain charitable contributions) do to help reduce poverty? In coming years, more proactive standards will undoubtedly be implemented.

Codes of conduct related to international financing activities have also been an active topic. In June 2003 ten banks from seven countries formally adopted the so-called Equator Principles, which are voluntary guidelines for managing social and environmental issues arising in financing development projects. The principles were developed by the banks with assistance from the World Bank and its private sector arm, the International Finance Corporation (IFC).

There is plenty to find limiting in the Equator Principles statement. For example, it does not explicitly disallow investments in the most ecologically sensitive environments where almost any investments could cause irreparable harm. And even given these limits, to be meaningful such standards ultimately will need to come with sanctions for those who breach them. But while no panacea, voluntary standards are much better than no standards at all. Adhering to a public and transparent set of principles improves governance, and allows for a legitimate role of other stakeholders. Again, this can be a commitment device: The hypocrisy of claiming to adhere to principles that one then ignores may be a worse public relations failure than flouting social norms with no pretensions to being high minded.

Also, farsighted business managers of companies with international operations who want to make a difference should give serious consideration to investing in Sub-Saharan Africa. In 2050 there will be 1.7 billion people in Sub-Saharan Africa—significantly more than in China (projected to have less than 1.5 billion people in 2050). Companies that invest in Africa have a chance to get in on the proverbial ground floor. If American, European, and Japanese companies would start thinking about this market the way they did China's in the 1980s, there is a good chance that a virtuous cycle of self-fulfilling expectations can get started. Africa has a great future, and an investment pioneer has a chance to do well while doing good.

European companies have long been given some encouragement to work with Africa, and the African Growth and Opportunity Act (AGOA) makes it easier than ever for American companies to do so (see http://www.agoa.gov/).

ON DOING WELL AND DOING GOOD

Businesses are increasingly pairing with many NGOs in implementing "fair trade" and other projects intended to make progress on poverty reduction while enhancing their corporate images.

Douglas Holt of Said Business School, Oxford; John Quelch of Harvard Business School; and Earl Taylor of Marketing Science Institute point out that model behavior can bring market power and suggest that companies "treat 'anti-globals' as customers." Of course this has to be done credibly. British Petroleum (BP) was criticized for its Beyond Petroleum campaign because it wasn't squaring with what people saw as most of the company's activities. Holt, Quelch, and Taylor argue that, "To be credible global companies' social responsibility efforts must show that the companies have harnessed their ample resources to benefit society."

In some cases, businesses have found that by doing good they can do very well indeed. Procter & Gamble's (P&G) Health Sciences Institute recently developed and tested its PuR Water Purifier, which significantly reduced diarrheal illness in trials in Guatemala. Residents pour a small packet of powdered chemicals into a container of water and within minutes it separates out contaminants. The water is then filtered through a cloth to provide cleaner, safer drinking water. The cost is about 10 cents for ten liters (or about two and a half gallons) of water. P&G partnered with the International Council of Nurses and the U.S. Centers for Disease Control (CDC), and is working to develop partnerships with NGOs and others to bring the product to the field. P&G has given the packets free to the Sudanese refugee camps in Chad, and garnered some invaluable free publicity in return.

In a partnership between CARE and Cable & Wireless, CARE detailed its needs for improved communications in humanitarian and emergency operations, and C&W developed portable telecommunications kits that met these requirements. The company also benefited by testing innovative products under extremely demanding circumstances.

Hewlett-Packard is developing a more affordable PC that can be used by several children at once, each working independently with their own keyboard and mouse, piloted for use in schools in South Africa.

No doubt there are many other such opportunities; and opening up many lines of communication between business and NGOs can help to generate new ideas. There are many other valuable contributions that companies can make; here are a few:

- Technology transfer. A growing number of companies also help with transfer of technology and sharing of skills. Companies can train employees in developing countries or help develop training programs even in countries where they do not have any operations. You can partner with appropriate technology groups such as Techno-Serve or EnterpriseWorks, or work in higher-tech areas such as the partnerships with Grameen described earlier in the book.
- Farmer-to-farmer assistance. The most traditional form of such assistance is in the field of agriculture. The U.S. Farmer-to-Farmer Program began in 1985 in the Farm Bill, which provided an outlet for American farmers to share their expertise with farmers in the rest of the world. USAID's Office of Private and

Voluntary Cooperation (PVC) manages the program. Thousands of farmers, managers, engineers, and others participate in Farmer-to-Farmer and similar programs. Volunteers in Overseas Cooperative Assistance (VOCA) initiated the Farmer-to-Farmer program in 1985, and it remains one of the most active groups as part of ACDI-VOCA (having merged with the former International Cooperative Development Association in 1997). Currently, ACDI-VOCA runs Farmer-to-Farmer programs in numerous developing and transition countries including Armenia, Bolivia, Cambodia, and Uganda, among others. In addition, ACDI-VOCA has many other international activities including co-op development, assistance with natural resource management, and food aid. The group offers numerous volunteer opportunities. You can find out more about ACDI-VOCA at http://www.acdivoca.org/acdivoca/Acdiweb2.nsf/.

- Partner chambers of commerce. It is often easier for businesses to act together in associations than as individual firms. In the developing world, chambers of commerce and similar groupings are now emerging. Forming a partner chamber of commerce could be an effective strategy for business-to-business (B2B) assistance of the type that can help end global poverty.

You can in some cases build on existing relationships. For example, there are joint Chamber of Commerce groupings, such as ones that connect the United States with Mexico and Pacific Rim countries. This is something to consider if you are interested in making a business impact on poverty. Of course, once a country takes off toward development there are more opportunities and more reasons for creating these partnerships. But pioneering efforts with Africa could lead to a major impact. You can probably get assistance from bilateral agencies, such as USAID or the new Millennium Challenge Account in the United States. Most have well-established arms to help energize the private sector in Africa and other low-income countries. Small companies can also take part in B2B assistance. You can work with small and medium-sized enterprises in a developing country to which you have close connections.

Business has begun actively contributing to the struggle against poverty in a way that few imagined only a decade ago. Your company can play a vital role both in its normal business operations and through special activities and programs that can frequently lead to outcomes that help pay for themselves.

SOME CLOSING WORDS

THE END OF GLOBAL POVERTY

This book has shown why poverty is a trap, explained what the poor need to escape poverty traps, and described some of the most innovative and effective strategies now being used in the world's poorest regions to help people escape from the bondage of extreme poverty. The struggle to end global poverty is an epic drama in which we all play a supporting role.

We live in a special moment in history. There are real reasons for optimism. Economic growth is fairly high, technological progress and the spread of new technologies around the world is rapid, market efficiencies are improving, democracy and freedoms are reaching an ever-larger number of people, and measurable progress has been made toward ending global poverty. In one very possible future, we could virtually end extreme poverty in the next quarter century.

But a different and far worse future is also all too possible. We could still lose the struggle to end global poverty. This is a time of dramatic change, and social and economic patterns have not become set. In the developing world, instead of gaining new rights and freedoms, the poor could find themselves subjected to wider abuses and denial of basic rights. Hundreds of millions of people could sink further into hunger and disease, with large regions of the world trapped in poverty indefinitely. Elites in the developing world, aided negligently by global business, could view globalization as an opportunity to exploit the poor more effectively. Stifled by debt, the poorest countries could enter into a new period of stagnation. Worst of all, as the natural environment continues to deteriorate, all of the benefits of improved knowledge and productivity could be exhausted just in the effort to compensate. Frustrated by growing gaps between images of the distant developed world and the close-by realities of impoverishment, peoples could be driven to false promises of demagogues, whose policies could enslave and impoverish them further.

In developed countries, a growing focus on the war on terrorism to the exclusion of other social objectives, and a frustration with the slow pace of progress, could lead to a loss of resolve. The struggle to end extreme poverty is strongly complementary with the struggle against terrorism, but in budgets around the world these goals seem to be in competition with each other. While a failure to achieve the Millennium Development Goals by the 2015 target date could lead to a renewed commitment, it could also lead to discouragement.

In the Cold War, governments in the "Third" (or developing) World were asked to choose between alliance with the First World, led by the United States, or with the Second World, led by the Soviet Union. Now the question is posed in a different way. Not which of two worlds will poor countries ally themselves with, but whether the rich and poor will become two worlds, separate and unequal, sowing the seeds of future international conflict, a growing allure of terrorist groups, global environmental destruction, spread of disease without regard to borders, and continued human misery among the poor.

With the end of the Cold War came less willingness on the part of the rich countries to tolerate repressive regimes whose policies either neglected or worsened poverty. The spread of freedom and democracy has been a very constructive factor in reducing poverty. But the end of the Cold War also led to less interest in assisting some of the poorest countries in the world, particularly in Africa. In the first few years of the new millennium there has been a shift in rhetoric and some modest increases in public funding. But more funding is needed, and, at least as important, we need to do better targeting of both government and citizen sector aid to the best programs that effectively improve the lives of the poorest.

If the priority for aid is to end extreme poverty, then we need to focus attention on what the poor need, what capabilities and assets they lack, and what local and global forces are holding them back. Aid could have more impact on extreme poverty if approached with the perspective that helping people and local communities helps their countries to get stronger and their economies to grow. We can hope that by helping a country's government agencies or private sector we will stimulate growth and efficiency and thereby help the poor. But we cannot focus on this hope to the exclusion of working with the organizations best situated to providing the poor with the keys to capability and assisting the escape from poverty traps. This is needed more than ever in the poorest countries far from the centers of world growth.

While we still grapple with how to accelerate growth in countries such as Kenya, Zambia, Bolivia, and Pakistan, we have learned a great deal about how to improve the lives of poor people even when growth is low. We can do this by helping the poor gain the keys to capability that they need to escape from poverty traps. In so doing, we improve the breadth of the human resources of the country and thus indirectly help to strengthen and improve the markets and institutions needed for successful development. Once the keys to capability have spread as widely as possible throughout a country, the people themselves, through their own institutions and reform efforts, will then be better positioned to determine the most effective development strategies for their own context.

Successful cases of development usually involve a unique, local response to local constraints that outsiders are not in a good position to understand. Few recent examples of highly successful development, which are concentrated in Asia, correspond to simple reliance on the invisible hand. Market incentives play a key role, but so do effective government and a dynamic citizen sector, working in concert. Local development strategies can be worked out with foreign advice—but they must be locally owned in fact as well as in name, and carried out on local terms. The World Bank, bilateral agencies, and NGOs all have roles to play—but to reach those living in extremely poor countries the old model of seeking to influence elites to follow the popular theories of the moment will have to be discarded in favor of strategies for helping to provide the keys to capability at the community level, and assisting, not insisting, on particular policies. China and India made many economic mistakes but ultimately moved slowly but steadily toward better institutions and faster growth as a result of charting their own course through the rocky shoals of social and economic transformation. China, like South Korea and Taiwan before it, learned much from the West about institutions as well as technologies, but adjusted these to their own circumstances in a way that only they could know best. Development strategies for today's impoverished regions can also be better attuned and tailored to local constraints.

Despite progress in understanding some of the key sources of growth and the role of institutions in improving market efficiency, remarkably little is known about how to design and implement policies to ensure that growth in the developing world effectively lifts the poor out of poverty. It is one thing to understand that some of the institutions found in developed countries are more effective at stimulating growth than those of developing countries, but quite another to effectively change these institutions. The policies of the countries that have experienced the most rapid poverty reduction— China is a particularly striking example—often look very different from the prescriptions of aid agencies such as USAID. The development strategies followed by successful countries are quite varied and have generally been designed and built locally to circumvent local constraints. And in all countries we are left with the problem of how to help those poor who, for whatever reasons, have benefited little from whatever growth their country has achieved. We cannot wait to find all the explanations of growth and development; instead, we should do better at finding and funding programs that can help the poor to help themselves, where they are, on their own terms—even if they aren't fortunate enough to live in a high-growth economy.

In the world of policymaking as much as in the world at large, the voices of the rich can be heard loud and clear while those of the poor barely register. The poor countries, and the poor themselves, now need a larger voice in World Bank and other development decision-making. Currently, the World Bank is governed by one-dollar-one-vote, giving control to rich country donors. As a first step to expanding the voice of the governed, the World Bank could create an advisory council comprised largely of people from developing countries who have made a difference in the lives of the poor, such as leading social entrepreneurs. Rather than using ad hoc committees to address controversial issues, this would be a permanent body, though with a rotating membership selected by an independent and transparent process. The council would need guarantees of independence and full access to information and staff assistance, and would make public recommendations, and control a steadily growing share of the budget. This would go a long way to restoring credibility. But ultimately, the one-dollar–one-vote structure of World Bank decision-making will have to give way to a more people-friendly formula.

The Internet changes many things. It makes information cheaper and easier to find. It enables groups to organize. In the fight against poverty, it enables donors large and small to identify programs that fit their values and ideas about what can work. Donor clubs can be formed. Citizens can now bypass traditional development agencies and organizations and work directly with the communities they would like to assist. With these changes come risks as well as rewards: The possibilities of scams multiply. But, carried out wisely, there are new opportunities to enable a wide public in developed and developing countries to follow program developments actively. Virtual visits to programs become more realistic. Evaluation data put on the web (with careful controls on confidentiality and accuracy) can help potential supporters or donors check claims of evaluation. Researchers at universities and elsewhere can volunteer to do studies for NGOs on condition that they are done independently and rigorously, and these studies can be made widely available. What better way to energize people around the world to participate in ending poverty?

We must emphasize more than ever the need to get the greatest poverty reduction impact per aid dollar spent, and this means that objective, rigorous, and independent evaluation should be a condition of funding. Innovation is critical, and must be encouraged, but donors need to greatly scale-up funding for programs of proven effectiveness, and not overemphasize funding "innovative" programs simply for the sake of appearing innovative.

Donors must not avoid the kind of serious research that can prove some programs haven't worked, simply because they fear they would look bad if it were discovered they had funded an unsuccessful program.

At the same time donors should consider greater emphasis on decentralized discovery of effective poverty strategies and the diffusion of these ideas. Many of the experiences described in this book suggest that very useful strategies for ending poverty can be developed by practitioners in the field. Rather than relying on a few elite thinkers in locations such as universities and the World Bank or other international organizations to develop programs, people working with the poor and often the poor themselves can generate useful innovations by reflecting on problems faced by the poor, trying out new strategies based on these insights, and then learning from their mistakes to improve their programs. For example, prizes and awards for effective poverty activities can motivate people to experiment with their new ideas or show how existing programs can be scaled up, drawing attention to those that show the most promise and demonstrated effectiveness, and then in turn attracting additional funds from donors who learn about the program through publicity about the award. Innovative programs may be designed and run by local governments, but often NGOs in the citizen sector take the lead. Such groups can sometimes carry out high-impact programs at startlingly low costs.

Like "value investing" in the stock market, or the "moneyball" search in professional sports for overlooked players making the biggest impact on games won per player salary spent, we can make more rapid progress against poverty with better methods. We can do this by developing strategies that start with first principles about the fundamental nature of poverty and the predicaments of poverty traps, finding new ways of identifying overlooked programs with high impact per dollar spent on poverty in the multidimensional sense used in this book, using more rigorous program evaluations such as randomized trials that are designed and implemented in tandem with the program at every step, and engaging the public—the value of a taxpaying and charity-giving public that demands focus, accountability, and effectiveness on the central goal of ending poverty cannot be overstated. Such a strategy involves putting aside preconceptions, starting from first principles, and evaluating programs unflinchingly. We can and should do this whatever the size of the poverty budget that we have to work with, even as we continue to give generously and to lobby government for a more reasonable level of funding for ending global poverty.

Every era has its compelling moral issues. For Ralph Waldo Emerson it was slavery. He would have preferred to contemplate, and to discuss philosophy with his friends. But in the end, Emerson felt he had to risk everything to take a very public stand against slavery at a time when it was perceived as an extreme and inflammatory position. Today's compelling issue is poverty. In an age of such overflowing abundance, there is no justification for those of us who have been so blessed to stand by while others suffer the most terrible deprivations. In one way, to take a stand on poverty is easy: it is hard to find anyone who admits to being "for" poverty. But it takes risks to stand against farm subsidies and textile protection, and to call for more spending on aid, and more restrictions to preserve the global environment so that the poor in the developing world do not suffer further. To effectively end poverty will require some sacrifices, even though the ultimate benefits will be great for us all. The struggle to end global poverty should also transcend all political calculations. Republican and Democrat; Conservative, Liberal, and Labor—all should find ways to put aside their other differences and unite for this urgent cause.

There are other compelling issues. One of the most important is preservation of the environment, and I understand that some put it in the first position. But there is more synergy than tradeoff. Sometimes, to solve environmental problems you have to solve poverty, poverty that is leading the poor to carve unsustainable farms in rainforests, burn unclean fuels, cut environmentally needed trees for cooking fires, and overuse the soil to have more food that particular year when they so desperately need it. And poverty is worsened by climate change that expands deserts, causes more severe weather and more frequent flooding, worsens erosion, and now threatens to submerge heavily populated coastal areas.

Terrorism is another pressing problem. Muhammad Yunus, founder of the Grameen Bank that assists the poor in Bangladesh, said, "One of the major causes of terrorism is poverty." Certainly, ending extreme poverty will not completely end terrorism. Terrorist leaders are often wealthy, or middle-class and well educated. But making a full effort to end poverty will surely help. Undereducated people who sense that they have no other future are more willing recruits as foot soldiers for terrorist leaders who make false promises. The existence of gross disparities in wealth, and such unnecessary suffering, is not the only source of alienation among many young people in the developing world, but it is one important source. Efforts of the rich countries on behalf of the poor are key to winning "hearts and minds." Within as well as across countries, extremes in relative inequality will also need to be addressed, for gross inequality in itself, whether deprivations such as hunger and illiteracy are found or not, can also have adverse effects on society, the economy, and individual well-being, ultimately leading to its own forms of absolute deprivation. Of course there are many other demands on our attention and our budgets. But despite many spending pressures we still have plenty of resources to end global poverty if we can summon the political will to spend them, and to spend them wisely.

When we have finally ended global poverty, the world will still have to face other issues. But I hope that we will never lose sight of the great strides we made to eliminate so much unnecessary premature death, hunger, malnourishment, exposure to the elements, easily treatable illness, illiteracy, vulnerability, lack of opportunity, and powerlessness. In the far future humanity might look back and say that was our greatest achievement.

To end global poverty will require everyone's help. The next step is yours.

NOTES AND REFERENCES

INTRODUCTION

Scale of global poverty: World Bank, *World Development Report: Attacking Poverty,* World Development Report 2000/2001, New York: Oxford University Press, 2000.

Child health information: World Health Organization (WHO) websites, http://www.who.int/en/ and http://www.who.int/child-adolescent-health/ and the Global Health Council website, http://www.globalhealth.org/view_top.php3?id=25.

For a map of child deaths around the world see: http://www.unsystem.org/scn/Publications/AnnualMeeting/SCN31/approach.pdf

For an ILO fact sheet on child labor: http://www.ilo.org/public/english/bureau/inf/childlabour/factssheet.htm.

For other references on poverty see: UNDP, *Human Development Report 2003,* http://www.undp.org/hdr2003/; and earlier years.

UN Food and Agriculture Organization (FAO) November 2003 report, "The State of Food Insecurity in the World," available at http://www.fao.org/.

Gary Fields, *Distribution and Development: A New Look at the Developing World,* MIT Press, 2001.

Andrew McKay and David Lawson, "Assessing the Extent and Nature of Chronic Poverty in Low Income Countries: Issues and Evidence," *World Development,* vol. 31, no. 3, March 2003: 425–39.

Andy McKay and Bob Baulch, "How Many Chronically Poor People Are there in the World? Some Preliminary Estimates," Chronic Poverty Research Centre (CPRC) Working Paper No 45, Chronic Poverty Research Centre, 2003. Website: http://www.chronicpoverty.org/.

David Hulme and Andrew Shepherd, "Conceptualizing Chronic Poverty," *World Development,* vol. 31, no. 3, March 2003: 403–23.

For optimistic assessments of the impact of trade and growth on global poverty see David Dollar and Art Kraay, "Growth Is Good for the Poor," *Journal of Economic Growth,* September, 7, no. 3, pp. 195–225, 2002, and David Dollar and Art Kraay, "Trade, Growth, and Poverty," *The Economic Journal,* vol. 114, no. 493, 2004: F22-F49(1). A caveat stressed by Dani Rodrick is that the poorest countries have the poorest data.

For world population data see Population Reference Bureau, *2004 World Population Data Sheet,* available at http://www.prb.org/Template.cfm?Section=PRB&template=/Content/ContentGroups/Datasheets/2004_World_Population_Data_Sheet.htm.

For recent estimates of poverty declines at one dollar per day (1993 purchasing power parity), see: UNDP, *Human Development Report 2002,* New York: Oxford University Press, 2002; and Chen, Shaohua and Ravallion, Martin, "How Have the

World's Poorest Fared Since the Early 1980s?" *World Bank Policy Research Working Paper* No. 3341, June 10, 2004.

For a wide-ranging analysis of problems of extreme poverty, see Partha Dasgupta, *An Inquiry into Well-Being and Destitution,* Oxford: Oxford University Press, 1993.

For a skeptical view of the extent of poverty reduction in South Asia and elsewhere based on statistical considerations, see Sanjay G. Reddy and Thomas W. Pogge, "How Not to Count the Poor," working paper, Columbia University, 2003.

On the sense of giving something back:

Bill Shore, *The Cathedral Within: Transforming Your Life by Giving Something Back,* New York: Random House, 1999.

Peter D. Hart Research Associates, "New Leadership for a New Century: Key Findings from a Study on Youth Leadership and Community Service," Washington, DC, 1998.

On the Bread for the World poll, see http://www.bread.org/media/archives/2002_July_29_Alliance.html

See also Mary McGrory, Hungry for Justice, *The Washington Post,* August 1, 2002, available at http://www.washingtonpost.com/ac2/wp-dyn?pagename=article&contentId=A29055-2002Jul31&notFound=true.

Another representative poll is the February 2001 survey by the Program on International Policy Attitudes, http://www.pipa.org/OnlineReports/BFW/finding3.html.

PART I. EXTREME POVERTY: THE CRUELEST TRAP

CHAPTER 1. POVERTY TRAPS
AND THE EXPERIENCE OF THE POOR

The Predicament of the Poorest of the Poor: Why It's a Trap

Stephen C. Smith, "The Organizational Comparative Advantage of NGOs in Eradicating Extreme Poverty and Hunger: Strategy for Escape from Poverty Traps," presented at the Conference on the Role of NGOs in Achieving the Millennium Development Goals, Washington, DC: George Washington University, May 12–13, 2004.

Muhammad Yunus of the Grameen Bank notes that poverty traps are set by the rich. Interview with author, Sept. 29, 2003. See also Mohammad Yunus, *The Millennium Development Goals: We Can Really Do It* (Dhaka: Grameen Bank pamphlet, 2002).

Cornell professor and child labor expert Kaushik Basu observed in his textbook *Analytical Development Economics* (Cambridge: MIT Press, 1997) that the term "poverty trap" suggests that there is a way out.

I have not tried to report comprehensively all types of traps. Some traps not discussed here include (a) neighborhood traps, in which being surrounded the poor conspires to keep you poor as well; (b) social norms traps: there can be harmful social norms as well as beneficial ones, but each carry momentum of their own; and (c) corruption traps, in which when everyone expects corruption all feel compelled to participate in it, at least to pay bribes.

For general reading about the poverty traps described in the book:

Karla Hoff and Joseph Stiglitz, "Modern Economic Theory and Development," in Gerald Meier and Joseph Stiglitz, eds., *Frontiers in Development Economics,* New York: Oxford University Press, 2001.

Karla Hoff, "Beyond Rosenstein-Rodan: The Modern Theory of Underdevelopment Traps," http://orion.forumone.com/ABCDE/files.fcgi/137_hoff.pdf, paper presented at the Annual Bank Conference on Development Economics, World Bank, Washington DC, 2001.

Michael P. Todaro and Stephen C. Smith, *Economic Development*, 9th Edition, Reading, MA: Addison-Wesley, 2005. Chapters 4, 5, 6, 7, 8.

Debraj Ray, *Development Economics*, Princeton, NJ: Princeton University Press, 1998.

Andrew McKay and Bob Baulch, "How Many Chronically Poor People Are there in the World? Some Preliminary Estimates," Chronic Poverty Research Centre, CPRC Working Paper No. 45, 2003.

Michael R. Carter and Julian May, "One Kind of Freedom: Poverty Dynamics in Post-Apartheid South Africa," *World Development*, vol. 29, no. 12, pp. 1987–2006.

Child labor traps

Kaushik Basu, "Child Labor: Cause, Consequence, and Cure, with Remarks on International Labor Standards," *Journal of Economic Literature*, vol. 37, no. 3, 1083–1120, September 1999.

Oded Galor and Joseph Zeira, "Income Distribution and Macroeconomics," *Review of Economic Studies*, vol. 60, no. 1 (January 1993): 35–52.

Illiteracy traps

Jean-Marie Baland and James A. Robinson, "Is Child Labor Inefficient?" *Journal of Political Economy*, vol. 108, no. 1 (August 2000): 663–79.

Jacoby, Hanan G., "Borrowing Constraints and Progress Through School: Evidence from Peru," *Review of Economics and Statistics*" (1994): 151–160.

Working capital traps

Abhijit V. Banerjee and Andrew Newman, "Poverty, Incentives, and Development," *American Economic Review Papers and Proceedings*, vol. 84, no. 2, May 1994: 211–220.

Abhijit V. Banerjee and Andrew Newman, "Occupational Choice and the Process of Development," *Journal of Political Economy*, vol. 101, no. 2, April 1993: 274–298.

Beatriz Armendriz de Aghion and Jonathan Morduch, *The Economics of Microfinance*, Cambridge, MA: MIT Press, 2005.

Maitreesh Ghatak and Timothy W. Guinnane, "The Economics of Lending with Joint Liability: A Review of Theory and Practice," *Journal of Development Economics*, vol. 60, no. 1, October 1999: 195–228.

Uninsurable risk traps

Frederick J. Zimmerman and Michael R. Carter, "Asset Smoothing, Consumption Smoothing and the Reproduction of Inequality under Risk and Subsistence Constraints," *Journal of Development Economics*, vol. 71, no. 2, August 2003: 233–60.

Debraj Ray, *Development Economics*, Princeton, NJ: Princeton University Press, 1998, chs. 12, 13, 14.

Marcel Fafchamps, *Rural Poverty, Risk and Development,* Cheltenham, UK; Northampton, MA: E. Elgar, 2003.

Debt bondage traps

Arnab K. Basu, "Oligopsonistic Landlords, Segmented Labor Markets, and the Persistence of Tied-Labor Contracts," *American Journal of Agricultural Economics,* vol. 84, no. 2, May 2002: 438–53.

Arnab K. Basu and Nancy H. Chau, "Targeting Child Labor in Debt Bondage: Evidence, Theory, and Policy Implications," *World Bank Economic Review,* vol. 17, no. 2, 2003: 255–81.

Roger L. Ransom and Richard Sutch, *One Kind of Freedom: The Economic Consequences of Emancipation,* 2d edition. New York: Cambridge University Press, 2001.

Kevin Bales, *Disposable People: New Slavery in the Global Economy,* Berkeley: University of California Press, 2000.

Debraj Ray, *Development Economics,* Princeton, NJ: Princeton University Press, 1998, chapter 14.

Free the Slaves: http://www.freetheslaves.net/.

Information traps

Stephen C. Smith, "Organizational Comparative Advantages of NGOs in Eradicating Extreme Poverty and Hunger: Strategy for Escape from Poverty Traps," presented at the Conference on the Role of NGOs in Achieving the Millennium Development Goals, Washington, DC: George Washington University, May 12–13, 2004.

Undernutrition and illness traps

Partha Dasgupta and Debraj Ray, "Inequality as a Determinant of Malnutrition and Unemployment: Theory," *Economic Journal,* vol. 96, no. 384, December 1986: 1011–34.

Partha Dasgupta and Debraj Ray, "Inequality as a Determinant of Malnutrition and Unemployment: Policy," *Economic Journal* vol. 97, no. 385, March 1987: 177–88.

Partha Dasgupta, *An Inquiry into Well-Being and Destitution,* Oxford: Oxford University Press, 1993.

Low skill traps

Karla Hoff, "Beyond Rosenstein-Rodan: The Modern Theory of Underdevelopment Traps," http://orion.forumone.com/ABCDE/files.fcgi/137_hoff.pdf, paper presented at the Annual Bank Conference on Development Economics, World Bank, Washington DC, 2001.

Kremer, Michael, "The O-Ring Theory of Economic Development," *Quarterly Journal of Economics,* vol. 108, no. 3 August 1993: 551–75.

Daron Acemoglu, "Training and Innovation in an Imperfect Labour Market," *Review of Economic Studies,* vol. 64, no. 3, July 1997: 445–64.

Abhijit V. Banerjee and Andrew Newman, "Occupational Choice and the Process of Development," *Journal of Political Economy,* vol. 101, no. 2, April 1993: 274–298.

Oded Galor, and Zeira, Joseph, "Income Distribution and Macroeconomics," *Review of Economic Studies,* vol. 60, January 1993: 35–52.

Jyotsna Jalan, and Martin Ravallion, "Geographic Poverty Traps? A Micro Model of Consumption Growth in Rural China," *Journal of Applied Econometrics*, vol. 17, no. 4, July-August 2002: 329–46.

High fertility traps

Michael P. Todaro and Stephen C. Smith, *Economic Development*, 9th Edition, Reading, MA: Addison-Wesley, 2005, chap. 6.

Partha Dasgupta, "The Population Problem: Theory and Evidence," *Journal of Economic Literature*, vol. 33, no. 4, December 1995: 1879–1902.

Higher fertility is also associated with lower growth; see, e.g., Robert J. Barro, *Determinants of Economic Growth: a Cross-country Empirical Study*, Cambridge, MA: The MIT Press, 1997.

Subsistence traps

Shahe Emran and Forhad Shilpi, "Marketing Externalities, Multiple Equilibria, and Market Development," paper presented at the Northeast Universities Development Conference, Boston, MA: Boston University, September 2001, revised in 2004.

Farm erosion traps

Michael P. Todaro and Stephen C. Smith, *Economic Development*, 9th Edition, Reading, MA: Addison-Wesley, 2005, chap. 10.

Charles Perrings, "An Optimal Path to Extinction? Poverty and Resource Degradation in the Open Agrarian Economy," *Journal of Development Economics*," vol. 30, 1989: 1–24.

Sylwester, Kevin, "Simple Model of Resource Degradation and Agricultural Productivity in a Subsistence Economy," *Review of Development Economics*, vol. 8, no. 1, February 2004: 128–40.

Bekele Shiferaw and Stein T. Holden, "Resource Degradation and Adoption of Land Conservation Technologies in the Ethiopian Highlands: A Case Study in Andit Tid, North Shewa," *Agricultural Economics*, vol. 18, no. 3, May 1998: 233–47.

Common property mismanagement traps

Bruce Larson, and David Bromley, "Property Rights, Externalities, and Resource Degradation: Locating the Tragedy," *Journal of Development Economics*, vol. 33, 1990: 235–262.

Michael P. Todaro and Stephen C. Smith, *Economic Development*, 9th Edition, Reading, MA: Addison-Wesley, ch 10.

Paul Seabright, "Managing Local Commons: Theoretical Issues in Incentive Design," *Journal of Economic Perspectives*, vol. 7, Fall 1993: 113–134.

N. S. Jodha, "Common Property Resources: A Missing Dimension of Development Strategies," World Bank Discussion Paper WDPI69, Washington, DC: World Bank, February 1995.

Collective action traps

Mancur Olson, *Logic of Collective Action: Public Goods and the Theory of Groups*, Cambridge, MA: Harvard University Press, 1971.

Paul Seabright, "Managing Local Commons: Theoretical Issues in Incentive Design," *Journal of Economic Perspectives,* vol. 7, Fall 1993: 113–34.

Criminality traps

Author interview with William Drayton, CEO of Ashoka, March 23, 2004.

Author interviews with World Vision staff, Ayacucho province, Peru, April 4, 2003.

Mental health traps

Economic models of undernutrition traps, suitably adapted, should be applicable to this type of trap.

Vikram Patel, et al., "Depression in Developing Countries: Lessons from Zimbabwe," *British Medical Journal,* vol. 322, 2001: 482–84.

Vikram Patel, "Poverty, Inequality and Mental Health in Developing Countries," in David Leon and Gill Walt, eds., *Poverty, Inequality and Health: An International Perspective,* New York: Oxford Univ. Press, 2000.

Block, Francis and Vijayendra Rao, "Terror as a bargaining Instrument: A Case Study of Dowry Violence in Rural India," *American Economic Review,* 92, 4, 1029–43, September 2002.

Myers, Jane E. and Carmen S. Gill, "Poor, Rural and Female: Under-Studied, Under-Counseled, More At-Risk," *Journal of Mental Health Counseling,* 26, 3k 2004.

Patel, Vikram, et al, "Women, Poverty and Common Mental Disorders in four Reconstructing Societites," *Social Science and Medicene,* 49, 11, 1461–1471, 1999.

Powerlessness traps

Ranjani K. Murthy and Lakshmi Sankaran, *Denial and Distress: Gender, Poverty, and Human Rights in Asia,* New York: Zed, 1999.

Mohammad Yunus, *The Millennium Development Goals: We Can Really Do It,* Dhaka: Grameen Bank, 2002.

Mohammad Yunus, Interview with author, Dhaka, Bangladesh, Sept. 29, 2003.

Conclusion of section on poverty traps

John D. Clark, *Worlds Apart. Civil Society and the Battle for Ethical Globalization,* Bloomfield, CT: Kumarian, 2003 (p. 51). Among other things Clark doubts the basic statistics on poverty, including some of the ones used in this book, such as the 1.2 billion people living on $1 per day.

Angus Deaton, "Is World Poverty Falling?" *Finance and Development,* International Monetary Fund, June 2002, vol. 39, no. 2.

Voices of the Poor

Except where otherwise noted, quotes of the poor are from *Voices of the Poor: Crying out for Change* and *Voices of the Poor: From Many Lands,* New York: Oxford University Press for the World Bank, 2000.

Voices from Ethiopia: These quotes are from *Voices of the Poor: Crying out for Change,* 2000, Box 2.3, p. 33, box 12.1, p. 269.

A Holistic Understanding of Poverty

The importance of assets
Michael R. Carter and Christopher B. Barrett, "The Economics of Poverty Traps and Persistent Poverty: An Asset-based Approach," BASIS-Collaborative Research Support Program, Department of Agricultural and Applied Economics, Madison: University of Wisconsin, November 2004.

Michael R. Carter and Julian May, "Poverty, Livelihood and Class in Rural South Africa," *World Development*, vol. 27, no. 1, 1999: 1–20.

Michael R. Carter and Julian May, "One Kind of Freedom: Poverty Dynamics in Post-Apartheid South Africa," *World Development*, vol. 29, no. 12, pp. 1987–2006.

Extreme Poverty as Deprivation of Capabilities

The quote from the man from Ghana is also drawn from the *Voices of the Poor* study, ibid.

On capability to function, see Amartya Sen, *Development as Freedom,* New York: Alfred Knopf, 1999; the quote is from page 14. A more technical analysis is found in Amartya Sen, *Commodities and Capabilities,* Amsterdam, Netherlands: North Holland, 1985.

For an application to poverty measurement see Sanjay G. Reddy, "The 'Index Number Problem' and Poverty Monitoring: The Unique Advantages of a Capability Approach," working paper, Columbia Univ., 2003.

Abhijit Banerjee, Angus Deaton, and Esther Duflo. "Wealth, Health, and Health Services in Rural Rajasthan," working paper, Economics Department, Cambridge, MA: Massachusetts Institute of Technology, May, 2004.

On the multidimensional nature of poverty see also: World Bank, *World Development Report: Attacking Poverty,* World Development Report 2000/2001, New York: Oxford University Press, 2000.

For details of poverty measures, see Michael P. Todaro and Stephen C. Smith, *Economic Development,* 9th Edition, Reading, MA: Addison-Wesley, 2005, chapters 2 and 5; Gary Fields, *Distribution and Development: A New Look at the Developing World,* MIT Press, 2001; and Amartya Sen and James E. Foster, *On Economic Inequality,* 2nd Ed., New York: Oxford/Clarendon, 1997.

Common Characteristics of the Poor

United Nations Development Program, *Human Development Report,* (2002), New York: Oxford, 2002, also available at http://www.undp.org/hdr2002/.

World Bank, *World Development Report: Attacking Poverty* World Development Report 2000/2001, New York: Oxford University Press, 2000.

Michael Todaro and Stephen C. Smith, *Economic Development,* 9th Edition, Reading, MA: Addison-Wesley, 2005, chap. 5.

Gary Fields, *Poverty, Inequality, and Development,* New York: Cambridge University Press, 1980.

Does Inequality Matter?

On relationships between relative inequality and absolute deprivation, see Amartya Sen, *Development as Freedom,* New York: Alfred Knopf, 1999, esp. pp. 20–24, 87–90, and 107–110. Sen cites Adam Smith on consumption and standards on p. 71.

Torsten Persson and Guido Tabellini, "Is Inequality Harmful for Growth?" *American Economic Review*, vol. 84, no. 3, June 1994: 600–621.

Debraj Ray, *Development Economics*, Princeton, NJ: Princeton University Press, 1998, chs. 6–8.

Michael Todaro and Stephen C. Smith, *Economic Development*, 9th Edition, Reading, MA: Addison-Wesley, 2005, chap. 5.

For papers showing the long-term rise in world inequality see:

Lant Pritchett, "Divergence, Big Time," *Journal of Economic Perspectives*, vol. 11, no. 3, 1997: 3–18.

Francois Bourguignon and Christian Morrisson, "Inequality among World Citizens: 1820–1992," *American Economic Review*, vol. 92, no. 4, September 2002: 727–44.

For a statistical assessment that world inequality is continuing to rise in recent years, see Branko Milanovic, "True World Income Distribution, 1988 and 1993: First Calculation Based on Household Surveys Alone," *Economic Journal*, vol. 112, no. 476, January 2002: 51–92.

For an opposing statistical assessment that global income inequality has fallen overall in recent years, see Xavier Sala-i-Martin, "The Disturbing 'Rise' in World Income Inequality," working paper, Columbia University, http://www.columbia.edu/~xs23/papers/GlobalIncomeInequality.htm, and "The World Distribution of Income," http://www.columbia.edu/~xs23/papers/WorldDistribution.htm

For his reply to Sala-I-Martin, see Branko Milanovic, "The Ricardian Vice: Why Sala-i-Martin's Calculations of World Income Inequality are Wrong," working paper, Washington: Carnegie Endowment, 2003, paper available at http://econwpa.wustl.edu/eps/hew/papers/0305/0305003.pdf.

CHAPTER 2. THE KEYS TO CAPABILITY: EIGHT KEYS TO ESCAPING POVERTY TRAPS

Health and nutrition for adults to work
and children to grow to their potential.

Food and Agriculture Organization (FAO), *The State of Food Insecurity in the World*, Rome, Italy: UN Food and Agriculture Organization, November 2003, available at http://www.fao.org/.

Laura E. Caulfield, Mercedes de Onis, Monika Blössner and Robert E. Black, "Undernutrition as an Underlying Cause of Child Deaths Associated with Diarrhea, Pneumonia, Malaria and Measles," *American Journal of Clinical Nutrition*, vol. 80, no. 1, July 2004: 193–98. An earlier study in *The Lancet* presented evidence of an even higher impact.

Food and Agriculture Organization (FAO), *Dimensions of Need, An Atlas of Food and Agriculture, on the 50th Anniversary of the FAO*, 1995, Rome, Italy: UN Food and Agriculture Organization, available at http://www.fao.org/.

Ann Florini with Neal Spivack, *Food on the Table: Seeking Global Solutions to Chronic Hunger*, New York: United Nations Association-USA, 1987.

Statistics on health and nutrition of the poor: World Bank, *World Development Report: Attacking Poverty* World Development Report 2000/2001, New York: Oxford University Press, 2000. World Bank, *World Development Report 1993: Health*, New York: Oxford University Press, 1993.

World Health Organization, *World Health Report,* Geneva, Switzerland: World Health Organization, 2001.

Basic education to build the foundations of self-reliance

Kaushik Basu and James E. Foster, "On Measuring Literacy," *Economic Journal,* vol. 108, no. 451, November 1998: 1733–49.

Michael Todaro and Stephen C. Smith, *Economic Development,* 9th Edition, Reading, MA: Addison-Wesley, chap. 8.

Paolo Friere, *Pedagogy of the Oppressed,* New York: Seabury Press, 1970.

Kaushik Basu, "Child Labor: Cause, Consequence, and Cure, with Remarks on International Labor Standards," *Journal of Economic Literature,* vol. 37, no. 3, September 1999: 1083–1120.

Jean-Marie Baland and James A. Robinson, "Is Child Labor Inefficient?" *Journal of Political Economy* vol. 108, no. 4, August 2000: 663–79.

Yuko Tauchi, "Who decides? Introducing Literacy to Preliterate Societies: Pros and Cons," http://www.ntu.edu.au/education/csle/student/tauchi/tauchi0.html.

A useful UN-ILO report on child labor may be found at: http://www.ilo.org/dyn/declaris/DECLARATIONWEB.DOWNLOAD_BLOB?Var_DocumentID=1566.

Credit and basic insurance for working capital and defense against risk

Mohammad Yunus, *Banker to the Poor, Micro Lending and the Battle Against World Poverty,* New York: PublicAffairs /Perseus, 1999.

Beatriz Armendariz de Aghion and Jonathan Morduch, *The Economics of Microfinance,* Cambridge: MIT Press, 2005.

Stephen Smith, *Case Studies in Economic Development,* 2d Ed., Boston, MA: Addison-Wesley-Longman, 1997, ch 5.

"MFIs serve only 11 percent of the world's 240 million poorest families"; Sam Daley-Harris, et al., "State of the Microcredit Summit Campaign Report, 2002, available at: http://www.microcreditsummit.org/pubs/reports/socr/2002/socr02_en.pdf.

Abhijit V. Banerjee, Timothy Besley, and Timothy W. Guinnane, "Thy Neighbor's Keeper: The Design of a Credit Cooperative with Theory and a Test," *Quarterly Journal of Economics,* vol. 109, no. 2, May 1994: 491–515.

Jonathan Morduch, "The Microfinance Promise," *Journal of Economic Literature,* vol. 37, no. 4, Dec. 1999.

Marguerite S. Robinson, *The Microfinance Revolution: Sustainable Finance for the Poor,* Washington, DC: The World Bank, 2001.

Elisabeth H. Rhyne, *Mainstreaming Microfinance: How Lending to the Poor Began, Grew, and Came of Age in Bolivia,* Kumarian Press, 2001.

Maitreesh Ghatak and Timothy W. Guinnane, "The Economics of Lending with Joint Liability: A Review of Theory and Practice," *Journal of Development Economics,* vol. 60, no. 1, October 1999: 195–228.

Siwan Anderson and Jean-Marie Baland, "The Economics of ROSCAS and Intrahousehold Resource Allocation," *The Quarterly Journal of Economics,* vol. 117, no. 3, August 2002: 963–995.

Robert M. Townsend, "Risk and Insurance in Village India," *Econometrica,* vol. 62, no. 3 May 1994: 539–91.

Christopher Udry, "Risk and Saving in Northern Nigeria," *American Economic Review,* vol. 85, no. 5, December 1995: 1287–1300.

Access to functioning markets for income
and opportunities to acquire assets

Mozambique bureaucracy: 2002 World Bank *World Development Report,* New York:
Oxford University Press, 2002.

Land reform: Michael P. Todaro and Stephen C. Smith, *Economic Development,*
9th Edition, Reading, MA: Addison-Wesley, 2005, chap. 9.

Amartya Sen, *Development as Freedom,* New York: Knopf 1999

Abhijit V. Banerjee, Paul J. Gertler, and Maitreesh Ghatak, "Empowerment and Efficiency: Tenancy Reform in West Bengal," *Journal of Political Economy,* vol. 110,
April 2002: 239–280.

Timothy Besley and Robin Burgess, "Land Reform, Poverty Reduction, and
Growth: Evidence from India," *Quarterly Journal of Economics,* vol. 115, no. 2, May
2000: 389–430.

Access to the benefits of new technologies for higher productivity

For the uneven access and use of new technologies around the world, a map showing
the global distribution of technology innovators and adapters, as well as the technol-
ogy-excluded regions, is available in Jeffrey Sachs, "A New Map of the World," *Imag-
ining Tomorrow: Rethinking the Global Challenge,* Kamalesh Sharma, ed. reprinted
in *The Economist,* June 24, 2000, http://www.cid.harvard.edu/cidinthenews/articles/
Sachs_on_globalisation.htm.

Paolo Friere, *Pedagogy of the Oppressed,* New York: Seabury Press, 1970.

Useful information can be found at the websites of NGOs specializing in technology for poverty alleviation, in particular:

TechnoServe website: www.technoserve.org.

EnterpriseWorks: http://www.enterpriseworks.org/.org.

A non-degraded and stable environment
to ensure sustainable development

World Resources Institute, 2001 *World Resources Report,* Washington: World Resources Institute, 2001. This biannual report contains useful information on the environment and development.

World Bank, *World Development Report 2003, Sustainable Development in a Dynamic World: Transforming Institutions, Growth, and Quality of Life,* New York:
Oxford University Press, 2003.

Jan Vandemoortele, "The MDGs and Requirements for Pro-Poor Policies," presented at the Conference on the Role of NGOs in Achieving the Millennium Development Goals, Washington, DC: George Washington University, May 12–13, 2004.

Stephen C. Smith, *Case Studies in Economic Development,* 2nd Ed., Boston: Addison-Wesley-Longman, 1997, chaps. 11, 12.

Paul Seabright, Managing Local Commons: Theoretical Issues in Incentive Design," *Journal of Economic Perspectives,* vol. 7, Fall 1993: 113–34.

John Clark, cited by Jennifer Brinkerhoff, *Partnership for International Development: Rhetoric or Results,* Boulder, CO: Lynne Reiner, 2002.

Robin Broad and John Cavanagh, *Plundering Paradise: The Struggle for the Environment in the Philippines,* Berkeley: University of California Press, 1994.

Phillip J. Cooper and Claudia Maria Vargas, *Implementing Sustainable Development:
From Global Policy to Local Action,* Lantham MD: Rowman and Littlefield (2004).

Kibera, Nairobi, Kenya, discussed on UN-Habitat webpage, http://www.unhabitat.org.

Personal empowerment to gain
freedom from exploitation and torment

Kevin Bales, *Disposable People: New Slavery in the Global Economy,* Berkeley: University of California Press, 2000.

Vikram Patel, et al., "Depression in Developing Countries: Lessons from Zimbabwe," *British Medical Journal,* no. 322, 2001: 482–4.

Vikram Patel, "Poverty, Inequality and Mental Health in Developing Countries," in David Leon and Gill Walt, eds., *Poverty, Inequality and Health: An International Perspective,* Oxford, UK: Oxford University Press, 2000.

Community empowerment to ensure
effective participation in the wider world

Rosabeth Moss Kanter: *On the Frontiers of Management,* Boston, MA: Harvard Business Review Book, 1997. See especially Part IV, pp. 131–32, and her chapter on "Power failure in management circuits," pp. 135–157.

"All too often poor people report experiencing law and law enforcement not as a means to a better life, but as obstacles." *Voices of the Poor: Crying out for Change* and *Voices of the Poor: From Many Lands* New York: Oxford University Press for the World Bank, 2000, p. 54.

John Clark: cited by Jennifer Brinkerhoff, *Partnership for International Development: Rhetoric or Results,* Boulder, CO: Lynne Reiner, 2002.

PART II. ESCAPING THE CRUEL TRAP OF POVERTY:
HOW THE POOR ARE GAINING THE KEYS TO CAPABILITY

How the Programs Featured in the Book Were Selected

Identification of exemplary programs relies on a combination of rigorous statistical and qualitative case study methods tempered by judgment. Although chosen with care, for every program covered there are very many others that are at least as good. I have attempted to identify effective strategies and programs that get the most leverage for the greatest number in breaking out of various kinds of poverty traps. Each selected program had to clearly help develop one of the eight keys to capability and assist families in sustainably escaping from poverty. Within these strategies, I try to feature highly effective programs, which demonstrate organizational tactics for getting the most sustainable benefits of the strategy for the fewest costs. In addition, I try to feature particularly promising recent innovations. The selection process is still experimental and subject to qualification. I used a combination of quantitative and qualitative screens.

A first major screen for programs included in the book is the existence of rigorous research, mainly but not only using randomized trial methods, published in peer-review journals, and showing substantial positive impact. These were identified through standard database searches, including EconLit and ProQuest. The list was augmented by a search for working papers reporting on impact studies meeting rigorous methodological standards, and currently in the peer review process, or forthcoming in refereed journals. In some cases, active studies were identified through expert interviews.

A second screen is the winning of juried prizes awarded to poverty programs (in the broad sense of this book), including the UN Equator Prize, World Habitat Award, World Bank Development Marketplace awards, the Belgium-based King Baudouin International Development Prize, the Global Development Network (GDN) Japan Award for Most Innovative Development Project, and the Pro-Poor Innovation Challenge Award sponsored by the Consultative Group to Assist the Poorest (CGAP). It is possible that "political" considerations influence selections, so such awards should be appraised with caution.

The third selection process began with a set of preliminary choices of NGOs based on existing ratings systems, augmented with a review of available program evaluations and recommendations by specialists. For a U.S.-based PVO/NGO to be selected as a candidate program sponsor, it had to score at minimum levels on major rating agencies' key criteria. I required the organization to meet the Council of Better Business Bureaus (CBBB) Standards for Charitable Solicitations, described at http://www.give.org/standards/cbbbstds.asp. I required a grade of B or better from the American Institute of Philanthropy (AIP) Charity Rating Guide & Watchdog Report. A number of charities were added to this initial list as a result of high ratings from other published charity reports.

The result was a list of 27 U.S.-based international NGOs for initial consideration. I then interviewed the chief of evaluation (or closest equivalent position) of each selected NGO who agreed to participate. I asked them to identify highly effective poverty programs within their field of expertise not only of their own organization, but also of peer NGOs. I placed high weight on the frequency of citations of programs of other organizations by their peers. The method was designed to be roughly analogous to that used in the U.S. National Academy of Sciences rankings of academic departments, which are based on interviews and questionnaires of key authorities in the relevant fields. Many of the interviews were conducted in person, others by phone, and a few by e-mail. Some refused to consent to the interview, or to identify a position equivalent to (or supervising equivalent tasks as) a director of evaluation, or to reply to inquiries, and these NGOs were dropped from the study.

Additional U.S. and Europe-based organizations not on the initial list were interviewed on the basis of a concentration of such citations. In addition, many of the developing country-based NGOs included in the book were cited by U.S.-based NGOs in the interviews, though most passed other screens as well. I want to underline the caveats: First, I viewed these experimental interviews as a pre-test for a full-scale study I hope to undertake in coming years; ideally, many other analysts will also take up this general approach. Second, an apparent tendency for interviewees to name well-known organizations is a potential concern. Third, an effective organization is not the same as an effective program. This is a search for promising programs, with the next step being to convince organizations identified by qualitative screens to participate in randomization studies of these programs—but that is for further research. As a result, the interview-based selection strategy is not a verified, let along rigorous, indicator of effectiveness in itself.

Some programs that met my criteria were not included in the book, for reasons of space, to avoid including too many programs that were too similar to each other, or simply for lack of time and resources to investigate them adequately.

For background on program evaluation see:

Martin Ravallion, "The Mystery of the Vanishing Benefits: An Introduction to Impact Evaluation," *World Bank Economic Review,* vol. 15, no. 1, 2001: 115–140.

World Bank, *Evaluation and Poverty Reduction: Proceedings from a World Bank Conference,* Washington, DC: World Bank 2000: 193–203.

Michael Kremer, "Randomized Evaluations of Educational Programs in Developing Countries: Some Lessons." *American Economic Review Papers and Proceedings.* vol. 93, no.2, May 2003: 102–106.

Judy Baker, *Evaluating the Impact of Development Projects on Poverty: A Handbook for Practitioners,* World Bank, 2000, http://poverty.worldbank.org/library/view/3376/.

Gary Burtless, "The Case for Randomized Field Trials in Economic and Policy Research," *Journal of Economic Perspectives,* vol. 9, no. 2, 1995: 63–84.

James J. Heckman and Jeffrey A. Smith, "Assessing the Case for Social Experiments," *Journal of Economic Perspectives,* vol. 9, no. 2, 1995: 85–110.

John Newman, Laura Rawlings, and Paul Gertler, "Using Randomized Control Designs in Evaluating Social Sector Programs in Developing Countries," *The World Bank Research Observer,* vol. 9, no. 2, 1994: 181–201.

G. Prennushi, G. Rubio, and K. Subbarao, "Monitoring and Evaluation," in World Bank, *A Sourcebook for Poverty Reduction Strategies,* Washington, DC: World Bank, 2000.

For a survey on participatory evaluation see, Edward T. Jackson, "The Front-End Costs and Downstream Benefits of Participatory Evaluation," in O. Feinstein and R. Picciotto, eds., *Evaluation and Poverty Reduction: Proceedings from a World Bank Conference.* Operations Evaluation Department, Washington, DC: World Bank, 2000: 115–26.

Several important randomization experiments are currently being conducted by Poverty Action Lab, at www.povertyactionlab.org and by Dean Karlan at www.wws.princeton.edu/~dkarlan.

CHAPTER 3. HEALTH, NUTRITION, AND POPULATION

On South Africa's Roundabout Outdoor Playpump (Merrygoround), see the Roundabout website at roundaboutoutdoor.org and http://www.roundabout.co.za/main.htm.

For further information, see World Bank Human Development Findings 218 Nov. 2002, http://www.worldbank.org/afr/findings/english/find218.pdf.

Also see http://www.changemakers.net/journal/03july/roundabout.cfm.

TASO: Stephen C. Smith, *Case Studies in Economic Development* (New York: Longman, 1993). TASO now has a website at http://www.tasouganda.org/.

CARE in Ethiopia. For further details see Marcie Rubardt, "CARE International's Community-Based Distribution Program in Eastern Ethiopia Increases Contraceptive Use," NGO Networks for Health, *At A Glance,* no. 8, December 2002, http://www.dec.org/pdf_docs/PNACS821.pdf. Note that in this case the evaluation was not sufficiently rigorous to attribute the reported gains entirely to the program. Also draws on interviews and CARE-Ethiopia, "Project Progress to Date: Major Achievements of the Project (February 2002–September 2004)."

International Christelijk Steunfonds Africa (ICS). See ICS, *Primary School Deworming Programme Evaluation Findings,* Nairobi: ICS, n.d.

Details on the impact of deworming are found in Michael Kremer and Edward Miguel, "Worms: Identifying Impacts on Education and Health in the Presence of Treatment Externalities," *Econometrica,* vol. 72, no. 1, January 2004: 159–217.

Michael Kremer and Edward Miguel, "The Illusion of Sustainability," *National Bureau of Economic Research Working Paper 10324,* Cambridge, MA: NBER, February 2004.

Cost of treatment: Partnership for Child Development, "The Cost of Large-Scale School Health Programs which Deliver Anthelmintics in Ghana and Tanzania, *Acta Tropica,* vol. 73, 1999: 183–204, cited in Kremer and Miguel, *Worms.*

Surge in enrollments with above-age students: *New York Times,* April 4, 2004, p. A01. See also "Free Primary Education and Poverty Reduction: The Case of Kenya, Lesotho, Malawi and Uganda," from the Scaling Up Poverty Reduction: A Global Learning Process, and Conference in Shanghai, May 25–27, 2004, available at http://www.worldbank.org/wbi/reducingpoverty/docs/FullCases/PDFs%2011–13–04/East%20Africa%20univ%20primary%20ed.pdf.

John Strauss and Duncan Thomas, "Health, Nutrition, and Economic Development," *Journal of Economic Literature,* vol. 36, 1998: 766–817.

Partha Dasgupta, "The Population Problem: Theory and Evidence," *Journal of Economic Literature,* vol. 33, no. 4, December 1995: 1879–1902.

Lant Pritchett, "Desired Fertility and the Impact of Population Policies," *Population and Development Review,* vol. 20, no. 1, March 1994.

CHAPTER 4. BASIC EDUCATION

Pratham's Accelerated and Computer-Assisted Primary Learning in India

Abhijit Banerjee, Shawn Cole, Esther Duflo, and Leigh Linden. "Remedying Education: Evidence from Two Randomized Experiments in India," Poverty Action Lab Paper No. 4, Cambridge, MA: MIT, September 17, 2003, available at http://econ-www.mit.edu/faculty/download_pdf.php?id=677 or http://www.povertyaction-lab.com/papers/banerjee_cole_duflo_linden.pdf.

Abhijit Banerjee, Esther Duflo and Leigh Linden. "Computer-Assisted Learning: Evidence from A Randomized Experiment," Poverty Action Lab Paper No. 5, Cambridge, MA: MIT, October, 2003 http://www.povertyactionlab.com/papers/banerjee_duflo_linden.pdf.

Information on ICICI Bank, which is also involved with microfinance activities, can be found at: http://www.icicibank.com/pfsuser/aboutus/overview/overview.htm.

No impact was found on language skills, perhaps understandable since these were math games, but nevertheless disappointing in that no "spillovers" from the program to interest in school and learning more generally seemed to have been found. Perhaps in the future the program can introduce other games that build language skills as well.

Pathways out of Poverty:
Progresa, Southern Mexico

Secretaría de Desarrollo Social (SEDESOL), Government of Mexico, Programa de Educación, Salud, y Alimentación (PROGRESA), 2001, http://www.progresa.gob.mx.

John Hoddinott and Emmanuel Skoufias, "Preliminary Evidence on the Impact of PROGRESA on Consumption," paper presented at the American Economic Association annual meetings, New Orleans, January 2001.

T. Paul Schultz, The Impact of PROGRESA on School Enrollment, paper presented at the American Economic Association annual meetings, New Orleans, January 2001.

John Hoddinott and Jere R. Behrman, "Program Evaluation with Unobserved Heterogeneity, Selective Implementation and Imperfectly Targeted Beneficiaries: The Mexican PROGRESA Impact on Child Nutrition," paper presented at the Northeast Universities Development Conference, Boston University, September 2001.

Emmanuel Skoufias and Susan W. Parker, with comments by Jere R. Behrman, and Carola Pessino, "Conditional Cash Transfers and Their Impact on Child Work and Schooling: Evidence from the PROGRESA Program in Mexico," *Economia: Journal of the Latin American and Caribbean Economic Association*, vol. 2, no. 1, Fall 2001.

Emmanuel Skoufias, Benjamin Davis, and Sergio de la Vega, "Targeting the Poor in Mexico: An Evaluation of the Selection of Households into PROGRESA," *World Development* vol. 29, no. 10, October 2001: 1769–84.

Emmanuel Skoufias and Bonnie McClafferty, "Is PROGRESA Working? Summary of the Results of an Evaluation by IFPRI," http://www.ifpri.org/themes/progresa/synthesis.htm.

Evelyne Rodriguez, "Some Notes on Changing Social Policy: Mexico's Experience," World Bank Safety Net Primer Launch, December 2003, http://www.worldbank.org/wbi/socialsafetynets/courses/dc2003/pdfppt/rodriguez.pdf

Jere Behrman, Piyali Sengupta, and Petra Todd, "Progressing through PROGRESA: An Impact Assessment of a School Subsidy Experiment," http://www.ifpri.org/themes/progresa/education.htm.

BRAC's Nonformal Primary Education Solution

BRAC's webpage provides useful information on their schools at: http://www.brac.net/edf.htm.

John Quelch and Nathalie Laidler, *BRAC*, Harvard Business School Case Study, Boston: HBS, July 2003.

Catherine H. Lovell, *Breaking the Cycle of Poverty: The BRAC Strategy*, West Hartford: Kumarian Press, 1992.

Shahidur R. Khandker, Baqui Khalily, *The Bangladesh Rural Advancement Committee's Credit Programs: Performance and Sustainability*, Washington, D.C.: World Bank, 1996.

Sidebar: When Education Reform is Less than Meets the Eye

More on Poverty Reduction Strategy Papers (PRSPs), including Uganda's PEAP, can be found at: http://www.imf.org/external/np/prsp/prsp.asp or http://poverty.worldbank.org/prsp/.

World Bank three-year review of PRSPs: Poverty Reduction Strategy Papers—Progress in Implementation, http://www.worldbank.org/poverty/strategies/progrep.htm.

Christian Aid, "Ignoring the Experts: Poor people's exclusion from poverty reduction strategies," http://www.christian-aid.org.uk/indepth/0110prsp/prsp.htm.

Nancy Alexander, "PRSPs and the Vision Problems of the International Financial Institutions," Washington, DC, Citizens' Network on Essential Services, January 2004.

A recent and positive assessment of the UPE impact can be found at "Free Primary Education and Poverty Reduction: The Case of Kenya, Lesotho, Malawi and Uganda," from the Scaling Up Poverty Reduction: A Global Learning Process, and Conference in Shanghai, May 25–27, 2004, available at http://www.worldbank.org/

wbi/reducingpoverty/docs/FullCases/PDFs%2011–13–04/East%20Africa%20univ
%20primary%20ed.pdf.

IMF video: Uganda—A Different Drummer: http://www.imf.org/external/mmedia/
view1.asp?eventId=54&file=1.

NGOs such as Alternative Information and Development Centre, Third World
Network, and Africa Action have long criticized the impact they observe of "cost-re-
covery" programs, often part of Structural Adjustment packages, on children's health
and education status in Africa.

Ritva Reinikka and Jakob Svensson, "Local Capture: Evidence from a Central
Government Transfer Program in Uganda," *Quarterly Journal of Economics*, May
2004: 679.

Giving Children a CHANCE:
Save the Children's Nonformal Primary Schools in Uganda

Save the Children: http://www.savethechildren.org/. Uganda programs: http://www.
savethechildren.org/countries/africa/uganda.asp.

Heather Greer, *Strong Beginnings: The Making of a Village School*, STC, Education office, n.d.

Yolande Miller Grandvaux and Karla Yoder, *A Literature Review of Community
Schools in Africa*, Washington DC: USAID, Bureau for Africa, Office of Sustainable
Development, 2002.

CHAPTER 5. GIVING CREDIT FOR POVERTY REDUCTION, AND INSURING OPPORTUNITY

Sam Daley-Harris, State of the Microcredit Summit Campaign Report, http://www.
microcreditsummit.org/pubs/reports/socr/2002/socr02_en.pdf, 2002.

Jonathan Morduch, "The Microfinance Promise," *Journal of Economic Literature*, vol. 37, no. 4, December 1999.

Maitreesh Ghatak and Timothy W. Guinnane, "The Economics of Lending with
Joint Liability: A Review of Theory and Practice," *Journal of Development Economics*, vol. 60, no. 1, October 1999: 195–228.

Beatriz Armendriz de Aghion and Jonathan Morduch, *The Economics of Microfinance*, Cambridge, MA: MIT Press, 2005.

Monique Cohen, "Evaluating Microfinance's Impact: Going Down Market," *Evaluation and Poverty Reduction: Proceedings from a World Bank Conference*, Washington, DC: World Bank 2000: 193–203.

Marguerite S. Robinson, *The Microfinance Revolution: Sustainable Finance for
the Poor*, Washington, DC: The World Bank, 2001.

Making Credit Institutions People-worthy:
The Grameen Bank of Bangladesh

Grameen website: http://www.grameen-info.org/.

Stephen C. Smith, *Case Studies in Economic Development*, 2d edition, Reading,
MA: Addison-Wesley-Longman, 1997, chap. 5.

Mohammad Yunus, *Banker to the Poor: Micro Lending and the Battle Against
World Poverty*, New York: PublicAffairs/Perseus, 1999.

Muhammad Yunus, *Grameen II,* Pamphlet, Dhaka, Bangladesh: Grameen Bank, 2001.

Daniel Pearl, "Grameen Bank, Which Pioneered Loans For the Poor, Has Hit a Repayment Snag," *Wall Street Journal,* November 27, 2001. Available at http://online.wsj.com/public/resources/documents/pearl112701.htm.

Building and Social Housing Foundation, *Presentation of the World Habitat Awards, World Habitat Day 1998,* Dubai, UAE, Leicestershire, UK: Building and Social Housing Foundation, 1998.

Banking on the Village: FINCA in Uganda

FINCA website: http://villagebanking.org/.

On commercialization of MFIs: Robert Peck Christen and Deborah Drake, *Commercialization: The New Reality of Microfinance?* West Hartford, CT: Kumarian, 2002; Elisabeth H. Rhyne, *Mainstreaming Microfinance: How Lending to the Poor Began, Grew, and Came of Age in Bolivia,* Kumarian Press, 2001.

Integrating Credit with Health: Project Hope, Ecuador

Stephen C. Smith, "Village Banking and Maternal and Child Health: Evidence from Ecuador and Honduras," *World Development,* vol. 30, no. 4, April 2002: 707–723.

Project Hope, "Project Hope's Village Banking and Income Generation Project," Millwood, VA: Project Hope, 1994.

Project Hope, website: http://www.projecthope.org/.

Rosalia Rodriguez-Garcia, James Macinko, and William Waters, eds., *Microenterprise Development for Better Health Outcomes,* in Contributions to Economics and Economic History, Westport, CT: Greenwood, 2001.

The Model T of Microfinance: The ASA Alternative

Daniel Pearl, "Grameen Bank, Which Pioneered Loans For the Poor, Has Hit a Repayment Snag," *Wall Street Journal,* November 27, 2001.

Nimal A. Fernando and Richard L. Meyer, "ASA—The Ford Motor Model of Microfinance," *Finance for the Poor,* Manila: Asian Development Bank, vol. 3, no. 3, June 2003.

Mostaq Ahmmed, *Key to Achieving Sustainability: Simple and Standard Microfinance Services of ASA,* Dhaka, Bangladesh: Prominent Printers, 2002.

Sidebar: Insurance against Poverty

Stefan Dercon, ed., *Insurance against Poverty,* New York: Oxford University Press, 2004.

World Bank's activities in the insurance field: http://web.worldbank.org/WBSITE/EXTERNAL/NEWS/0,contentMDK:20125678~menuPK:34457~pagePK:34370~piPK:34424~theSitePK:4607,00.html

Food for Work Program, Bangladesh: Stephen C. Smith, *Case Studies in Economic Development,* 2d Edition, Reading, MA: Addison-Wesley-Longman, 1997, chapter 7.

Emanuela Galasso, Martin Ravallion, and Agustin Salvia, "Assisting the Transition from Workfare to Work: Argentina's Proempleo Experiment," World Bank Development Economics Research Group, Washington, DC: World Bank, see also http://

poverty.worldbank.org/files/11255_Martin-PROEMPLEO-Evaluation.pdf and http://
www.microfinancegateway.org/microinsurance/provide_long.htm#a

Timothy J. Besley and Stephen Coate, "Workfare versus Welfare: Incentive Arguments for Work Requirements in Poverty Alleviation Programs," *American Economic
Review,* vol. 82, 1992: 249–261.

CHAPTER 6. BOTTOM-UP MARKET DEVELOPMENT:
ASSETS AND ACCESS FOR THE POOR

Frontiers of Poverty Reduction:
BRAC's Targeting the Ultrapoor Program

Imran Matin, *Stories of Targeting: The BRAC Targeting the Ultrapoor Program,*
BRAC Research and Evaluation Division report, Dhaka, Bangladesh: BRAC, 2003.

Imran Matin and David Hulme, "Programs for the Poorest: Learning from the
IGVGD Program in Bangladesh," *World Development,* vol. 31, no. 3, March 2003:
647–65.

Quotes from BRAC founder Fazle Hasan Abed are from author interviews conducted in Dhaka in September 2003.

Several recent internal studies of the TUP program are useful references: "Towards
a Profile of the Ultra Poor in Bangladesh: Findings from CFPR/TUP Baseline Survey"
(2004); "Combining Methodologies for Better Targeting of the Extreme Poor: Lessons
from BRAC's CFPR/TUP Programme" (2004); "Exploring Changes in the Lives of the
Ultra Poor: An Exploratory Study on CFPR/TUP Members" (2004); "Engaging Elite
Support for the Poorest: BRAC's Experience with the Ultra Poor Programme" (2004).
These and other studies are available online from http://www.eldis.org/.

John Quelch and Nathalie Laidler, *BRAC,* Harvard Business School Case Study,
July 2003.

BRAC, *Briefing on BRAC Health Program,* Dhaka: BRAC, 2003.

Creating Markets the Poor Need while Funding Poverty Alleviation:
BRAC Enterprises

Most of the information on BRAC Enterprises is drawn from field interviews.

John Quelch and Nathalie Laidler, *The BRAC and Aarong Commercial Brands,*
Harvard Business School Case Study, Boston: HBS, July 2003.

Shahidur R. Khandker and Baqui Khalily, *The Bangladesh Rural Advancement
Committee's Credit Programs: Performance and Sustainability,* Washington, DC:
World Bank, 1996.

On the value of growth for the poor in most cases, see David Dollar and Aart
Kraay, "Growth Is Good for the Poor," *Journal of Economic Growth,* vol. 7, no. 3,
September 2002: 195–225.

Public Service:
Self-Employed Women's Association (SEWA) in India

You can read about Self-Employed Women's Association (SEWA) at their website.
http://sewa.org/, and http://sewa.org/aboutus/index.htm.

For further background, see John Blaxall, "India's Self-Employed Women's Association (SEWA): Empowerment through Mobilization of Poor Women on a Large

Scale," presented at the World Bank conference on Scaling Up Poverty Reduction, Shanghai May 25–27, 2004, available at http://www.worldbank.org/wbi/reducing-poverty/docs/FullCases/India%20PDF/India%20SEWA.pdf.

Cooperation at Work: KDB in Kerala, India

On the role of cooperatives, see Johnston Birchall, *The Role of Cooperatives in Achieving the Millennium Development Goals,* Geneva: United Nations-International Labor Organization, 2004.

The story of KDB is beautifully told by T. M. Thomas Isaac, Richard W. Franke, and Pyaralal Raghavan, *Democracy at Work in an Indian Industrial Cooperative. The Story of Kerala Dinesh Beedi,* Ithaca, NY: ILR Press, 2000. I also draw from:

Gaurang Mitu Gulati, T. M. Thomas Isaac, and William A. Klein, "When a Workers' Cooperative Works: The Case of Kerala Dinesh Beedi," *UCLA Law Review* vol. 49, 2002: 1417.

Sumit Joshi and Stephen C. Smith, "An Endogenous Group Formation Theory of Cooperatives and Cooperative Networks," George Washington University Discussion Paper, Washington DC, George Washington University, October 2004.

Stephen C. Smith, "Network Externalities and Co-operative Networks: Stylized Facts and Theory," chapter 7 of *Ownership and Governance of Enterprises,* Laixiang Sun, ed., New York: Palgrave/Macmillan, 2003.

Stephen C. Smith, "Network Externalities and Co-operative Networks: A Comparative Case Study of Mondragon and La Lega With Implications for Developing and Transition Countries," chapter 8 of *Ownership and Governance of Enterprises,* Laixiang Sun, ed., New York: Palgrave/Macmillan, 2003.

CHAPTER 7. ACCESS TO NEW TECHNOLOGIES AND THE SKILLS TO USE AND BENEFIT FROM THEM

Job One—Providing the Tools to Create Stable Jobs: The Small Enterprise Assistance Fund

For more information on SEAF see http://www.seaf.com.

Small Enterprise Assistance Fund, *The Development Impact of Small and Medium Enterprises,* Washington, DC: SEAF, 2003.

Victoria Kids has a U.S. website at http://www.victoriakids.com/. SWMS can be found on the web at http://www.swms-sac.com/.

A Worthwhile Endeavor

The website for Endeavor may be found at: http://www.endeavor.org/

Grameen's Phone Ladies: Fighting Poverty with Telecom and Computing in Bangladesh

Information on Grameen's phone ladies was drawn from interviews. Other information comes from a World Bank short case study on the phone ladies, Subhash Bhatnager, Anikita Dervan, Magui Moreno Torres, and Parameeta Kanungo, "Grameen Telecom: The Village Phone Program," available at http://poverty.worldbank.org/files/14648_Grameen-web.pdf.

See also Grameen Telecom's website at: http://www.grameen-info.org/grameen/gtelecom/index.html.

Technology with a Subtext: Music Videos
Subtitling in Village Television in India

For more information see http://web.worldbank.org/WBSITE/EXTERNAL/NEWS/ 0,contentMDK:20135702~menuPK:141310~pagePK:36880~piPK:141922~theSite PK:4607,00.html, or http://web.worldbank.org/WBSITE/EXTERNAL/OPPORTUNI-TIES/GRANTS/DEVMARKETPLACE/0,contentMDK:20100393~menuPK:214469~ pagePK:180691~piPK:174492~theSitePK:205098,00.html.

Peas in a Pod—Better Products and Better Marketing:
TechnoServe and Partners in Tanzania

Most of the information on TechnoServe is drawn from field interviews. Other information comes from the TechnoServe website: www.technoserve.org.

Information on the International Crops Research Institute for the Semi-Arid Tropics ICRISAT can be found at www.icrisat.org/.

Also see the websites for Catholic Relief Services, at http://www.catholicrelief.org/ and Lutheran World Relief, at http://www.lwr.org/.

CHAPTER 8. SUSTAINING THE ENVIRONMENT OF THE POOR
Honey Care and Africa Now in Kenya

Most of the information presented on Honey Care and Africa Now is drawn from field interviews.

Africa Now, *New Beekeeping Opportunities for Small Holder Farmers,* Kisumu, Kenya: Africa Now, n.d.

For more on programs to introduce basic oil seed technology, see e.g., Tristi Nichols, "End-of-Term Evaluaton, Manica Oil Seed Food Security Initiative," Washington, DC: Africare; and see EnterpriseWorks: http://www.enterpriseworks.org/.

Another leasing activity, in Uganda, is described at http://www.basis.wisc.edu/live/ rfc/cs_09c.pdf.

Sustaining the Forest Life: Suledo Forest Community, Tanzania

Hakan Sjoholm and Shabani Luono, "The Green Forest Pastures of Suledo: Maasai Communities Organize to Save the Forests and Secure their Livelihoods, *Forests Trees and People Newsletter,* no. 46, September 2002.

Consultancy Report, "Supporting the Suledo Forest Community to Secure their Rights to Village Land," mimeo, n.d.

Field interviews, July 2003.

Preserving Forests and Livelihoods in Costa Rica

You can find FUNDECOR on the web at http://www.fundecor.org.

For more on the King Baudouin Foundation International Development Prize see http://www.kbprize.org/english/prize/prize.htm.

Gram Vikas Rural Health and Environment Program, India

The Gram Vikas website is found at http://www.gramvikas.org/.

Food Security and a Greener Urban Environment: Heifer International in the Lima Slums

Field interviews, April 2003.

Heifer International Peru, *Agricultura Ecologica en el Medio y Bajo Piura: Una Alternativea de Desarrollo Sostenible,* Lima: Heifer International Peru, 2003.

Heifer program information can be found on their website at http://heifer.org/.

CHAPTER 9. DIGNITY AND EMPOWERMENT FOR THE POOR AND VOICELESS

Bidding Poverty ADEW: The innovative campaigns of ADEW in Egypt

ADEW's website is: http://www.adew.org/

Association for the Development and Enhancement of Women, *To Be or Not to Be: Egyptian Women's Legal Existence,* pamphlet, Cairo, Egypt: ADEW, n.d.

Association for the Development and Enhancement of Women, *Women Are Full Citizens Too,* pamphlet, Cairo, Egypt: ADEW, n.d.

Association for the Development and Enhancement of Women, *Marginalized Women in the Spotlight,* pamphlet, Cairo, Egypt: ADEW, n.d.

Field visits conducted in June 2002.

Lifeline: The Child Helpline, India

Child Helpline's website is: http://www.childlincindia.org.in/aboutus08.htm.

Jeroo Billimoria's work is also described in David Bornstein, *How to Change the World. Social Entrepreneurs and the Power of New Idea,* New York: Oxford University Press, 2004.

For more on the Helpline franchise approach see http://www.citizenbase.org/cstudies/partnerships.html.

Sidebar: Human Rights for the Poor in Cambodia

LICADHO website is found at: http://www.licadho.org/

The Bridges to Justice webpage is found at: http://www.ibj.org/.

BRAC Legal Education and Group Action in Rural Bangladesh

In addition to materials on BRAC cited earlier, see BRAC's webpage on activities related to legal training at: http://www.brac.net/edp_main.html.

Human Rights Center, Chiapas Mexico

The English language version of the HRC webpage, Fray Bartolomé de Las Casas, A.C., is now available at http://www.laneta.apc.org/cdhbcasas/Ingles/.

See also, "The War of Attrition in Chiapas," *Human Rights Brief,* vol. 7, no. 3, available at http://www.wcl.american.edu/hrbrief/07/3thewar.cfm.

For recent accounts of cases examined by HRC, see http://www.laneta.apc.org/cdhbcasas/Ingles.

Enlace Civil, "Intensification of the War Climate in Chiapas," Press Communique, August 27, 2002, http://www.globalexchange.org/countries/mexico/chiapas/334.html.

CHAPTER 10. COMMUNITY EMPOWERMENT AND DEVELOPMENT

Women's Voices Make a Difference: An Experiment in West Bengal, India

Esther Duflo and Raghabendra Chattopadhyay, "Women as Policy Makers: Evidence from a Randomized Policy Experiment in India," *Econometrica,* vol. 72, no. 5, September 2004: 1409–43.

Professor Duflo has posted some interesting follow-up papers on her website: http://econ-www.mit.edu/faculty.

Sidebar: Empowerment is Electrifying— Possibilities of Rural Electrification

The photo of the earth at night can be seen at http://antwrp.gsfc.nasa.gov/apod/ap001127.html. It is also on the cover of Michael P. Todaro and Stephen C. Smith, *Economic Development,* 8th Edition, 2002, Reading, MA: Addison-Wesley.

For an example of a study of the impact of electrification, which unfortunately suffers from many of the methodological flaws common in such studies, see *Economic and Social Impact Evaluation Study of the Bangladesh Rural Electrification Program,* http://www.sari-energy.org/REBImpact.html.

Muhammad Yunus, *Information Technology to Eliminate Global Poverty,* Dhaka: Grameen Bank, 2002.

Grameen Shakti, *Promotion and Development of Renewable Energy Resources,* Dhaka: Grameen Shakti, n.d.

World Vision: Community Development in Peru

The World Vision website may be found at http://www.wvi.org/wvi/home.htm.

World Vision Peru, *Nuestras Mejores Practicas,* Lima: World Vision, 2001.

Sidebar: Entitled to Progress— Benefits of Titling to Squatters

Hernando de Soto, *The Other Path: The Economic Answer to Terrorism,* New York: Basic Books, 1989.

Jean Lanjouw and Philip I. Levy, "Untitled: A Study of Formal and Informal Property Rights in Urban Ecuador," *Economic Journal,* vol. 112, no. 482, October 2002: 986–1019.

Erica Field, "Entitled to Work: Urban Property Rights and Labor Supply in Peru," unpublished working paper, Department of Economics, Princeton University, Princeton, NJ: Princeton University, 2002.

Fernando Cantuarias and Miguel Delgado, "Peru's Urban Land Titling Program," presented at the World Bank conference on Scaling Up Poverty Reduction, Shanghai May 25–27, 2004, available at http://www.worldbank.org/wbi/reducingpoverty/docs/FullCases/LAC%20PDF/Peru%20Land%20Titling.pdf.

Preference for formal sector, steady jobs: Guy Pfefferman and Gary Fields, *Pathways out of Poverty,* Norwell: Kluwer Academic, 2003, page 5.

Land reform: Michael P. Todaro and Stephen C. Smith, *Economic Development,* 9th Edition, Reading, MA: Addison-Wesley, 2005, chap. 10.

Abhijit V. Banerjee, Paul J. Gertler, and Maitreesh Ghatak, "Empowerment and Efficiency: Tenancy Reform in West Bengal," *Journal of Political Economy*, vol. 110, April 2002: 239–280.

Timothy Besley and Robin Burgess, "Land Reform, Poverty Reduction, and Growth: Evidence from India," *Quarterly Journal of Economics*, vol. 115, no. 2, May 2000: 389–430.

Ajitava Raychaudhuri, "India: Lessons from the Land Reform Movement in West Bengal," presented at the World Bank conference on Scaling Up Poverty Reduction, Shanghai May 25–27, 2004, available at http://www.worldbank.org/wbi/reducing-poverty/docs/FullCases/India%20PDF/India%20West%20Bengal%20poverty.pdf.

Thomas C. Pinckney and Peter K. Kimuyu, "Land Tenure Reform in East Africa: Good, Bad, or Unimportant?" *Journal of African Economies*, vol. 3, 1994: 1–28.

Paul Collier and Jan Wellem Gunning, "Explaining African Economic Performance," *Journal of Economic Literature*, vol. 37, no. 1, 1999: 64–111.

Making Integrated Sustainable Development Work—
Africare in Uganda

Africare can be found on the web at Africare.org. The quote from Nelson Mandela is found on the Africare website.

Documents on evaluation are found at: http://63.220.11.81/icons/env/examples/africare.pdf.

CHAPTER 11. TEN STRATEGIES FOR INNOVATION IN ENDING GLOBAL POVERTY

On social entrepreneurship innovations see David Bornstein, *How to Change the World. Social Entrepreneurs and the Power of New Ideas*, New York: Oxford University Press, 2004.

PART III. WHAT YOU CAN DO TO HELP.
CHAPTER 12. FIRST STEPS
Learn More

On the nature of NGOs, Michael P. Todaro and Stephen C. Smith, *Economic Development*, 9th Edition, Reading, MA: Addison-Wesley, 2005, chapter 11, and Jennifer Brinkerhoff, Stephen C. Smith and Hildy Teegen, "Beyond the 'Non': The Strategic Space for NGOs in Development," conference on "The role of NGOs in Achieving the Millennium Development Goals," Washington DC: George Washington University, May 2004.

David Hulme and Michael Edwards NGOs, eds., *States and Donors: Too Close for Comfort?* New York: St. Martin's Press in Association with Save the Children Fund, 1997: 107–127.

Tim Brodhead, "NGOs: In One Year, Out the Other?" *World Development*. Ed. Anne Gordon Drabek, vol. 15 (Supplement 1987): 1–6.

Jonathan A. Fox and L. David Brown. *The Struggle for Accountability: The World Bank, NGOs and Grassroots Movements*. Cambridge, MA: MIT Press, 1998

Inge Kaul, "Global Public Goods: What Role for Civil Society?" *NonProfit and Voluntary Sector Quarterly,* vol. 30, no. 3 (2001): 588–602.

Marc Lindenberg and Coralie Bryant. *Going Global: Transforming Relief and Development NGOs.* Bloomfield, CT: Kumarian Press, 2002.

Lester M. Salamon, "The Rise of the Nonprofit Sector: A Global 'Associational Revolution'," *Foreign Affairs,* vol. 73, no. 4 (July 1999): 109–122.

Ann Florini, *The Coming Democracy: New Rules for Running a New World,* Island Press, 2003.

Bill Shore, *The Cathedral Within: Transforming your Life by Giving Something Back,* NY: Random House, 1999.

The Australia branches of World Vision and Oxfam Community Aid Abroad offer study tours, found respectively at http://www.worldvision.com.au/40HourFamine/study_tours.asp and http://www.caa.org.au/travel/.

The website for Heifer International tours is: http://www.heifer.org/get_involved/study_tours.htm.

Strategies for Giving

Contributing Wisely: Find Your Issue, Assess Your Talents

Council of Better Business Bureaus (CBBB) Wise Giving Alliance Standards for Charitable Solicitations: http://www.give.org/ standards/cbbbstds.asp.

American Institute of Philanthropy (AIP): http://www.charitywatch.org.

Charity Navigator: http://www.charitynavigator.org/index.cfm.

Independent Sector: http://www.independentsector.org/.

InterAction: http://www.interaction.org/.

Tracy Gary and Melissa Kohner, *Inspired Philanthropy: Your Step-by-Step Guide to Creating a Giving Plan* (San Francisco: Josse-Bass, 2002), offer a wealth of information and a number of useful exercises for helping you hone your giving plan. Highly recommended!

CHAPTER 13. FURTHER QUESTIONS

Lifestyle Changes: Would They Make Any Difference?

Howard D. Leathers, "The World Food Problem: It's All about Distribution (Isn't It?)," working paper, School of Agriculture, University of Maryland, 2003.

Should You Take Part in Child Sponsorship Programs?

InterAction describes its standards at: http://www.interaction.org/pvostandards/
Interviews with Ken Giunta, vice-president, InterAction.

Should You Focus on Relief Work or on Development?

International Rescue Committee: http://www.theirc.org/.

Should Development Assistance Be Provided by Multipurpose or Specialist Organizations?

Some of the basic issues particularly with respect to microfinance are raised in Stephen C. Smith, "Microcredit and Health Programs: To Integrate or Not to Integrate?" in Rosalia Rodriguez-Garcia, James Macinko and William Waters, eds., *Microenterprise Development for Better Health Outcomes* (in Contributions to Economics and Economic History), Westport, CT: Greenwood, 2001.

Protesting the International Financial Institutions: Does it Make Sense?

Meltzer Commission, *Report of the International Financial Institution Advisory Commission,* Washington, DC: U.S. Congress, 2000, available at http://www.house. gov/jec/imf/ifiac.htm.

For more on the debate over globalization, see Joseph Stiglitz, *Globalization and its Discontents* (New York: Norton, 2002); Stiglitz offers a skeptical appraisal of the impact of globalization, but ultimately finds a preponderance of benefits. Two recent pro-globalization books of note are Martin Wolf, *Why Globalization Works* (New Haven: Yale University Press, 2004); and Jagdish Bhagwati, *In Defense of Globalization* (New York: Oxford University Press, 2004). Critiques of globalization and its effects on poverty include John Cavanagh and Richard Barnet, *Global Dreams. Imperial Corporations and the New World Order* (New York: Simon and Schuster, 1994); and John Cavanagh, et al, *Alternatives to Economic Globalization* (San Francisco, CA: Berrett-Koehler 2002).

CHAPTER 14. STEPPING UP

Getting More Involved: Board and Advisory Group Membership

On the Carver policy governance model, see John Carver, *Boards That Make a Difference: A New Design for Leadership in Nonprofit and Public Organizations* (San Francisco: Jossey-Bass, 2nd edition, 1997). A very good short overview of the approach is found in John Carver and Miriam Carver, "Carver's Policy Governance Model in Nonprofit Organizations," available at http://www.carvergovernance.com/pg-np.htm.

Kim Wilson, *The Board Rules: Founding an MFI Board,* Baltimore: Catholic Relief Services, 2001.

David Korten's *The Post-Corporate World,* West Hartford: Kumarian Press 1999, offers suggestions for citizen involvement including through U.S. and developing country PVOs.

Invest with Poverty and Sustainable Development in Mind

Harris Interactive: http://www.harrisinteractive.com/expertise/reputation.asp.
Pax World Service: http://www.paxworld.org.
The Social Investment Forum: http://www.socialinvest.org.
Socially Responsible Investment Coalition: http://home.flash.net/~sric/.
Socialfunds.com: http://socialfunds.com.
U.K Social Investment Forum: http://www.uksif.org/J/Z/Z/jp/home/main/index.shtml). Canada Social Investment Organization website: http://www.socialinvestment.ca.

Partner Parishes and Faith-Based Initiatives

Catholic sister parishes: http://www.usccb.org/publishing/peace/service.htm.

Unitarian Universalist Association partner church council: http://www.uua.org/uupcc/.

David Beckmann and Art Simon, *Grace at the Table: Ending Hunger in God's World,* Paulist Press, 1999.

Religious and philosophical perspectives on working within organizations such as the World Bank to help end global poverty can be found in *Friday Morning Reflections at the World Bank* (Cabin John, MD: Seven Locks Press, 1991), including Christian, Muslim, Hindu, and humanist perspectives. Ismail Serageldin's essay, "The Justly Balanced Society: One Muslim's View," can be found in this collection.

Partner Clinics and Hospitals

A guide to volunteering in developing countries is found in James C. Cobey, *Guide to Volunteering Overseas* (Health Volunteers Overseas, 1997).

The HVO website is found at http://www.hvousa.org.

Photo of hospital sign published on *Lancet* website for the Jan. 3, 2004 issue.

Partner Clubs

The website for the Rotary International's polio eradication campaign is found at http://www.rotary.org/foundation/polioplus/.

Environmental Partnerships: Partnering NGOs

Sierra Club's "Beyond the Borders" program website is found at: http://www.sierraclub.org/beyondtheborders/.

The Climate Action Network's website is found at: http://www.climatenetwork.org/.

Dr. Richard Rice, Conservation International, interviews with author, June 2002, March 2003.

Sister Cities

For an introduction to sister cities programs, see http://www.sister-cities.org and http://www.unhabitat.org/press2000/documents/whd_sci.pdf

National and Multilateral Policy:
Making Your Voice Heard in the Corridors of Power

InterAction's website is found at: http://www.interaction.org.

Bread for the World's website is found at http://www.bread.org.

Jean Dreze and Amartya Sen, *Hunger and Public Action,* A UN-WIDER book, New York: Oxford University Press, 1989.

Robin Broad and John Cavanagh, *Plundering Paradise: The Struggle for the Environment in the Philippines,* Berkeley: University of California Press, 1994.

Jeffrey D. Sachs, "A New Global Consensus on Helping the Poorest of the Poor," speech delivered at the World Bank, Washington, DC, April 18, 1999. Sachs presented statistics from an earlier year on the per capita extent of U.S. aid that prompted me to calculate those presented in this section.

The Bush administration initiative on growth and poverty reduction in development countries, the Millennium Challenge Account (MCA), is run by the Millennium Challenge Corporation, and is found on the web at http://www.mca.gov/.

For some independent analyses of the MCA approach see:

Lael Brainard, Carol Graham, Steven Radelet, Nigel Purvis, and Gayle E. Smith, *The Other War: Global Poverty And The Millennium Challenge Account,* The Brookings Institution and the Center for Global Development, 2003.

Steve Radelet, Sarah Lucas, and Rikhil Bhavnani, "A Comment on the Millennium Challenge Account Selection Process," March 9, 2004, processed, Washington: CGD.

The Millennium Challenge Account: A New Vision for Development, InterAction, www.interaction.org/files.cgi/442_mcawhitepaper7.pdf.

Actively support international poverty reduction goals

United Nations Development Program, *Human Development Report 2003: Millennium Development Goals: A Compact Among Nations to End Human Poverty,* New York: Oxford University Press, 2003. http://hdr.undp.org/reports/global/2003/pdf/hdr03_complete.pdf.

"Little evidence that official aid has spurred growth": See William Easterly, *The Elusive Quest for Growth,* Cambridge, MA: MIT Press, 1999. For the January 2005 UN Millennium Project report, which was led by Jeffrey Sachs, *Investing in Development: A Practical Plan to achieve the Millennium Development Goals,* see http://www.unmillenniumproject.org.

Amartya Sen, *Development as Freedom,* New York: Alfred Knopf, 1999.

Nicholas Minot and Lisa Daniels, "Impact of Global Cotton Markets on Rural Poverty in Benin," Washington, DC: IFPRI Discussion Paper No. 48, November 2002: http://www.ifpri.org/divs/mtid/dp/mssdp48.htm.

The Oxfam International report, *Rigged Rules and Double Standards,* is found on the web at http://www.maketradefair.com/en/index.php?file=26032002105549.htm.

The Oxfam report on cotton subsidies, *Cultivating Poverty,* available at: http://www.oxfam.org/eng/pdfs/pp020925_cotton.pdf.

The Economist, "Special Report: The Cancun challenge"—World trade talks, *The Economist,* London, Sep. 6, 2003.

New York Times, "Harvesting Poverty," series found on the web at: nytimes.com/harvestingpoverty. The *New York Times* Editorial, "The Long Reach of King Cotton," published on August 5, 2003, page A14, is available at http://query.nytimes.com/gst/abstract.html?res=F20C1FFA355A0C768CDDA10894DB404482.

Warren Vieth, "U.S. Exports Misery to Africa With Farm Bill," *Los Angeles Times,* May 27, 2002.

Financial Times, "Sweet deals: 'Big Sugar' Fights Threats from Free Trade and a Global Drive to Limit Consumption." Feb 27, 2004.

Larger Volunteering Commitments and Career Avenues

The Peace Corps website can be found at http://www.peacecorps.gov.

Social Entrepreneurship

David Bornstein, *How to Change the World. Social Entrepreneurs and the Power of New Ideas,* New York: Oxford University Press, 2004.

Muhammad Yunus, *Halving Poverty by 2015: We Can Actually Make it Happen,* Commonwealth Lecture, 2003, Dhaka, Bangladesh: Grameen Bank, 2003.

Banker to the Poor, Micro Lending and the Battle Against World Poverty, New York: PublicAffairs/Perseus, 1999, is an interesting reflection by Mohammad Yunus, the Bangladeshi founder of the Grameen Bank, one of the organizations featured in *Ending Global Poverty.*

The Ashoka website can be found at: http://www.ashoka.org/home/index.cfm.
The Changemakers network sponsored by Ashoka can be found at http://www.changemakers.net/about.cfm.

Closer to Home: Poverty in America—a Brief Note

On recent U.S. poverty trends see Ceci Connolly and Griff Witte, "Poverty Rate Up 3rd Year In a Row; More Also Lack Health Coverage," *Washington Post*, Friday, August 27, 2004, Page A1.

The classic book on poverty within America is Michael Harrington's *The Other America* (New York: Penguin, 1962). An arresting participant-observer account of the plight of the working poor is Barbara Ehrenreich's *Nickel and Dimed: On (Not) Getting By in America* (New York: Metropolitan/Henry Holt, 2001).

What You Can Do to Help the Homeless, by Thomas Kenyon (Simon and Schuster, 1991), gives suggestions for U.S. action.

A Call to Citizen Action

Bread for the World Institute, *Are We On Track to End Hunger? Hunger Report 2004*, p. 12, Washington: Bread for the World Institute, 2004.

Kimberly Burge, "Make Hunger History," *Bread*, Washington, D.C.: Bread for the World, January 2005.

CHAPTER 15. WHAT BUSINESSES CAN DO

Adam Smith, *The Wealth of Nations*, New York: Knopf, 1991.

Adam Smith, *Theory of Moral Sentiments*, Knud Haakonssen, ed. New York: Cambridge University Press, 2002.

Working with Communities

Vijahendra Rao, "Price Heterogeneity and 'Real' Inequality: A Case Study of Prices and Poverty in Rural South India," *Review of Income and Wealth*, vol. 46, no. 2, June 2000: 201–11.

C. K. Pralahad and Allen Hammond, "Serving the Poor Profitably," *Harvard Business Review*, Sept. 2002.

C. K. Prahalad, *The Fortune at the Bottom of the Pyramid: Eradicating Poverty through Profits*, Philadelphia: Wharton School Press, 2004.

Rani Parker, e-mail correspondence with the author, July 2004. Parker is writing an article on how mining companies can more effectively work in partnerships in the communities in which they work.

Adopting a Code of Conduct

Douglas Holt, John A. Quelch and Earl Taylor, "How Model Behavior Brings Market Power," *Financial Times*, August 23, 2004.

Douglas Holt, John A. Quelch and Earl Taylor, "How Global Brands Compete," *Harvard Business Review*, September 1, 2004.

Michael Porter and Claas van der Linde, "Toward a New Conception of the Environment-Competitiveness Relationship," *Journal of Economic Perspectives*, vol. 9, no. 4, Autumn 1995, pp. 97–118.

Financial Times, Monday, November 29, 2004, special report section on responsible business. See in particular Alison Maitland, "Business Bows to Growing Pressures," page 1, and "Social Innovation Could Pay Useful Dividends," page 4.

Rainforest Alliance (RA): http://www.rainforest-alliance.org.

The UN Global Compact: http://www.unglobalcompact.org/Portal/Default.asp.

Fair Labor association: http://www.fairlabor.org. For the SW critique, see http://www.sweatshopwatch.org/swatch/headlines/1998/sw_fla.html.

Goodcorporation: http://www.goodcorporation.com/en.

Equator Principles: http://equatorprinciples.ifc.org/ifcext/equatorprinciples.nsf/Content/corepoints; http://equatorprinciples.ifc.org/ifcext/equatorprinciples.nsf/AttachmentsByTitle/EPFinal/$FILE/EPFinal.pdf.

Johannesburg World Summit on Sustainable Development, Business Action for Sustainable Development, 2002, described at http://europa.eu.int/comm/development/body/publications/courier/courier194/en/en_012_ni.pdf. See http://equatorprinciples.ifc.org/ifcext/equatorprinciples.nsf/content/corepoints; http://equatorprinciples.ifc.org/ifcext/equatorprinciples.nsf/AttachmentsByTitle/EPFinal/$FILE/EPFinal.pdf.

Hildy Teegen, "International NGOs as Global Institutions: Using Social Capital to Impact Multinational Enterprises and Governments." *Journal of Management,* 2003.

African Growth and Opportunity Act (AGOA): http://www.agoa.gov/.

On Doing Well and Doing Good

Douglas Holt, John A. Quelch and Earl Taylor, "Managing the Transnational Brand: How Global Perceptions Drive Value," in John A. Quelch and Rohit Deshpande, *The Global Market. Developing a Strategy to Manage Across Borders.*

Procter & Gamble's PuR Water Purifier, reported by the World Business Council for Sustainable Development (WBCSD):

http://www.wbcsd.org/plugins/DocSearch/details.asp?type=DocDet&DocId=2764.

The research study was published in the *Journal of Water and Health* in June 2003.

The CARE and Cable & Wireless partnership was drawn from Jennifer Brinkerhoff, *Partnership for International Development: Rhetoric or Results,* Boulder, CO: Lynne Reiner, 2002.

Hewlett-Packard's innovation in South Africa is reported in Alison Maitland, "Social Innovation Could Pay Useful Dividends," *Financial Times,* Monday, November 29, 2004, special report section on Responsible Business, page 4.

International Council of Nurses: http://www.icn.ch/.

The U.S. Centers for Disease Control (CDC): http://www.cdc.gov/.

TechnoServe: http://www.tns.org/home.html.

EnterpriseWorks: http://www.enterpriseworks.org/.

ACDI-VOCA: http://www.acdivoca.org/acdivoca/Acdiweb2.nsf/.

For an expansive vision of the widened role that business can play in ending poverty by "turning the poor into consumers," see C. K. Prahalad, *The Fortune at the Bottom of the Pyramid: Eradicating Poverty Through Profits,* Wharton School Press, 2004.

CHAPTER 16: SOME CLOSING WORDS: THE END OF GLOBAL POVERTY

David Lindauer and Lant Pritchett, "What's the big idea? The third generation of policies for economic growth." *Economia,* Fall 2002, pp. 1–39.

Amartya Sen, *Development as Freedom*, New York: Alfred Knopf, 1999.

William Easterly, *The Elusive Quest for Growth: Economists' Adventures and Misadventures in the Tropics*, Cambridge, MA: MIT, 2001.

For an examination of arguments and options for increasing the voice of developing countries (mainly their governments) in the World bank, see Nancy Birdsall, "Why It Matters Who Runs the IMF and the World Bank," Center for Global Development Working Paper 22, Washington: CGD, 2003, available at http://www.cgdev.org/Publications/index.cfm?PubID=22. More radical critics of the World Bank include Jubilee South (http://www.jubileesouth.org and 50 Years is Enough (http://www.50years.org).

Yingyi Qian, "How Reform Worked in China," in Dani Rodrik, editor, *In Search of Prosperity: Analytic Narratives on Economic Growth*, Princeton University Press, 2003, pp. 297–333. On local paths to development, see other articles in that volume, and also Dani Rodrik, *Rethinking Economic Growth in Developing Countries*, Luca d'Agliano Lecture, Octover 2004, and Dani Rodrik, Ricardo Hausmann and Andres Velasco, *Growth Diagnostics*, October 2004, at http://ksghome.harvard.edu/~drodrik/papers.html.

United Nations Development Program, *Human Development Report 2003: Millennium Development Goals: A Compact Among Nations to End Human Poverty*, New York: Oxford University Press, 2003.

NAME INDEX

Abed, Fazle Hasan, 66, 90, 94, 237
Acemoglu, Daron, 224
Acton, Lord, 42
Aghion, Beatriz Armendriz de, 223, 229, 236
Ahmed, Mostaq, 237
Alexander, Nancy, 235
Anderson, Siwan, 229

Baker, Judy, 232
Baland, Jean-Marie, 223, 229
Bales, Kevin, 224, 230
Banerjee, Abhijit V., 62, 63, 223, 224, 227, 229, 234, 242
Barrett, Christopher B., 226
Barro, Robert, 225
Basu, Arnab K., 223
Basu, Kaushik, 222, 223, 228
Baulch, Bob, 221, 223
Beckmann, David, 187, 245
Behrman, Jere R., 234, 235
Besley, Timothy, 229, 230, 237, 242
Bhatnager, Subhash, 239
Bhatt, Elaben, 97, 98
Bhavnani, Rikhil, 246
Billimoria, Jeroo, 130, 131, 241
Birchall, Johnston, 238
Birdsall, Nancy, 249
Blaxall, John, 238
Bloch, Francis, 226
Blossner, Monika, 228
Bono, 6
Bornstein, David, 241, 243, 247
Bourguignon, Francois, 227
Brainard, Lael, 246
Brinkerhoff, Jennifer, 230, 231, 243, 248
Broad, Robin, 198, 230, 246

Brodhead, Tim, 243
Bromley, David, 225
Brown, L. David, 243
Bryant, Coralie, 243
Burge, Kimberly, 247
Burgess, Robin, 229, 242
Burtless, Gary, 232
Bush, George W., 53, 193

Cantuarias, Fernando, 242
Carter, Michael R., 223, 226
Carver, John, 182
Carver, Miriam, 182
Caulfield, Laura E., 228
Cavanagh, John, 198, 230, 246
Chattopadhyay, Raghabendra, 139, 140, 241
Chau, Nancy H., 223
Chen, Shaohua, 5, 221
Choudhury, Shafiqual Haque, 85–86
Christen, Robert Peck, 236
Clark, John, 18, 226, 230, 231
Coate, Stephen, 237
Cohen, Monique, 236
Cole, Shawn, 62, 234
Collier, Paul, 242
Compaore, Blaise, 196
Cooper, Phillip J., 230
Covey, Stephen, 168

Daley-Harris, Sam, 13, 229, 236
Daniels, Lisa, 246
Dasgupta, Partha, 221, 224, 233
Davis, Benjamin, 234
Deaton, Angus, 18, 226, 227
Delgado, Miguel, 242
Dercon, Stefan, 237
Dervan, Anikita, 239

De Soto, Hernando, 146, 242
Dollar, David, 221, 238
Drake, Deborah, 236
Drayton, William, 130, 201, 202, 225
Dreze, Jean, 246
Duflo, Esther, 62, 63, 139, 140, 227,
   234, 241

Easterly, William, 246, 249
Edison, Thomas, 140
Edwards, Michael, 243
Ehrenreich, Barbara, 247
Emerson, Ralph Waldo, 217
Emran, Shahe, 225

Fafchamps, Marcel, 223
Feinstein, Osvaldo N., 233
Fernando, Nimal A., 237
Field, Erica, 146, 242
Fields, Gary 221, 227, 242
Florini, Ann, 228, 243
Ford, Henry, 85
Foster, Andrew, 224
Foster, James E., 227, 228
Fox, Jonathan A., 243
Franke, Richard W., 238
Franklin, Benjamin, 33
Freire, Paolo, 228, 230

Galabru, Kek, 131, 132
Galasso, Emanuela, 237
Galor, Oded, 223, 224
Garcias, Don Samuel Ruiz, 136
Gary, Tracy, 167, 168, 169, 243
Gertler, Paul, 229, 233, 242
Gill, Carmen S., 226
Giunta, Ken, 244
Ghatak, Maitreesh, 223, 229, 236, 242
Graham, Carol, 245
Grandvaux, Yolande Miller, 236
Greer, Heather, 235
Guinnane, Timothy W., 223, 229, 236
Gulati, Guarang Mitu, 101, 238
Gunning, Jan Wellem, 242

Hammond, Allan, 206, 247
Harrington, Michael, 247
Hart, Peter D., 222
Hausmann, Ricardo, 249
Heckman, James A., 232

Hoddinott, John, 234
Hoff, Karla, 222, 224
Holden, Stein, 225
Holt, Douglas, 210, 211, 248
Hulme, David, 221, 237, 243

Isaac, TM. Thomas, 238

Jacoby, Hanan, 223
Jackson, Edward, 233
Jalan, Jyotsna, 224
Jodha, N.S., 225
Joshi, Sumit, 238

Kaleeba, Noerine, 53
Kanter, Rosabeth Moss, 42–43, 231
Kanungo, Parameeta, 239
Karlan, Dean, 233
Kaul, Inge, 243
Kelly, Walt, 39
Kenyon, Thomas, 247
Khalily, Baqui, 235, 238
Khandker, Shahidur, 235, 238
Kimuyu, Peter K., 242
Klein, William, 238
Kohner, Melissa, 167, 168, 169, 243
Korten, David, 245
Kothari, Brij, 110
Kraay, Art, 221, 238
Kremer, Michael, 57, 58, 224, 232, 233

Laidler, Nathalie, 235, 238
Lanjouw, Jenny, 147, 242
Larson, Bruce, 225
Lawson, David 221, 222
Leon, David, 226
Levy, Philip, 147, 242
Lindauer, David, 249
Linden, Leigh, 62, 63, 234
Lindenberg, Marc, 243
Lovell, Catherine H., 235
Lucas, Sarah, 246
Luono, Shabani, 240

Macinko, James, 237
Mandela, Nelson, 153, 242
Massawe, William, 114
Matin, Imran, 237
May, Julian, 223, 226
McClafferty, Bonnie, 234

McGrory, Mary, 222
McKay, Andy, 221, 222, 223
Meyer, Richard L., 237
Meyers, Jane E., 226
Miguel, Edward (Ted), 58, 233
Milanovic, Branko, 228
Minot, Nicholas, 246
Morduch, Jonathan, 223, 229, 236
Morrisson, Christian, 227
Murthy, Ranjani K., 226

Newman, Andrew, 223, 224
Newman, John, 223
Nichols, Tristi, 240

O'Neill, Paul, 6
Olson, Mancur, 225
Onis, Mercedes de, 228

Parker, Rani, 207, 248
Parker, Susan W., 234
Patel, Vikram, 226, 230, 231
Pearl, Daniel, 84, 236, 237
Perrings, Charles, 225
Persson, Torsten, 227
Pessino, Carola, 234
Pfefferman, Guy, 242
Picciotto, Robert, 233
Pinckney, Thomas C., 242
Pogge, Thomas, 222
Porter, Michael, 208, 248
Prahalad, C.K., 206, 207, 247, 249
Prennushi, Giovanna, 223
Pritchett, Lant, 227, 234, 249
Purvis, Nigel, 246

Qian, Yingyi, 249
Quelch, John, 210–211, 235, 238, 248

Radelet, Steven, 246
Ransom, Roger L., 224
Rao, Vijayendra, 226, 247
Ravallion, Martin, 5, 221, 224, 232, 237
Rawlings, Laura, 233
Ray, Debraj, 222, 223, 224, 227
Raychaudhuri, Ajitava, 242
Reddy, Sanjay, 222, 227
Rehn, Harriet, 120

Reinikka, Ritva, 235
Rhyne, Elisabeth H., 229, 236
Rice, Richard, 190, 245
Robinson, James R., 223, 229
Robinson, Marguerite S., 229, 236
Rodriguez, Evelyne, 234
Rodriguez-Garcia, Rosalia, 237
Rodrik, Dani, 221, 249
Rubardt, Marcie, 233
Rubio Gloria, 233

Sachs, Jeffrey, 230, 246
Sala-I-Martin, Xavier, 228
Salamon, Lester, 243
Salvia, Agustin, 237
Sankaran, Lakshmi, 226
Seabright, Paul, 225, 230
Sen, Amartya, 25–26, 44, 194, 227, 229, 246, 249
Sengupta, Piyali, 235
Serageldin, Ismail, 187
Shaw, George Bernard, 41
Shepherd, Andrew, 221
Shiferaw, Bekele, 225
Shilpi, Forhad, 225
Shore, Bill, 222, 243
Shultz, T. Paul, 234
Simon, Art, 245
Sjoholm, Hakan, 240
Skoufias, Emmanuel, 234
Smith, Adam, 28, 205, 247
Smith, Rev. Christopher R., 186
Smith, Gayle E., 246
Smith, Jeffrey A., 232
Smith, Stephen C., 222, 224, 225, 227, 228, 229, 230, 233, 236, 237, 238, 241, 242, 243
Spivak, Neal, 228
Stiglitz, Joseph, 222
Strauss, John, 233
Subbarao, Kalanidhi, 233
Sun, Laixiang, 238
Sutch, Richard, 224
Svensson, Jakob, 235
Sylwester, Kevin, 225

Tattenbach, Franz, 121
Tauchi, Yuko, 229
Taylor, Earl, 210, 211, 248
Teegen, Hildy, 243, 248

Thomas, Duncan, 233
Todaro, Michael P., 222, 224, 225,
    227, 228, 229, 241, 242, 243
Todd, Petra, 235
Torres, Magui Moreno, 239
Townsend, Robert M., 229
Tse, Karen, 132

Udry, Christopher, 229

Vandemoortele, Jan, 40, 230
Van der Linde, Claas, 208, 248
Vargas, Claudia Maria, 230
Vega, Sergio de la, 234

Velasco, Andres, 249
Vieth, Warren, 246

Walt, Gill, 226
Waters, William, 237
Woods, Tiger, 90

Yoder, Karla, 236
Yunus, Mohammad, 17, 41, 75–78,
    107, 108, 109, 218, 222, 226, 229,
    236, 241, 247

Zeira, Joseph, 223, 224
Zimmerman, Frederick J., 223

SUBJECT INDEX

ACCION, 80
ACDI-VOCA, 212
Aid, official, 192–197
AIDS, 2, 33, 42, 52–54, 55, 193
AIDS Support Organization, The
   (TASO), 52–54, 157
Africa, Sub-Saharan, 1, 5, 6, 19, 39–40,
   42, 52, 54, 113, 210
Africa Now, 115–117, 147, 157
African Growth and Opportunities Act
   (AGOA), 210
Africare, 117, 145, 148–153, 156,
   157
Agricultural subsidies, harmful effects
   of, 195–197
Agriculture, developing countries, see
   farmers, poor
Alternativa Solidaria, 88
Alternative Gifts International, 173
Alternative Spring Break, 163
American Institute of Philanthropy
   (AIP), 70, 80, 145, 163
Amnesty International, 181
Angola, 2
Argentina, 23, 88, 106
Ashoka, 107, 130, 132, 201–202
Asia, East, 6, 147
Asia, South, 3, 37, 61, 89, 194
Assets of the poor, 24–25
Association for the Development and
   Enhancement of Women (ADEW),
   127–130, 145, 155, 157
Association for Social Advancement
   (ASA), 84–86

Bangladesh, 14, 38, 65–67, 84–86,
   89–97, 107–110, 132–134, 141
BASIX/KSB, 87

Better Business Bureau, see Wise Giving
   Alliance
Board and working group membership,
   181 184
BoardSource, 182
Bolivia, 105, 212
BRAC, 65–67, 80, 82, 86, 87, 89–97,
   132–134, 155, 156, 157, 173
Brazil, 65, 106
Bread for the World, 6, 187, 203
Burkina Faso, 2, 196–197
Burma, 198
Business initiatives, 205–212

Cable & Wireless, 211
Calvert Funds, 104, 185
Cambodia, 131 132, 212
Cambodian League for Promotion and
   Defense of Human Rights
   (LICADHO), 131–132
Capabilities to function approach,
   25–26
CARE, 54–56, 88, 181, 211
Catholic Church, 136, 187
Catholic Relief Services, 112, 176, 181,
   186
Center for Global Development, 193
Centers for Disease Control, U.S., 189,
   211
CHANCE program, 70–74
Charity Navigator, 70, 143, 145, 163
Chiapas, Mexico, 88, 134–136
Child labor, 2–3, 12, 64–65, 67, 95, 149
Childline Foundation, 130–131, 156
Child sponsorship, 174–176
Children International, 175
Chile, 106
China, 5, 198, 210, 215

Christian Children's Fund, 175
Church partnerships, 185–186
Climate Action Network, 190
Clinic partnerships, 188
Clubs, partner, 188–189
Codes of conduct, 208–210
Common property management, 16,
    117–120
Congo, 5
Conservation International, 190
Consultative Group to Assist the Poor
    (CGAP)
Cooperatives, 87, 98, 100–102, 113,
    116, 141, 212
Coptic Evangelical Organization for
    Social Services, 187
Corruption, 3, 23, 64–65
Costa Rica, 65, 121–122
Credit and credit constraints, 12, 13,
    35–36, 75–86
Criminality, 14

Debt bondage and slavery, 13, 132, 137,
    198
Debt, international, 178–179
Department for International
    Development (DFID), 80
Development Gateway Award, 108
Development strategies, 215
Deworming, 56–59, 156
Doctors without Borders, 188
Dominican Republic, 83, 186
Drop the Debt, 179

Economist magazine, 196
Ecuador, 82–84, 147
Education, for the poor, 3, 14, 34–35,
    61–74
Egypt, 127–130, 187
Electrification, 140–141
Empowerment, personal, 41–42
Empowerment, community, 42–45
Endeavor, 106–107, 156
Enlace Civil, 135
EnterpriseWorks, 117, 211
Environmental degradation and
    protection, 15–16, 39–41, 189–190,
    197
Environmental partnerships, 189–190

Equator Prize, see United Nations
    Equator Prize
Equator Principles, 209–210
Erosion, see environmental
    degradation
Ethiopia, 19, 54–56
Evaluation of programs, 7, 56–59,
    61–63, 65, 157, 162, 166, 167, 168,
    169, 174, 176, 180, 186, 216, 217,
    231–233, 234–235, 237, 241

Fair Labor Association, 209
Fair Trade Federation, 173
Fairtrade Labeling Organizations
    International, 173
Family planning, see fertility of the
    poor
Farmers, poor, 27, 36–38, 111–114,
    116, 121, 145, 148–153
Farmer-to-farmer assistance, 211–212
Fertility, of the poor, 15, 39–40, 54–56
Financial Times, 161, 186
Food, see also Undernutrition
Food, sufficiency of, 33, 145, 148–153
Food and Agriculture Organization
    (FAO), see United Nations Food and
    Agriculture
Organization
Ford Foundation, 104
Foundation for International
    Community Assistance (FINCA),
    79–82, 156, 176
Fray Bartolome Human Rights Center,
    136, 155, 162
Freedom from Hunger, 82
Free the Slaves, 14
Fundecor, 121–122, 156

Gates Prize, 66
Ghana, 82
Girls' Dreams Project, 127–130
Global Development Network Award,
    61
Global Exchange, 162
Global poverty, see Poverty
Global rich list, 162
Global Sullivan Principles, 209
Goodcorporation, 209
Gram Vikas, 122–123, 157

Grameen Bank 75–79, 80, 86, 87, 107–110, 141, 156, 173
Guatemala, 83
GuideStar, 163

Habitat for Humanity, 163
Haiti, 186
Health, of the Poor, 2, 14, 21–24, 49–59
Heifer International, 62, 93, 123–126, 144, 156, 162, 170, 181
Hewlett-Packard, 211
HIV-AIDS, see AIDS
Home ownership, 77, 79
Honduras, 83
Honey Care, 115–117, 156
Hospital partnerships, 188
Housing, 14, 40, 79
Human Rights and Legal Education program, 132–134
Human Rights Center, Chiapas, see Fray Bartolome Human Rights Center
Hunger, 2, 5, 193

ICICI Bank, 62, 87
Idealist.org, 198
Illiteracy, see Literacy
Income Generation for Vulnerable Group Development (IGVGD), 90, 91
India, 33, 86, 100–102, 110, 122–123, 130–131, 137, 139–140, 141–143
Inequality, 28–29
Information and poverty, 14
InterAction, 175, 192
International Bridges to Justice (IBJ), 132
International Business Leaders Forum, 206
International Christian Support Fund (ICS), 56–59, 157
International Crop Research Institute for the Semi-Arid Tropics (ICRISAT), 111
International Council of Nurses, 211
International Finance Corporation (IFC), 50, 210
International Food Policy Research Institute (IFPRI), 18, 65

International Monetary Fund, 68–69, 178
International Rescue Committee, 176
Islam, 186, 187
Investing, see Socially Responsible Investing

Jubilee movement, 178, 179, 187

Kamaiya Freedom Movement Mobilization Committee, 137
Kenya, 56–59, 115–117
Kerala Dinesh Beedi (KDB), 100–102, 157
Kibera, 40
King Baudouin International Development Prize, 53, 112,122, 173

Lake Victoria, 39
Land reform, 37–38, 147
Latin America and the Caribbean, 41, 134–135, 146–147
Leasing, as an approach to capital formation, 116–117
Leathers, Howard, 172
Letelier-Moffit Human Rights Award, Institute for Policy Studies, 136
Literacy, 3, 12, 34–35, 38, 62
Lutheran World Relief, 112

Malawi, 2, 70, 83
Mali, 2, 70, 196–197
Malnutrition, see undernutrition
Markets and market development, importance for the poor, 37–38, 89–102
Martin Ennals Award, 136
Masai, 117–120
Meltzer Commission, 179
Mennonite Central Committee, 173
Mental health of the poor, 16–17, 41–42
Mercy Corps, 185
Mexico, 63–65, 87–88, 106, 134–136
Micah Network, 187
Microcredit, see Microfinance
Microfinance, 13, 35–36, 66, 75–86, 144
Milkworx, 107

Millennium Challenge Account, 193, 212
Millennium Development Goals, 193–194, 206, 214
Millennium Project, see United Nations Millennium Project
Money magazine, 165
Mother-Child Day Care Center Services, 99, 156
Mozambique, 2, 37, 50

Nepal, 137
New York Life, 104
New York Times, 161, 196, 197
Niger, 2
Niwano Peace Prize, 136
Nobel Peace Prize, 136, 188
Nonformal Primary Education, 65–67, 70–74
Nutrition, see undernutrition

ONE Campaign, 192
Oportunidades, see Progresa
Overseas Cooperation Volunteers, 199
Oxfam International, 162, 195–196

Parasites, infectious, 2, 56–59
Pax World Service, 185
Peace Corps, 196, 199
Peru, 104–105, 123–126, 143–145, 146
Phone ladies, Grameen, 107–110, 157
Pigeon Peas Program, 111–114
Plan USA, 175
Playpump, see Roundabout Outdoor
Poor people, Characteristics of, 26–27
Poverty, scope and incidence of, 1–6
Poverty programs, 45, 47; see also specific programs
Poverty traps, 11–17
Powell, Colin, 53
Powerlessness, 3, 17
Pratham, 61–63, 157, 170
President's Award for Voluntary Action, 123
Presidential End Hunger Award, 123
Procter & Gamble PuR Water Purifier, 211
Productivity, 38–39
Program evaluation, see Evaluation of programs

Progresa, 63–65, 134, 156
Project Hope, 82–84, 188
Pro-Poor Innovation Challenge Award, 82
Public opinion polls, 7

Rainforest Alliance, 208–209
Red Cross/Red Crescent, 188
RESULTS, 192
Risk, 13, 24, 35–36, 86–88
Romania, 105, 186
Rotary International, 189
Roundabout Outdoor Playpump, 49–52, 157
Rural Health and Environment Program, 122–123
Rwanda, 2

Sahel, 40
Same Language Subtitling, 110
Sankalp, 137
Save the Children, 62, 70–74, 156, 175, 176, 188
Self-Employed Women's Association (SEWA), 87–88, 97–98, 100, 156, 157, 173
Selian Agricultural Research Institute, 112
Sierra Club Beyond the Borders, 189
Sierra Leone, 2
Simon Bolivar Prize, UNESCO, 136
Sister Cities International, 190–191
Slavery, see debt bondage and slavery
Slums, urban, 4, 40, 123–126, 127–130
Small Enterprise Assistance Fund (SEAF), 103–106, 156
Social Accountability International, 175
Social Entrepreneurship, 201–202
Social Investment Forum, 185
Socially Responsible Investing, 184–185
Society for International Development (SID), 161
South Africa, 49–52, 106–107
South Korea, 147, 215
Southwest Marbles and Stones, 104
Soviet Union, former, 19, 26, 41
Stitch Wise, 107
Subsistence traps, 15, 117, 150
Sudan, 32

Suledo Forest Community, 117–120, 156
Sweatshop Watch, 209
Swedish International Development Agency, 118
Synjuk Seng Samla Shnong (SSSS), 141–143, 156

Taiwan, 147, 215
Tanzania, 111–114, 117–120
Targeting the Ultrapoor Program, 89–93
TASO, see AIDS Support Organization
Technology, importance for the poor, 38–39, 103–114
TechnoServe, 111–114, 156, 157, 176, 211
Ten Thousand Villages, 173
Trade, effects of, 198
Transfair USA, 173
Transparency International, 65, 66
Travel Warnings, U.S. Dept. of State, 163

Uganda, 52–54, 68–69, 79–82, 99, 145, 148–153, 212
Undernutrition, 5, 14, 31–34
United Nations Children's Fund (UNICEF), 50, 62, 189
United Nations Development Program (UNDP), 4, 35, 193
United Nations Equator Prize, 115, 117, 152
United Nations Education, Scientific, and Cultural Organization (UNESCO), 99
United Nations Food and Agriculture Organization (FAO), 5, 32
United Nations Global Compact, 208, 209

United Nations Millennium Project, 194
United States, poverty in, 202–203
United States Agency for International Development (USAID), 32, 53, 80, 81, 88, 94, 206, 212
University degree programs, 199–200
Uruguay, 106

Victoria Kids, 104
Voices of the Poor study, see World Bank Voices of the Poor study
Voluntary Service Overseas, 199
Vulnerability, 3

Water, importance of clean and safe, 5, 33, 49–50
West Bengal, 139–140, 147, 155
Wise Giving Alliance, 143, 164, 176
World Affairs Council, 161
World Bank, 1, 18, 50, 68–69, 87, 178–180, 187, 210, 216
World Bank Development Marketplace, 50, 99, 110
World Bank Voices of the Poor study, 18–23, 41, 44
World Habitat Award, 79, 122
World Health Organization, 52, 189
World Neighbors, 181
World Relief, 186
World Trade Organization, 178
World Vision, 88, 143–145, 155, 162, 175, 181
Worldwatch Institute, 5
Worth magazine, 165

Zimbabwe, 54

About the Author

Stephen C. Smith is Professor of Economics at George Washington University, where he is Director of the Research Program on Poverty, Development, and Globalization, and Co-Coordinator of the GW International NGO Team (INGOT). Smith has been teaching courses on economic development with an emphasis on problems of poverty since 1983. He received his Ph.D. in economics from Cornell University and has been a Fulbright Research Scholar and a Jean Monnet Research Fellow. Smith is the co-author with Michael Todaro of a leading undergraduate text in the field, *Economic Development* (8th Ed., Addison-Wesley/Pearson, 2002). Smith served as organizer and then first director of GWU's International Development Studies Program in 1990–1996. He has also taught development economics at the State Department's Foreign Service Institute. Smith has done on-site work in developing countries on four continents, including Kenya, India, Peru, and former Yugoslavia. He has been a consultant for the World Bank, the International Labour Office (ILO, Geneva), the Small Enterprise Assistance Fund, and the World Institute for Development Economics Research (UN-WIDER, Helsinki), among other agencies.